DEATHLOK NATION

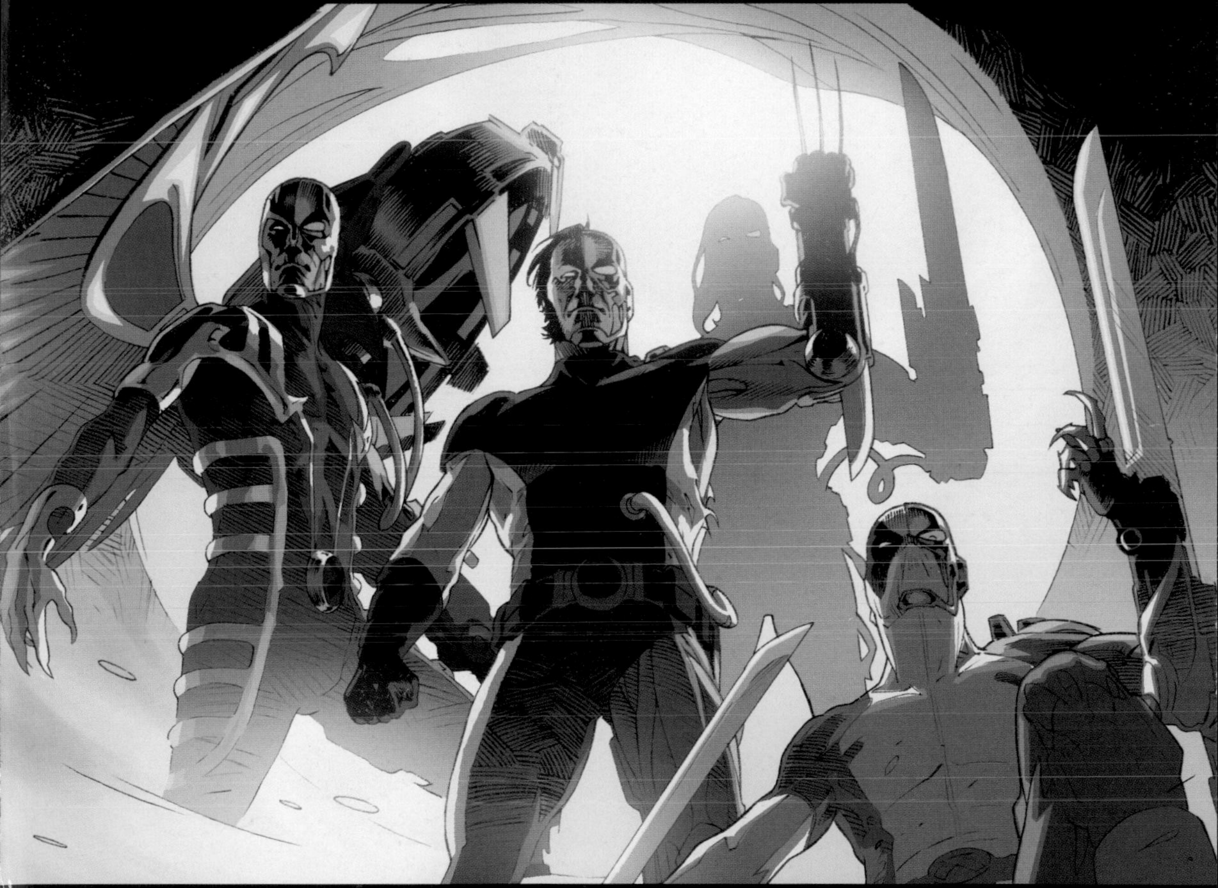

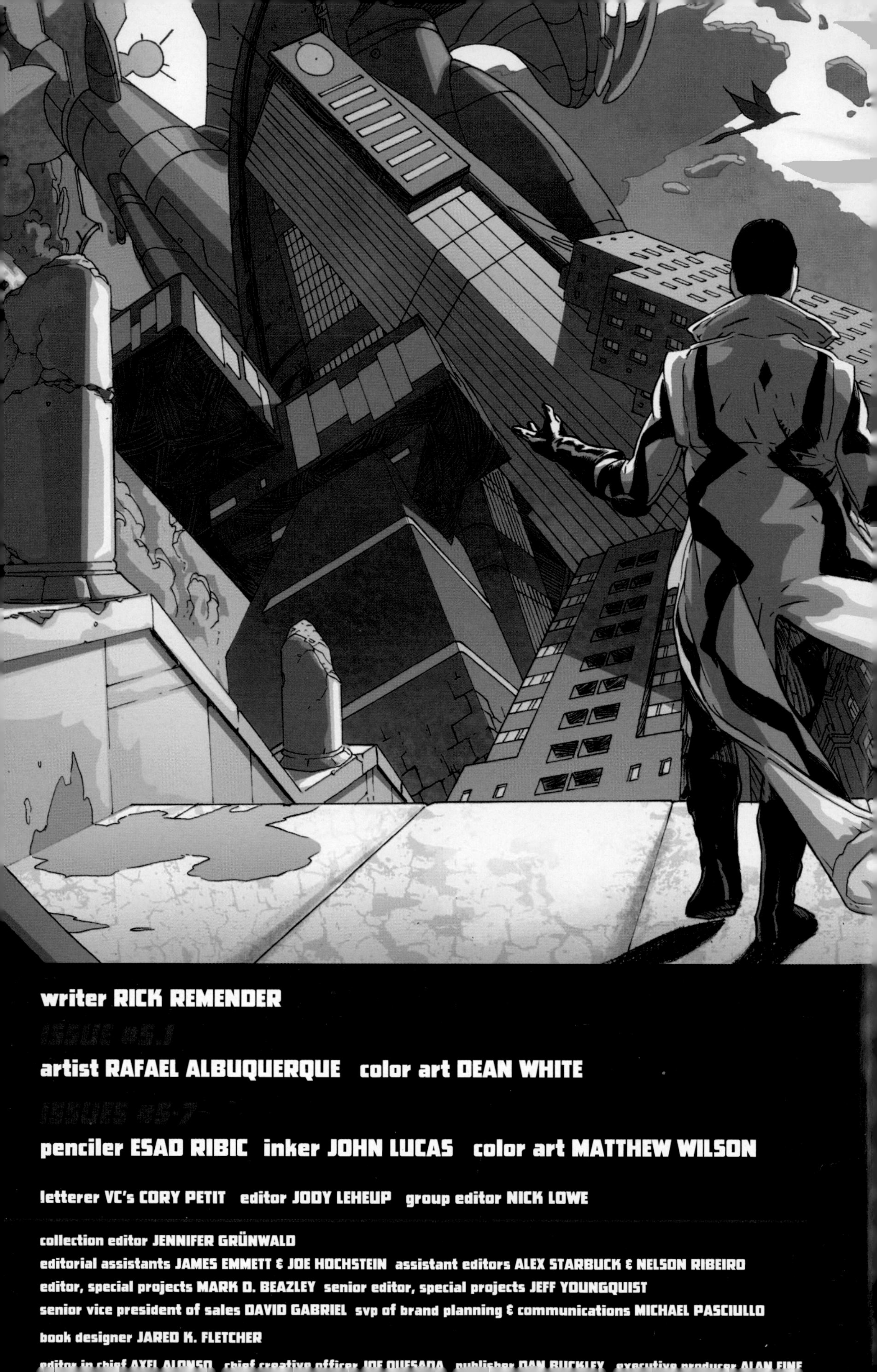

writer RICK REMENDER

ISSUE #5.1

artist RAFAEL ALBUQUERQUE color art DEAN WHITE

ISSUES #5-7

penciler ESAD RIBIC inker JOHN LUCAS color art MATTHEW WILSON

letterer VC's CORY PETIT editor JODY LEHEUP group editor NICK LOWE

collection editor JENNIFER GRÜNWALD
editorial assistants JAMES EMMETT & JOE HOCHSTEIN assistant editors ALEX STARBUCK & NELSON RIBEIRO
editor, special projects MARK D. BEAZLEY senior editor, special projects JEFF YOUNGQUIST
senior vice president of sales DAVID GABRIEL svp of brand planning & communications MICHAEL PASCIULLO
book designer JARED K. FLETCHER

editor in chief AXEL ALONSO chief creative officer JOE QUESADA publisher DAN BUCKLEY executive producer ALAN FINE

UNCANNY X-FORCE
DEATHLOK NATION

UNCANNY X-FORCE: DEATHLOK NATION. Contains material originally published in magazine form as UNCANNY X-FORCE #5-7 and #5.1, and X-MEN SPOTLIGHT. First printing 2011. ISBN# 978-0-7851-4856-2. Published by MARVEL WORLDWIDE, INC., a subsidiary of MARVEL ENTERTAINMENT, LLC. OFFICE OF PUBLICATION: 135 West 50th Street, New York, NY 10020. Copyright © 2011 Marvel Characters, Inc. All rights reserved. $19.99 per copy in the U.S. and $21.99 in Canada (GST #R127032852); Canadian Agreement #40668537. All characters featured in this issue and the distinctive names and likenesses thereof, and all related indicia are trademarks of Marvel Characters, Inc. No similarity between any of the names, characters, persons, and/or institutions in this magazine with those of any living or dead person or institution is intended, and any such similarity which may exist is purely coincidental. **Printed in the U.S.A.** ALAN FINE, EVP - Office of the President, Marvel Worldwide, Inc. and EVP & CMO Marvel Characters B.V.; DAN BUCKLEY, Publisher & President - Print, Animation & Digital Divisions; JOE QUESADA, Chief Creative Officer; JIM SOKOLOWSKI, Chief Operating Officer; DAVID BOGART, SVP of Business Affairs & Talent Management; TOM BREVOORT, SVP of Publishing; C.B. CEBULSKI, SVP of Creator & Content Development; DAVID GABRIEL, SVP of Publishing Sales & Circulation; MICHAEL PASCIULLO, SVP of Brand Planning, X Communications; JIM O'KEEFE, VP of Operations & Logistics; DAN CARR, Executive Director of Publishing Technology; JUSTIN F. GABRIE, Director of Publishing & Editorial Operations; SUSAN CRESPI, Editorial Operations Manager; ALEX MORALES, Publishing Operations Manager; STAN LEE, Chairman Emeritus. For information regarding advertising in Marvel Comics or on Marvel.com, please contact John Dokes, SVP Integrated Sales and Marketing, at jdokes@marvel.com. For Marvel subscription Inquiries, please call 800-217-9158. **Manufactured between 5/2/2011 and 5/30/2011 by R.R. DONNELLEY, INC., SALEM, VA, USA.**

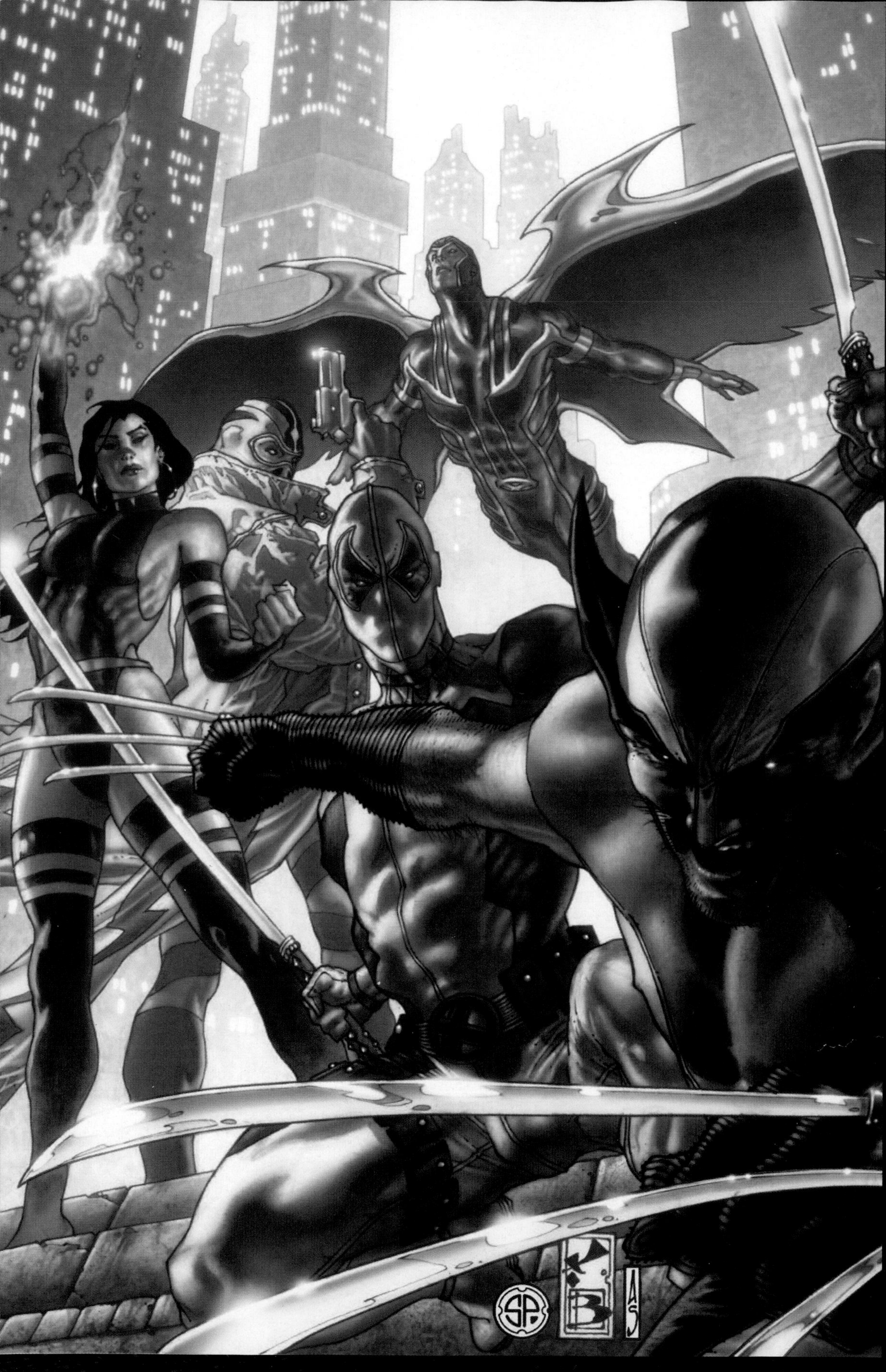

FIVE POINT ONE **05.1**

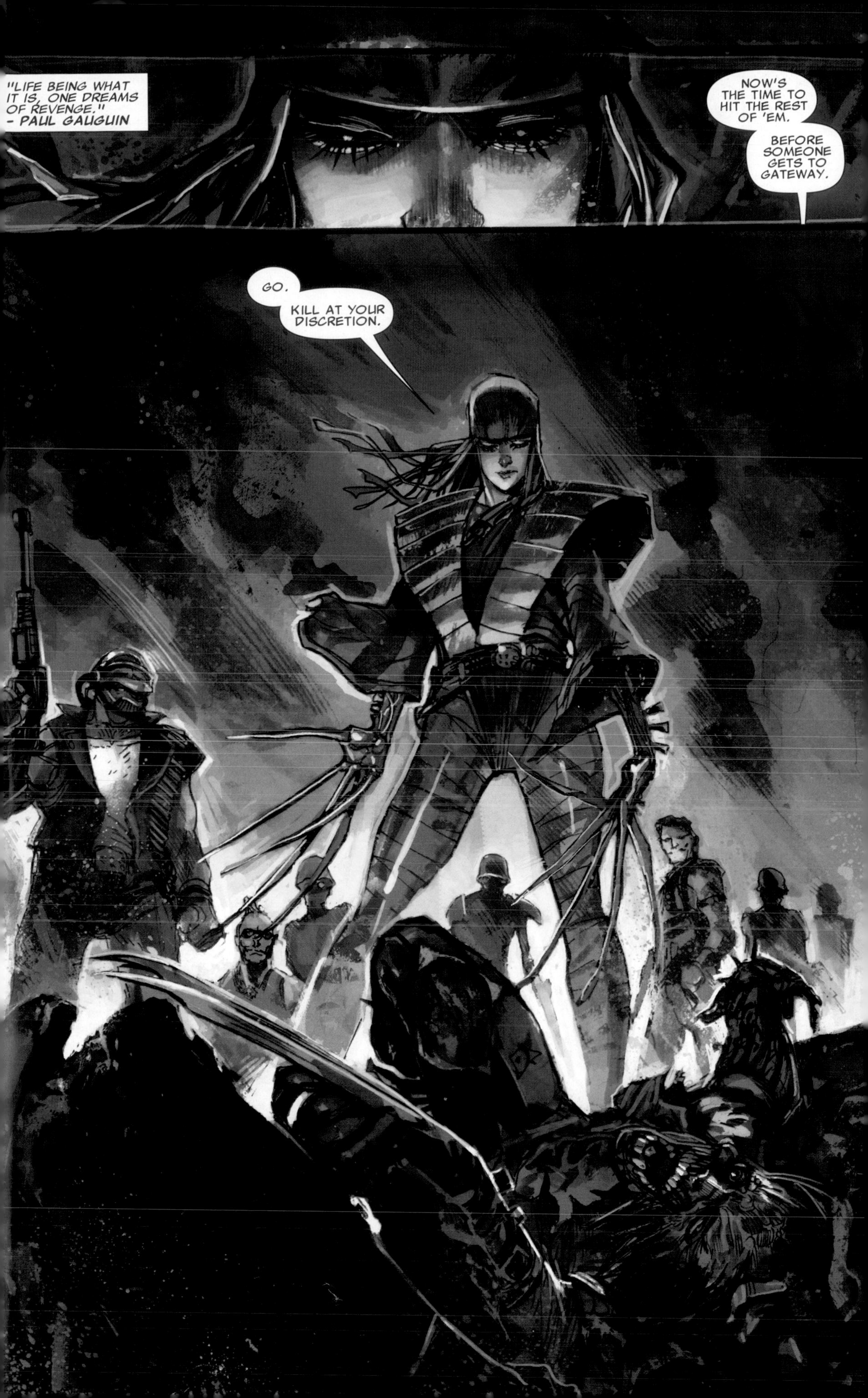
"LIFE BEING WHAT IT IS, ONE DREAMS OF REVENGE."
- PAUL GAUGUIN
NOW'S THE TIME TO HIT THE REST OF 'EM.
BEFORE SOMEONE GETS TO GATEWAY.
GO.
KILL AT YOUR DISCRETION.

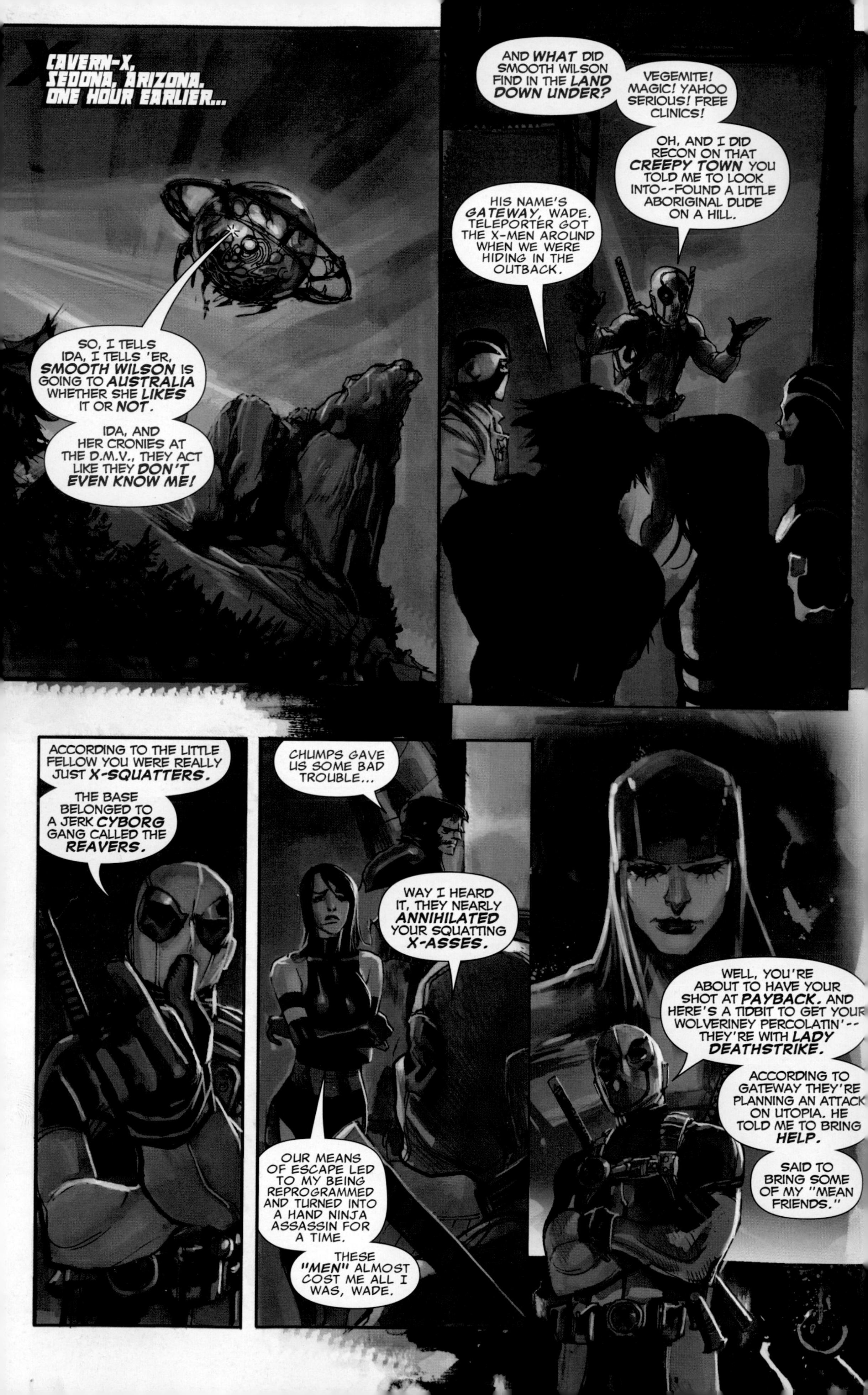
CAVERN-X, SEDONA, ARIZONA. ONE HOUR EARLIER...
SO, I TELLS IDA, I TELLS 'ER, SMOOTH WILSON IS GOING TO AUSTRALIA WHETHER SHE LIKES IT OR NOT.
IDA, AND HER CRONIES AT THE D.M.V., THEY ACT LIKE THEY DON'T EVEN KNOW ME!
AND WHAT DID SMOOTH WILSON FIND IN THE LAND DOWN UNDER?
VEGEMITE! MAGIC! YAHOO SERIOUS! FREE CLINICS!
OH, AND I DID RECON ON THAT CREEPY TOWN YOU TOLD ME TO LOOK INTO--FOUND A LITTLE ABORIGINAL DUDE ON A HILL.
HIS NAME'S GATEWAY, WADE. TELEPORTER GOT THE X-MEN AROUND WHEN WE WERE HIDING IN THE OUTBACK.
ACCORDING TO THE LITTLE FELLOW YOU WERE REALLY JUST X-SQUATTERS.
THE BASE BELONGED TO A JERK CYBORG GANG CALLED THE REAVERS.
CHUMPS GAVE US SOME BAD TROUBLE...
WAY I HEARD IT, THEY NEARLY ANNIHILATED YOUR SQUATTING X-ASSES.
OUR MEANS OF ESCAPE LED TO MY BEING REPROGRAMMED AND TURNED INTO A HAND NINJA ASSASSIN FOR A TIME.
THESE "MEN" ALMOST COST ME ALL I WAS, WADE.
WELL, YOU'RE ABOUT TO HAVE YOUR SHOT AT PAYBACK. AND HERE'S A TIDBIT TO GET YOUR WOLVERINEY PERCOLATIN'--THEY'RE WITH LADY DEATHSTRIKE.
ACCORDING TO GATEWAY THEY'RE PLANNING AN ATTACK ON UTOPIA. HE TOLD ME TO BRING HELP.
SAID TO BRING SOME OF MY "MEAN FRIENDS."

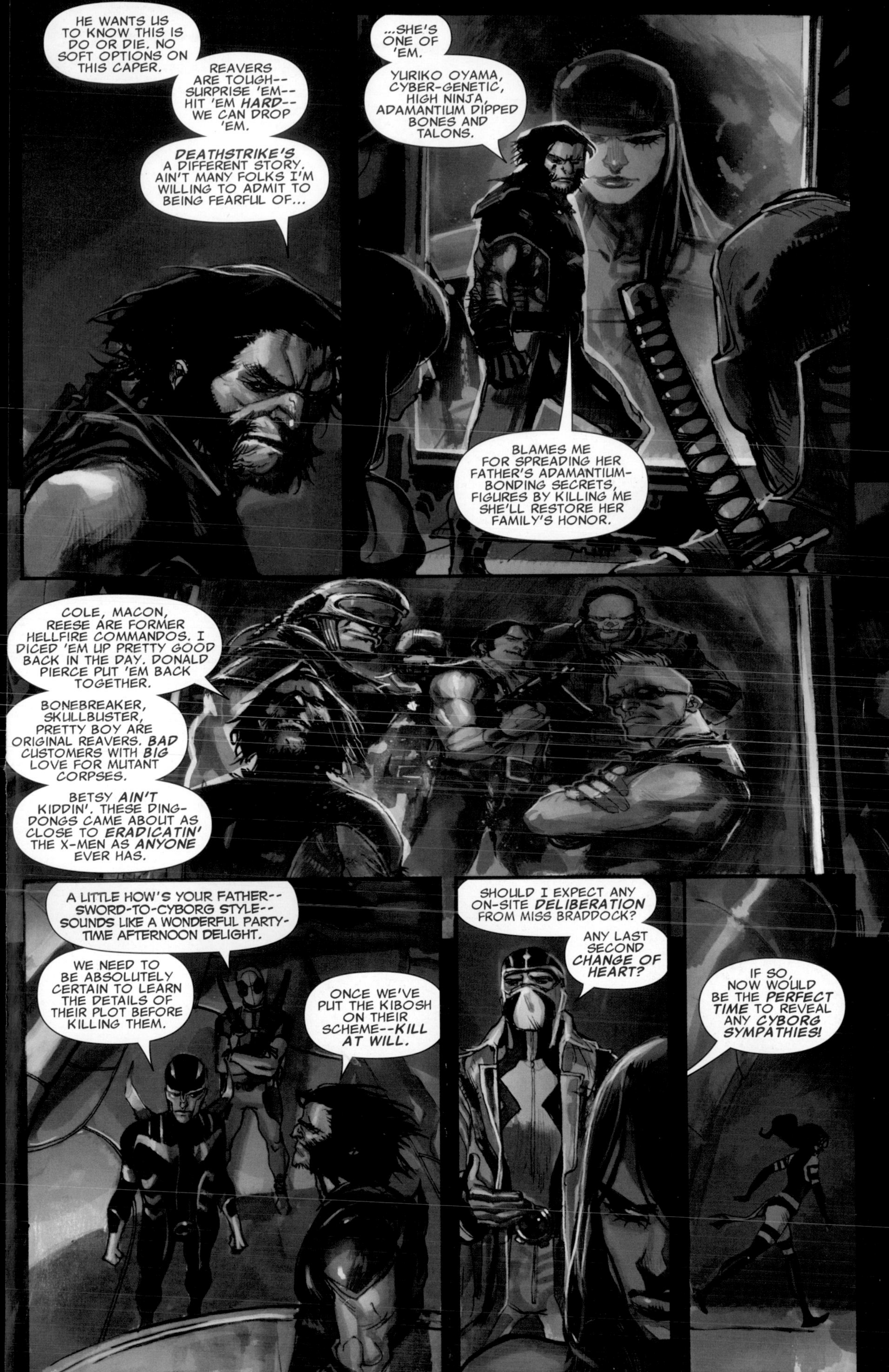
HE WANTS US TO KNOW THIS IS DO OR DIE. NO SOFT OPTIONS ON THIS CAPER.
REAVERS ARE TOUGH-- SURPRISE 'EM-- HIT 'EM HARD-- WE CAN DROP 'EM.
DEATHSTRIKE'S A DIFFERENT STORY. AIN'T MANY FOLKS I'M WILLING TO ADMIT TO BEING FEARFUL OF...
...SHE'S ONE OF 'EM.
YURIKO OYAMA, CYBER-GENETIC, HIGH NINJA, ADAMANTIUM DIPPED BONES AND TALONS.
BLAMES ME FOR SPREADING HER FATHER'S ADAMANTIUM-BONDING SECRETS, FIGURES BY KILLING ME SHE'LL RESTORE HER FAMILY'S HONOR.
COLE, MACON, REESE ARE FORMER HELLFIRE COMMANDOS. I DICED 'EM UP PRETTY GOOD BACK IN THE DAY. DONALD PIERCE PUT 'EM BACK TOGETHER.
BONEBREAKER, SKULLBUSTER, PRETTY BOY ARE ORIGINAL REAVERS. BAD CUSTOMERS WITH BIG LOVE FOR MUTANT CORPSES.
BETSY AIN'T KIDDIN'. THESE DING-DONGS CAME ABOUT AS CLOSE TO ERADICATIN' THE X-MEN AS ANYONE EVER HAS.
A LITTLE HOW'S YOUR FATHER-- SWORD-TO-CYBORG STYLE-- SOUNDS LIKE A WONDERFUL PARTY-TIME AFTERNOON DELIGHT.
WE NEED TO BE ABSOLUTELY CERTAIN TO LEARN THE DETAILS OF THEIR PLOT BEFORE KILLING THEM.
ONCE WE'VE PUT THE KIBOSH ON THEIR SCHEME--KILL AT WILL.
SHOULD I EXPECT ANY ON-SITE DELIBERATION FROM MISS BRADDOCK?
ANY LAST SECOND CHANGE OF HEART?
IF SO, NOW WOULD BE THE PERFECT TIME TO REVEAL ANY CYBORG SYMPATHIES!

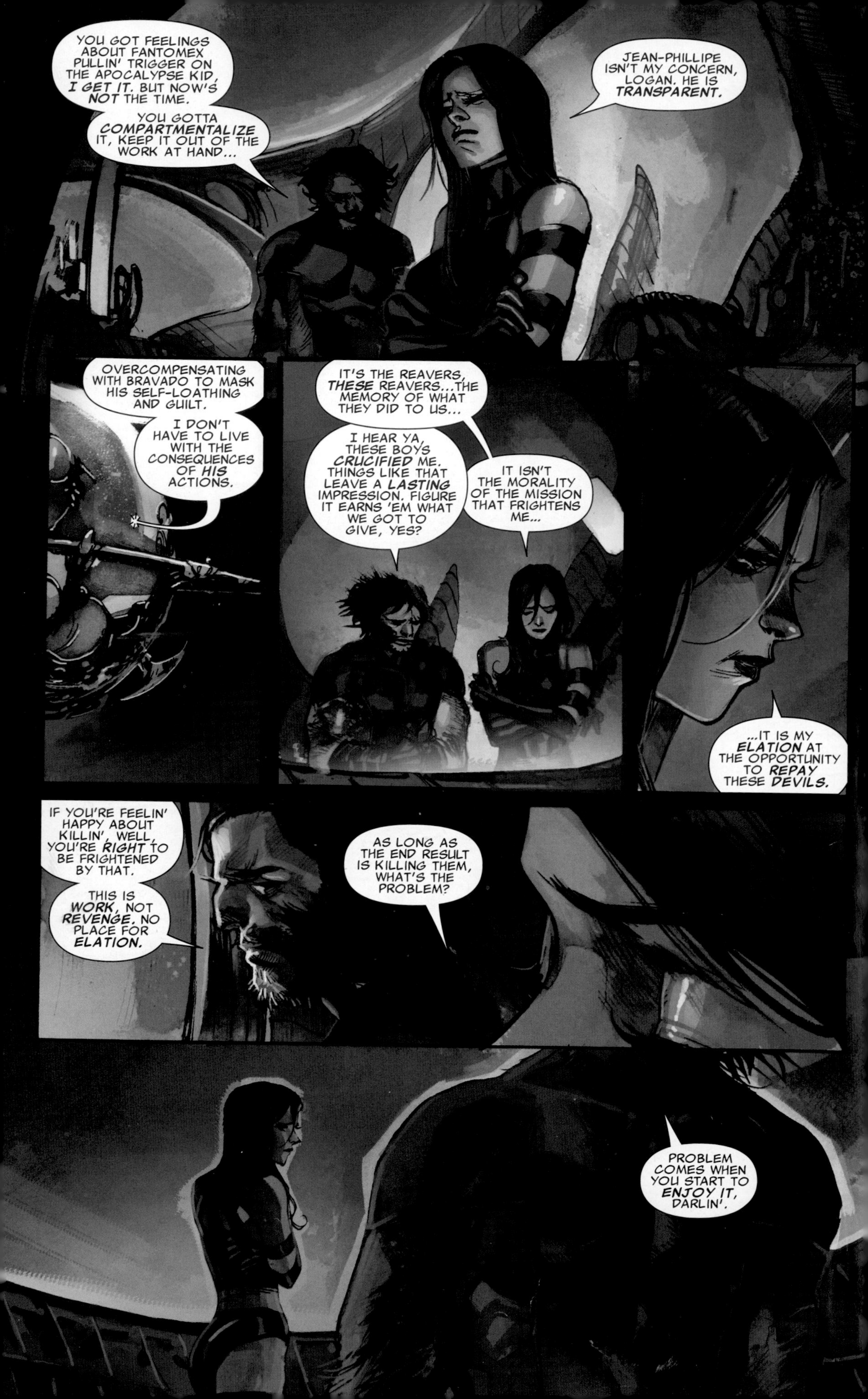

YOU GOT FEELINGS ABOUT FANTOMEX PULLIN' TRIGGER ON THE APOCALYPSE KID, I GET IT. BUT NOW'S NOT THE TIME.
YOU GOTTA COMPARTMENTALIZE IT, KEEP IT OUT OF THE WORK AT HAND...
JEAN-PHILLIPE ISN'T MY CONCERN, LOGAN. HE IS TRANSPARENT.
OVERCOMPENSATING WITH BRAVADO TO MASK HIS SELF-LOATHING AND GUILT.
I DON'T HAVE TO LIVE WITH THE CONSEQUENCES OF HIS ACTIONS.
IT'S THE REAVERS, THESE REAVERS...THE MEMORY OF WHAT THEY DID TO US...
I HEAR YA, THESE BOYS CRUCIFIED ME. THINGS LIKE THAT LEAVE A LASTING IMPRESSION. FIGURE IT EARNS 'EM WHAT WE GOT TO GIVE, YES?
IT ISN'T THE MORALITY OF THE MISSION THAT FRIGHTENS ME...
...IT IS MY ELATION AT THE OPPORTUNITY TO REPAY THESE DEVILS.
IF YOU'RE FEELIN' HAPPY ABOUT KILLIN', WELL, YOU'RE RIGHT TO BE FRIGHTENED BY THAT.
THIS IS WORK, NOT REVENGE. NO PLACE FOR ELATION.
AS LONG AS THE END RESULT IS KILLING THEM, WHAT'S THE PROBLEM?
PROBLEM COMES WHEN YOU START TO ENJOY IT, DARLIN'.

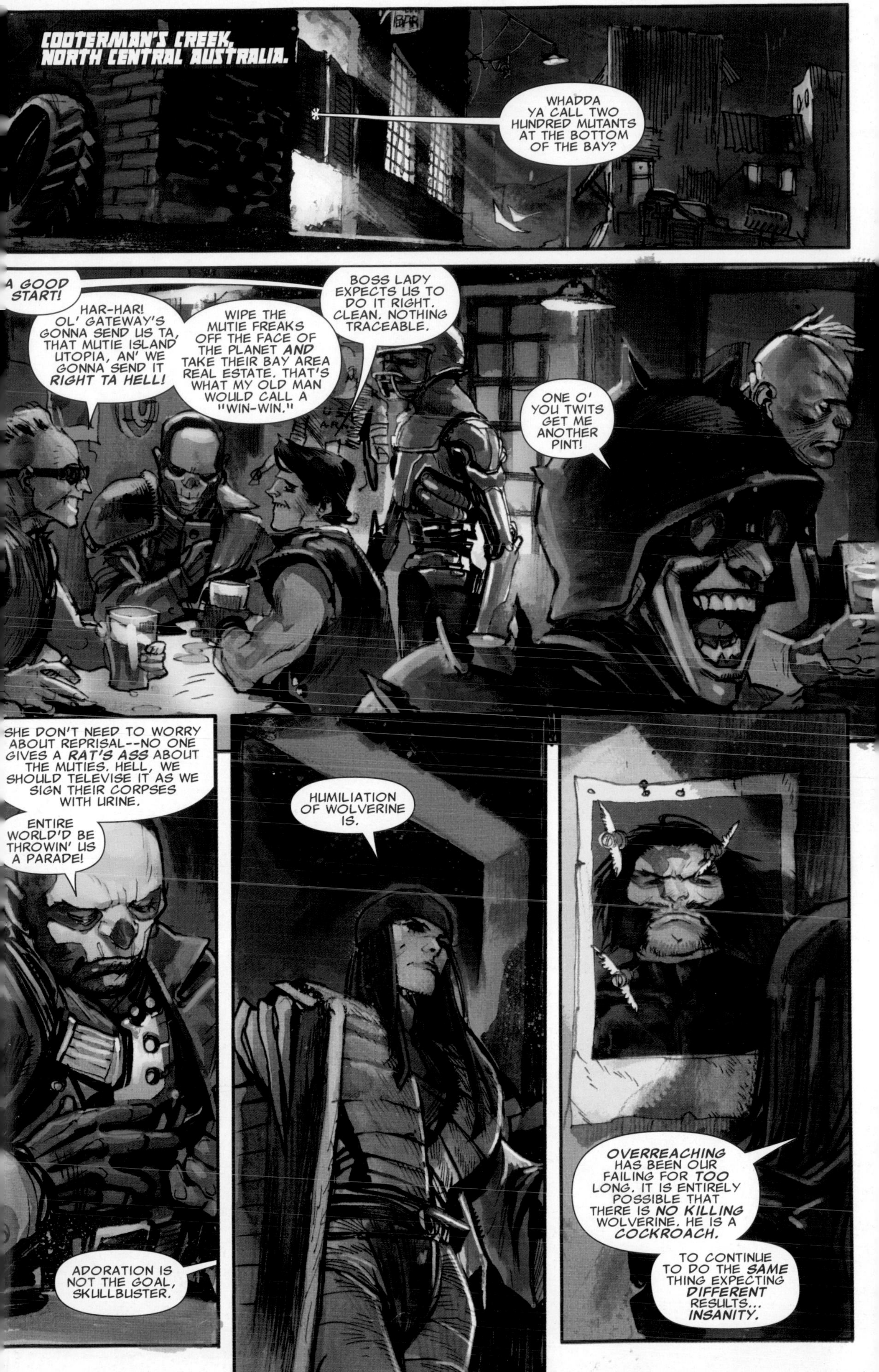
COOTERMAN'S CREEK, NORTH CENTRAL AUSTRALIA.
WHADDA YA CALL TWO HUNDRED MUTANTS AT THE BOTTOM OF THE BAY?
A GOOD START!
HAR-HAR! OL' GATEWAY'S GONNA SEND US TA THAT MUTIE ISLAND UTOPIA, AN' WE GONNA SEND IT RIGHT TA HELL!
WIPE THE MUTIE FREAKS OFF THE FACE OF THE PLANET AND TAKE THEIR BAY AREA REAL ESTATE. THAT'S WHAT MY OLD MAN WOULD CALL A "WIN-WIN."
BOSS LADY EXPECTS US TO DO IT RIGHT. CLEAN. NOTHING TRACEABLE.
ONE O' YOU TWITS GET ME ANOTHER PINT!
SHE DON'T NEED TO WORRY ABOUT REPRISAL--NO ONE GIVES A RAT'S ASS ABOUT THE MUTIES. HELL, WE SHOULD TELEVISE IT AS WE SIGN THEIR CORPSES WITH URINE.
ENTIRE WORLD'D BE THROWIN' US A PARADE!
ADORATION IS NOT THE GOAL, SKULLBUSTER.
HUMILIATION OF WOLVERINE IS.
OVERREACHING HAS BEEN OUR FAILING FOR TOO LONG. IT IS ENTIRELY POSSIBLE THAT THERE IS NO KILLING WOLVERINE. HE IS A COCKROACH.
TO CONTINUE TO DO THE SAME THING EXPECTING DIFFERENT RESULTS... INSANITY.

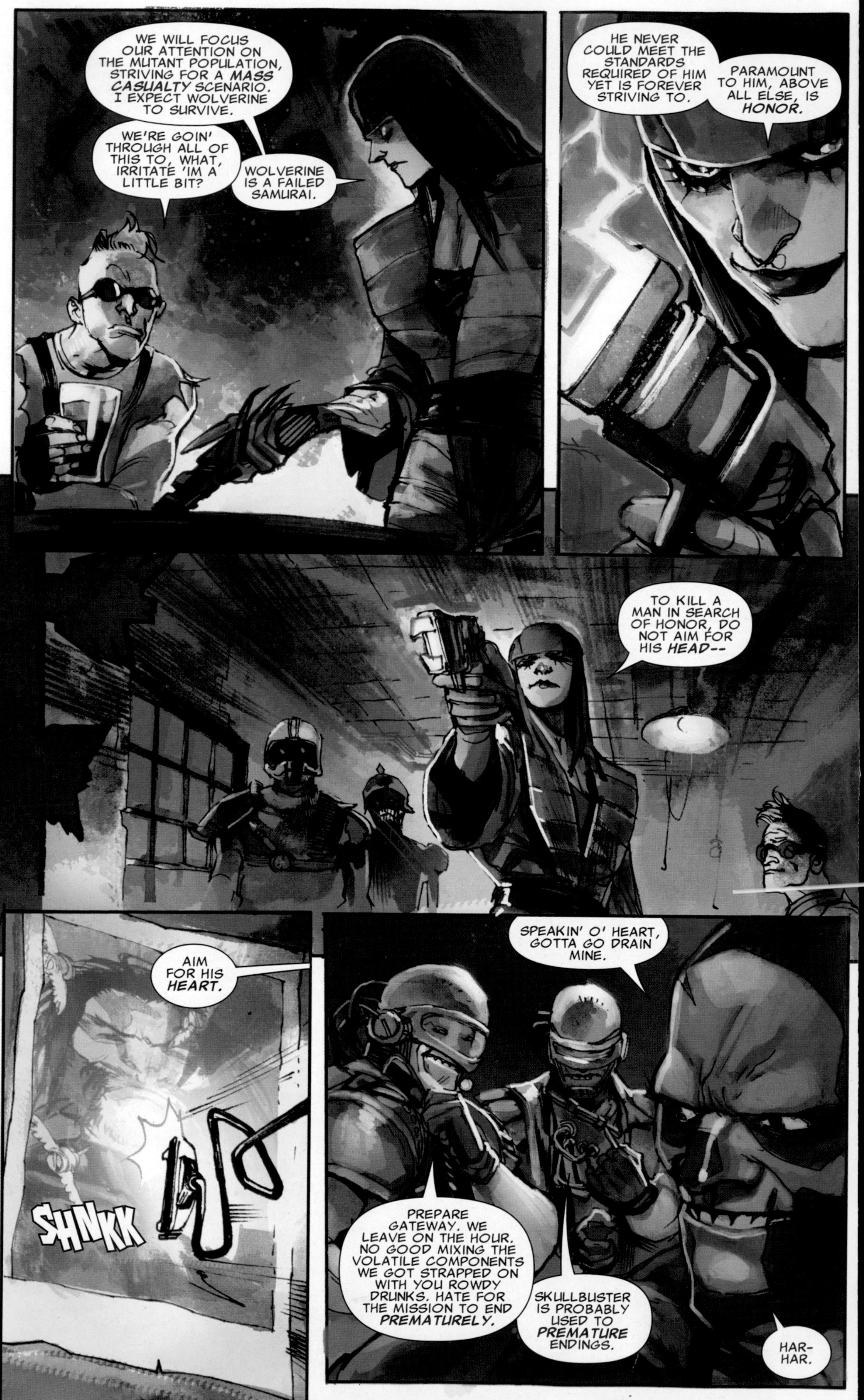

WE WILL FOCUS OUR ATTENTION ON THE MUTANT POPULATION, STRIVING FOR A MASS CASUALTY SCENARIO. I EXPECT WOLVERINE TO SURVIVE.
WE'RE GOIN' THROUGH ALL OF THIS TO, WHAT, IRRITATE 'IM A' LITTLE BIT?
WOLVERINE IS A FAILED SAMURAI.
HE NEVER COULD MEET THE STANDARDS REQUIRED OF HIM YET IS FOREVER STRIVING TO.
PARAMOUNT TO HIM, ABOVE ALL ELSE, IS HONOR.
TO KILL A MAN IN SEARCH OF HONOR, DO NOT AIM FOR HIS HEAD--
AIM FOR HIS HEART.
SHNKK
SPEAKIN' O' HEART, GOTTA GO DRAIN MINE.
PREPARE GATEWAY. WE LEAVE ON THE HOUR. NO GOOD MIXING THE VOLATILE COMPONENTS WE GOT STRAPPED ON WITH YOU ROWDY DRUNKS. HATE FOR THE MISSION TO END PREMATURELY.
SKULLBUSTER IS PROBABLY USED TO PREMATURE ENDINGS.
HAR-HAR.

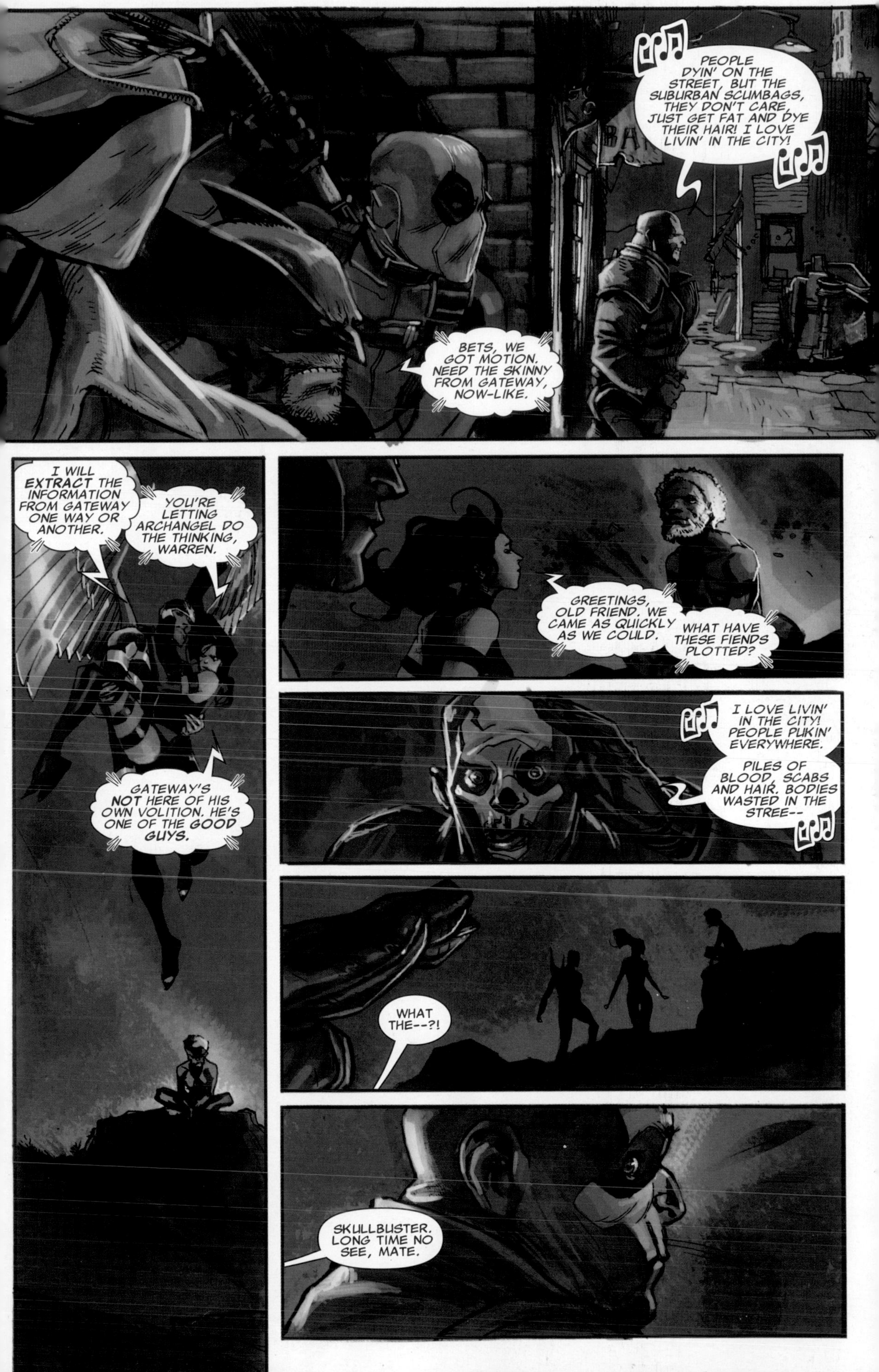
PEOPLE DYIN' ON THE STREET, BUT THE SUBURBAN SCUMBAGS, THEY DON'T CARE, JUST GET FAT AND DYE THEIR HAIR! I LOVE LIVIN' IN THE CITY!
BETS, WE GOT MOTION. NEED THE SKINNY FROM GATEWAY, NOW-LIKE.
I WILL EXTRACT THE INFORMATION FROM GATEWAY ONE WAY OR ANOTHER.
YOU'RE LETTING ARCHANGEL DO THE THINKING, WARREN.
GATEWAY'S NOT HERE OF HIS OWN VOLITION. HE'S ONE OF THE GOOD GUYS.
GREETINGS, OLD FRIEND. WE CAME AS QUICKLY AS WE COULD.
WHAT HAVE THESE FIENDS PLOTTED?
I LOVE LIVIN' IN THE CITY! PEOPLE PUKIN' EVERYWHERE.
PILES OF BLOOD, SCABS AND HAIR. BODIES WASTED IN THE STREE--
WHAT THE--?!
SKULLBUSTER. LONG TIME NO SEE, MATE.

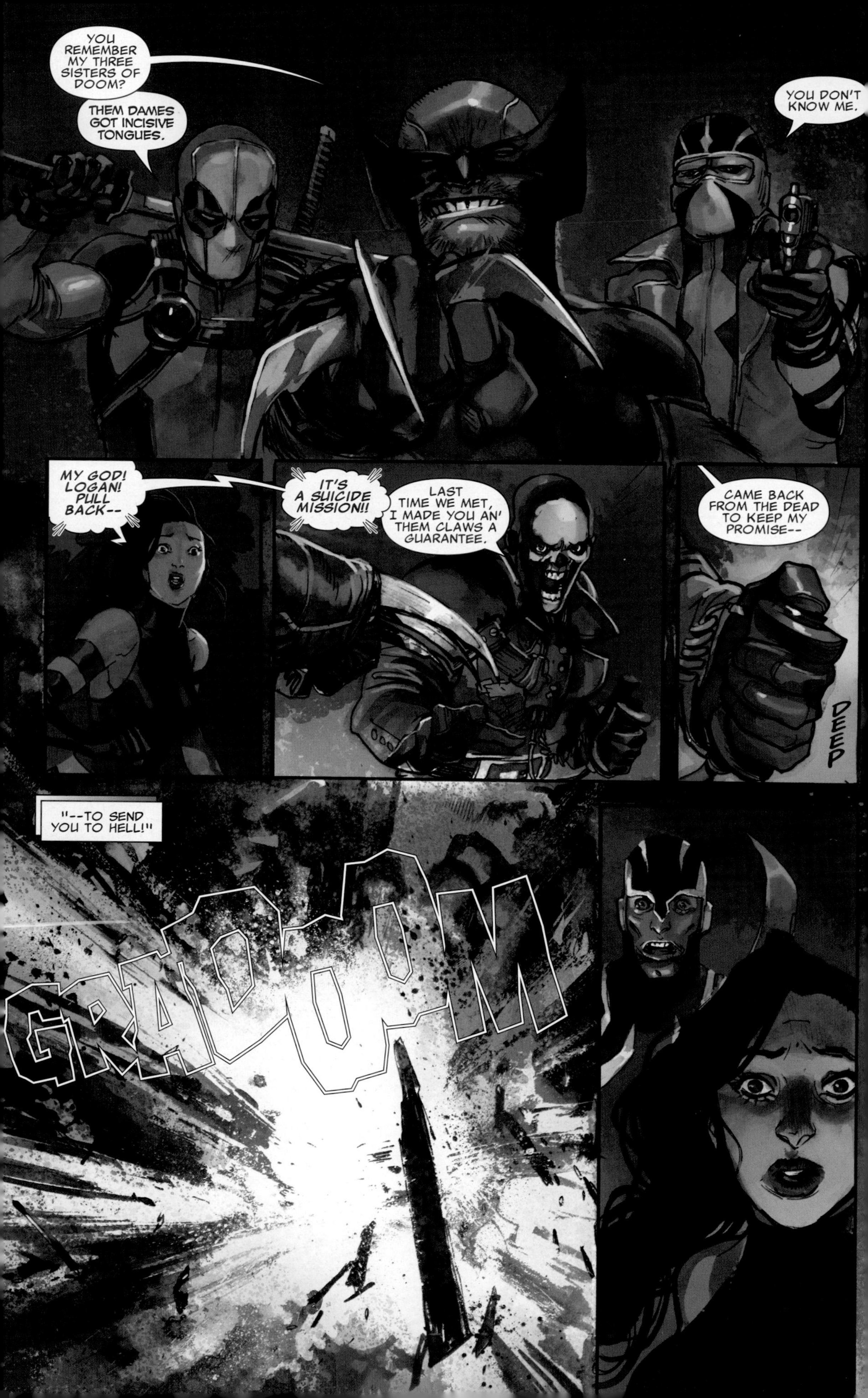
YOU REMEMBER MY THREE SISTERS OF DOOM?
THEM DAMES GOT INCISIVE TONGUES.
YOU DON'T KNOW ME.
MY GOD! LOGAN! PULL BACK--
IT'S A SUICIDE MISSION!!
LAST TIME WE MET, I MADE YOU AN' THEM CLAWS A GUARANTEE.
CAME BACK FROM THE DEAD TO KEEP MY PROMISE--
DEEP
"--TO SEND YOU TO HELL!"
GRADOOOM

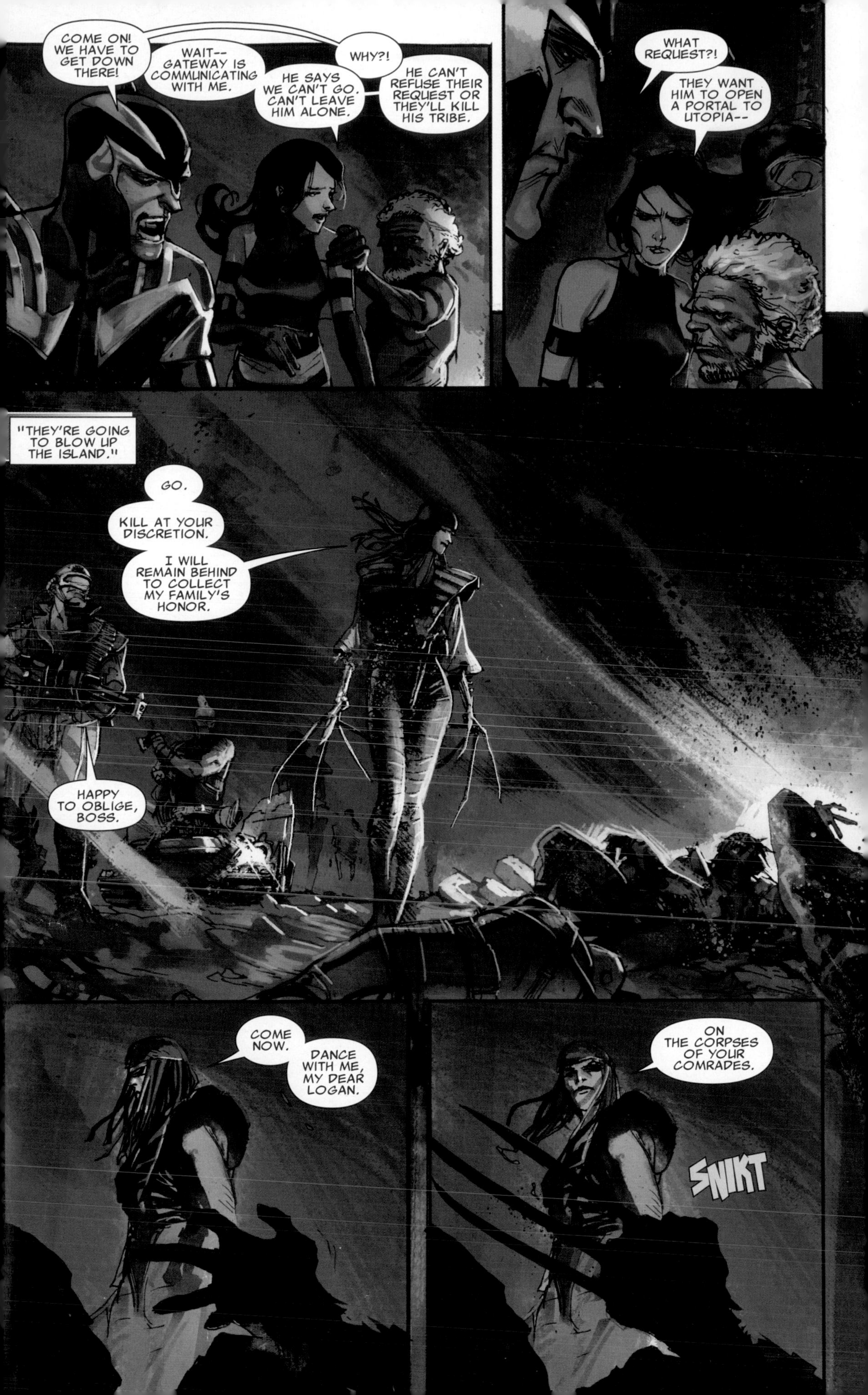
COME ON! WE HAVE TO GET DOWN THERE!
WAIT-- GATEWAY IS COMMUNICATING WITH ME.
WHY?!
HE SAYS WE CAN'T GO. CAN'T LEAVE HIM ALONE.
HE CAN'T REFUSE THEIR REQUEST OR THEY'LL KILL HIS TRIBE.
WHAT REQUEST?!
THEY WANT HIM TO OPEN A PORTAL TO UTOPIA--
"THEY'RE GOING TO BLOW UP THE ISLAND."
GO.
KILL AT YOUR DISCRETION.
I WILL REMAIN BEHIND TO COLLECT MY FAMILY'S HONOR.
HAPPY TO OBLIGE, BOSS.
COME NOW.
DANCE WITH ME, MY DEAR LOGAN.
ON THE CORPSES OF YOUR COMRADES.
SNIKT

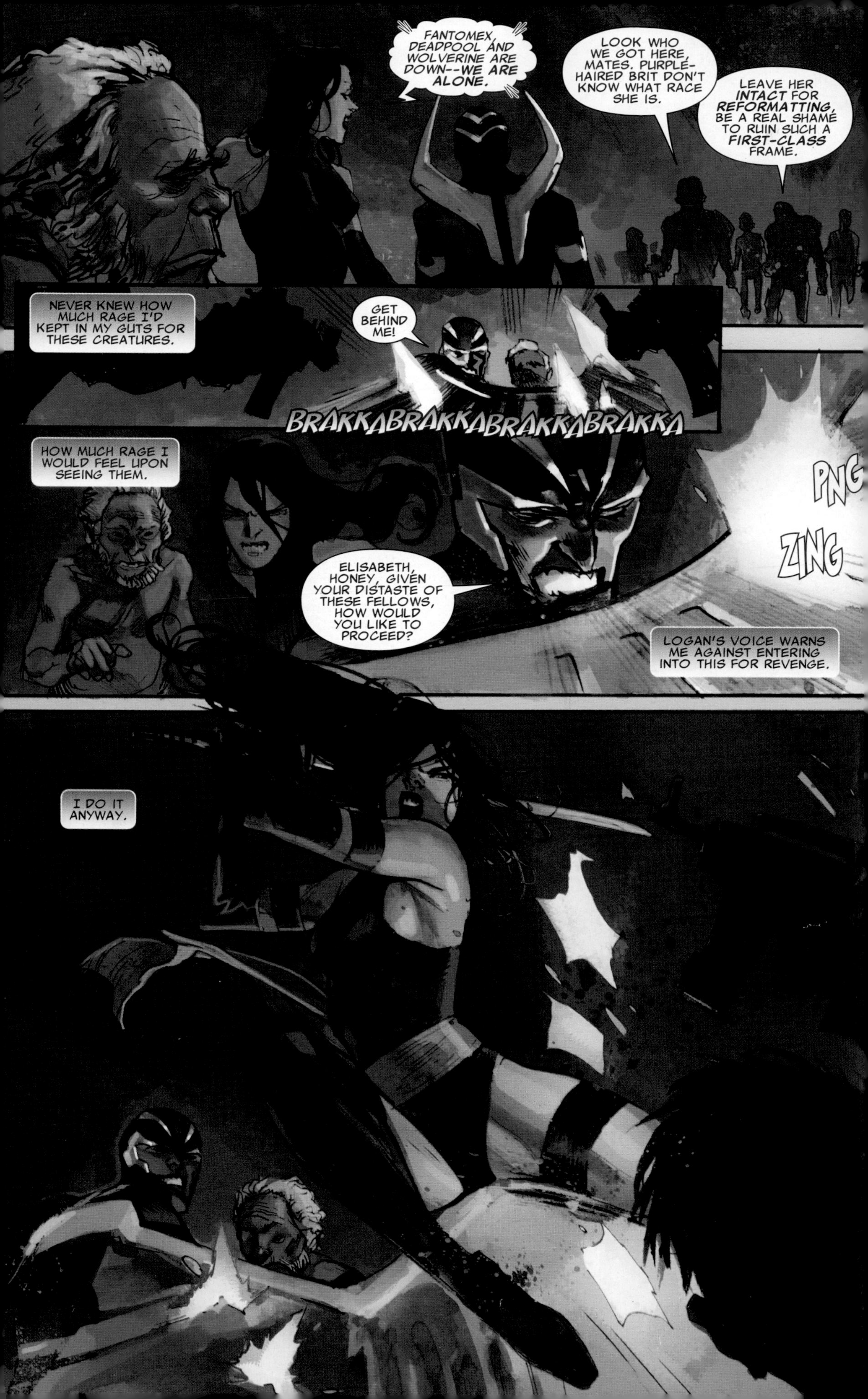
FANTOMEX, DEADPOOL AND WOLVERINE ARE DOWN--WE ARE ALONE.
LOOK WHO WE GOT HERE, MATES. PURPLE-HAIRED BRIT DON'T KNOW WHAT RACE SHE IS.
LEAVE HER INTACT FOR REFORMATTING, BE A REAL SHAME TO RUIN SUCH A FIRST-CLASS FRAME.
NEVER KNEW HOW MUCH RAGE I'D KEPT IN MY GUTS FOR THESE CREATURES.
GET BEHIND ME!
BRAKKABRAKKABRAKKABRAKKA
HOW MUCH RAGE I WOULD FEEL UPON SEEING THEM.
PNG
ZING
ELISABETH, HONEY, GIVEN YOUR DISTASTE OF THESE FELLOWS, HOW WOULD YOU LIKE TO PROCEED?
LOGAN'S VOICE WARNS ME AGAINST ENTERING INTO THIS FOR REVENGE.
I DO IT ANYWAY.

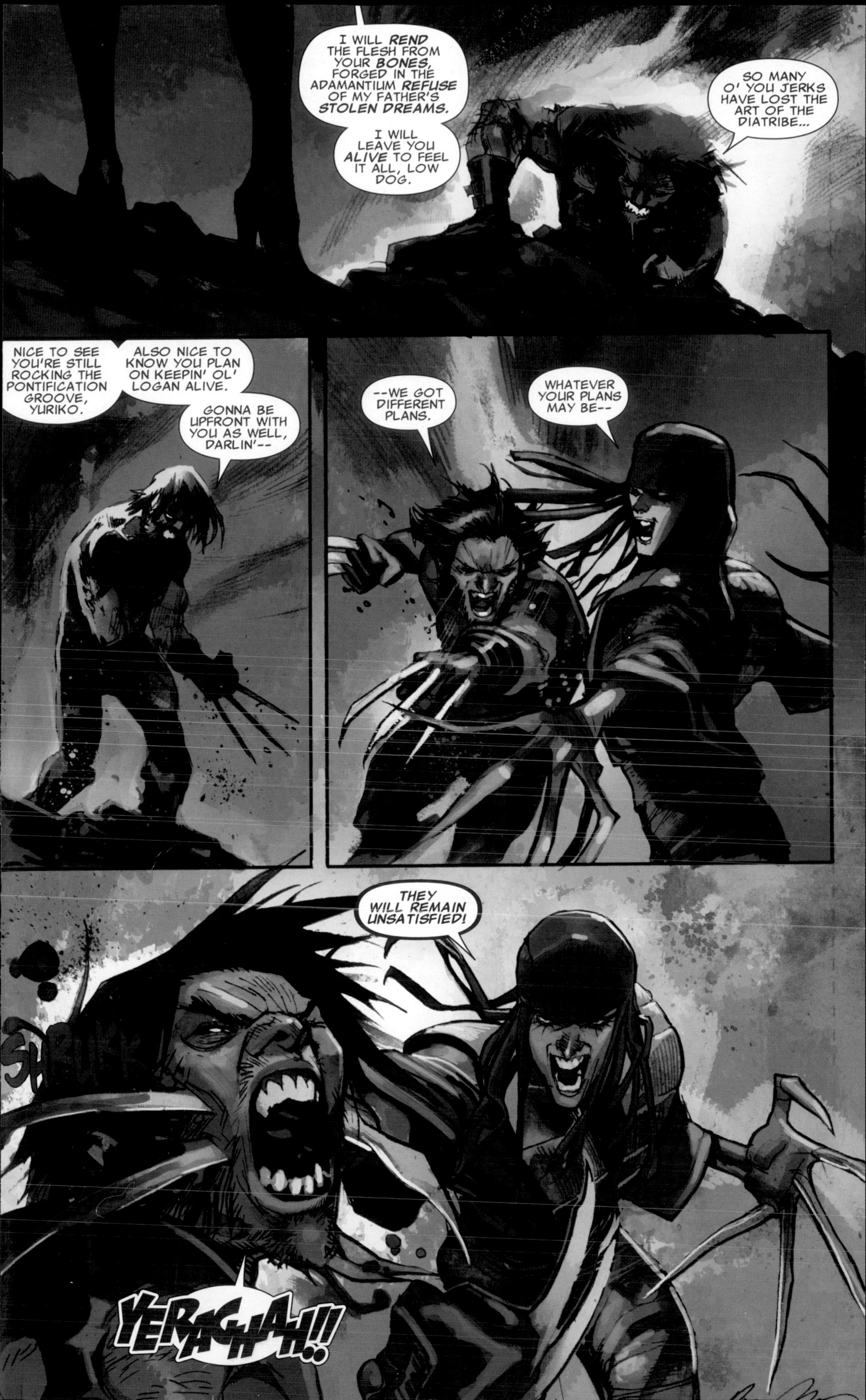
I WILL REND THE FLESH FROM YOUR BONES, FORGED IN THE ADAMANTIUM REFUSE OF MY FATHER'S STOLEN DREAMS.
I WILL LEAVE YOU ALIVE TO FEEL IT ALL, LOW DOG.
SO MANY O' YOU JERKS HAVE LOST THE ART OF THE DIATRIBE...
NICE TO SEE YOU'RE STILL ROCKING THE PONTIFICATION GROOVE, YURIKO.
ALSO NICE TO KNOW YOU PLAN ON KEEPIN' OL' LOGAN ALIVE.
GONNA BE UPFRONT WITH YOU AS WELL, DARLIN'--
--WE GOT DIFFERENT PLANS.
WHATEVER YOUR PLANS MAY BE--
THEY WILL REMAIN UNSATISFIED!
YERAGHAH!!

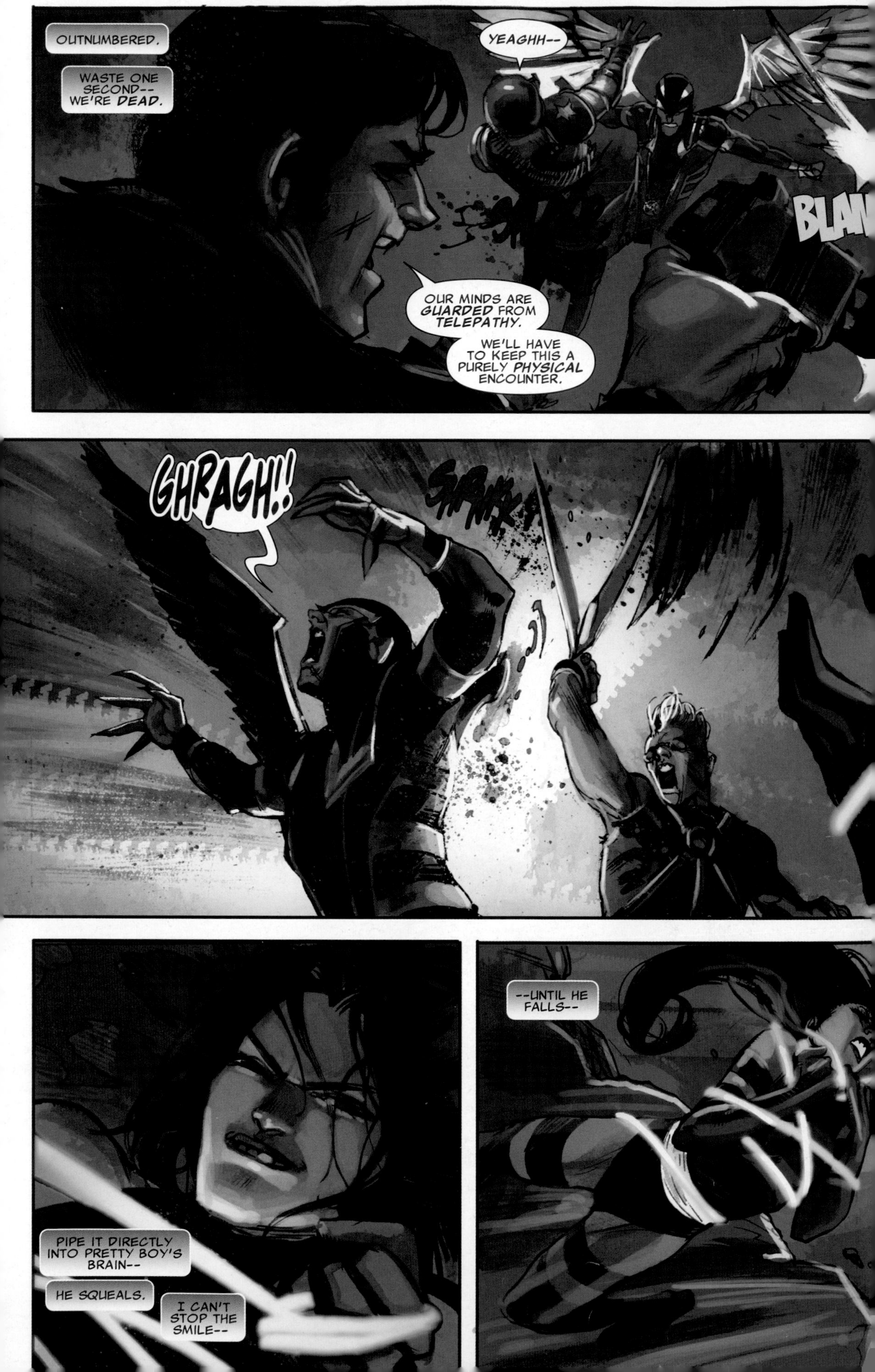
OUTNUMBERED.
WASTE ONE SECOND-- WE'RE DEAD.
YEAGHH--
BLAM
OUR MINDS ARE GUARDED FROM TELEPATHY.
WE'LL HAVE TO KEEP THIS A PURELY PHYSICAL ENCOUNTER.
GHRAGH!!
PIPE IT DIRECTLY INTO PRETTY BOY'S BRAIN--
HE SQUEALS.
I CAN'T STOP THE SMILE--
--UNTIL HE FALLS--

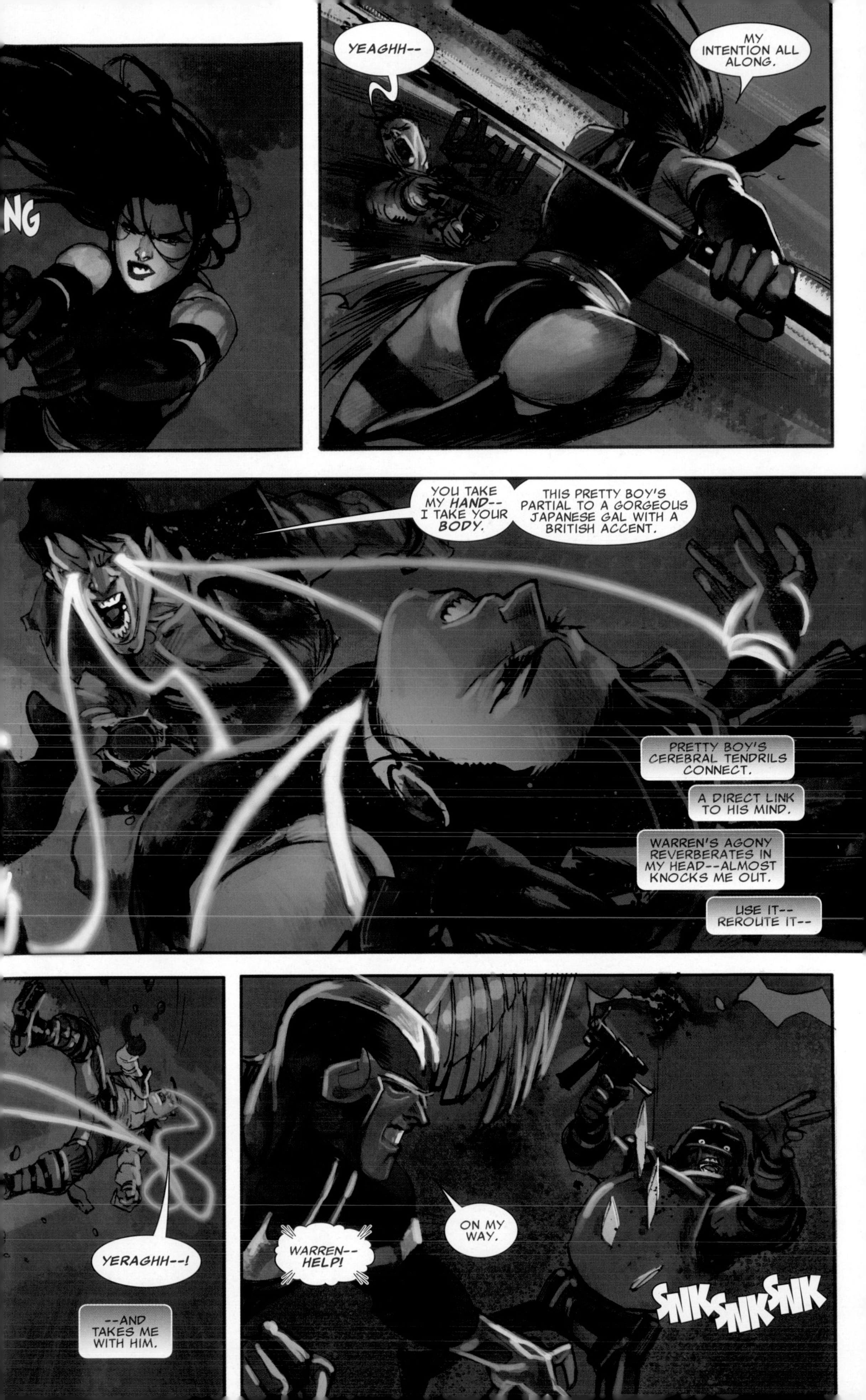
YEAGHH--
MY INTENTION ALL ALONG.
YOU TAKE MY HAND-- I TAKE YOUR BODY.
THIS PRETTY BOY'S PARTIAL TO A GORGEOUS JAPANESE GAL WITH A BRITISH ACCENT.
PRETTY BOY'S CEREBRAL TENDRILS CONNECT.
A DIRECT LINK TO HIS MIND.
WARREN'S AGONY REVERBERATES IN MY HEAD--ALMOST KNOCKS ME OUT.
USE IT-- REROUTE IT--
YERAGHH--!
--AND TAKES ME WITH HIM.
WARREN-- HELP!
ON MY WAY.
SNIKSNIKSNIK

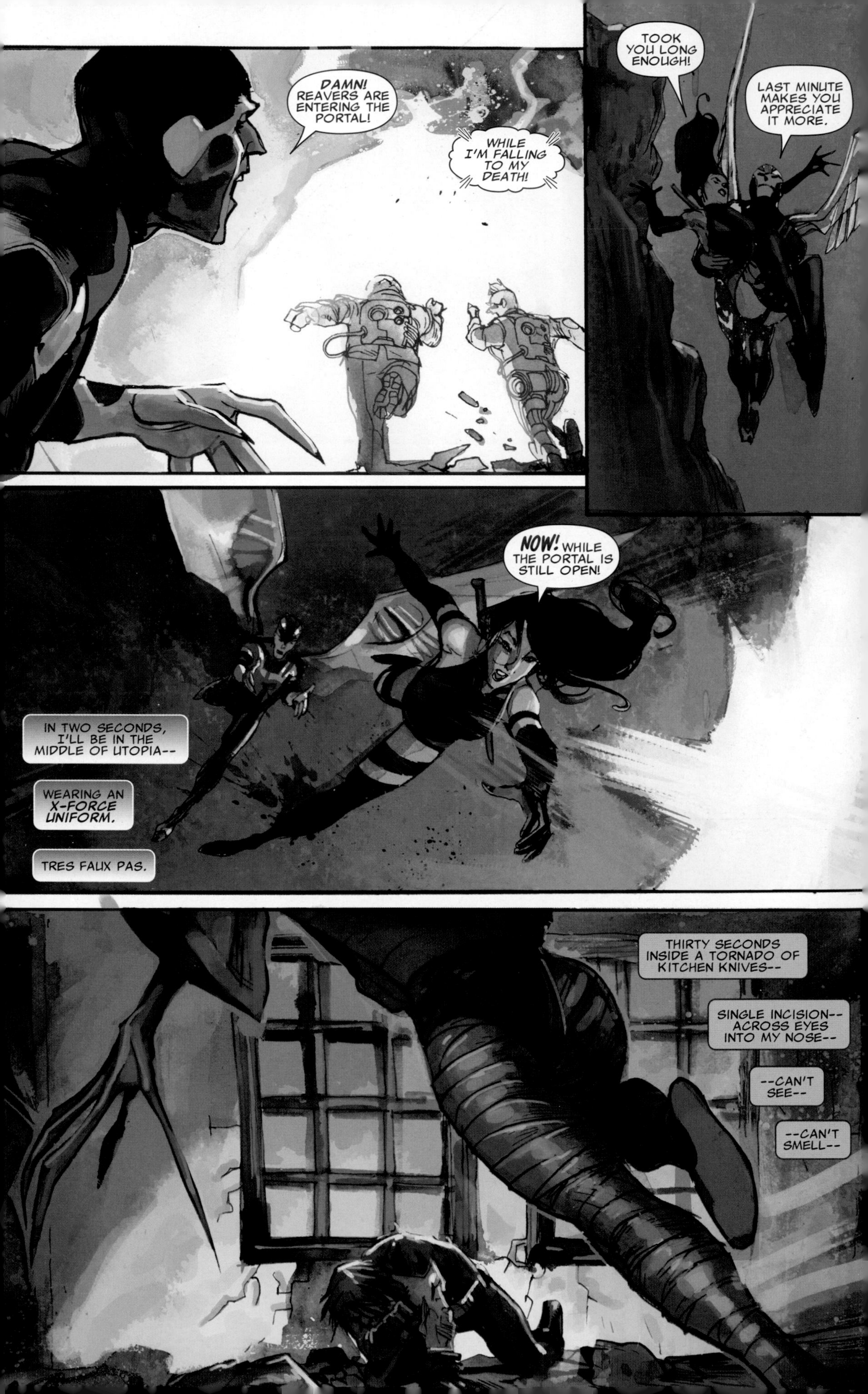
DAMN! REAVERS ARE ENTERING THE PORTAL!
WHILE I'M FALLING TO MY DEATH!
TOOK YOU LONG ENOUGH!
LAST MINUTE MAKES YOU APPRECIATE IT MORE.
NOW! WHILE THE PORTAL IS STILL OPEN!
IN TWO SECONDS, I'LL BE IN THE MIDDLE OF UTOPIA--
WEARING AN X-FORCE UNIFORM.
TRES FAUX PAS.
THIRTY SECONDS INSIDE A TORNADO OF KITCHEN KNIVES--
SINGLE INCISION--ACROSS EYES INTO MY NOSE--
--CAN'T SEE--
--CAN'T SMELL--

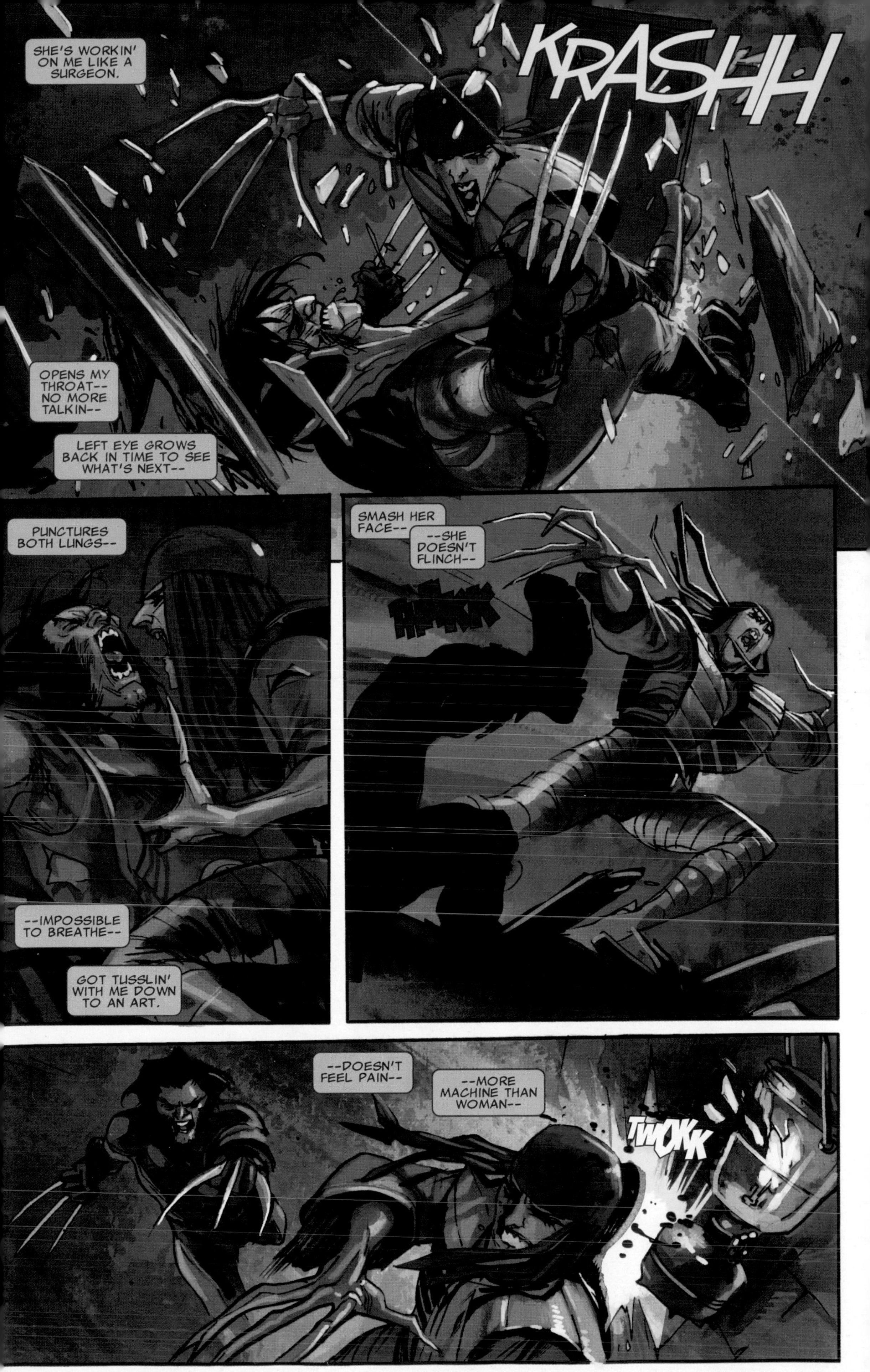
SHE'S WORKIN' ON ME LIKE A SURGEON.
KRASHH
OPENS MY THROAT--NO MORE TALKIN--
LEFT EYE GROWS BACK IN TIME TO SEE WHAT'S NEXT--
PUNCTURES BOTH LUNGS--
--IMPOSSIBLE TO BREATHE--
GOT TUSSLIN' WITH ME DOWN TO AN ART.
SMASH HER FACE--
--SHE DOESN'T FLINCH--
--DOESN'T FEEL PAIN--
--MORE MACHINE THAN WOMAN--
TWOKK

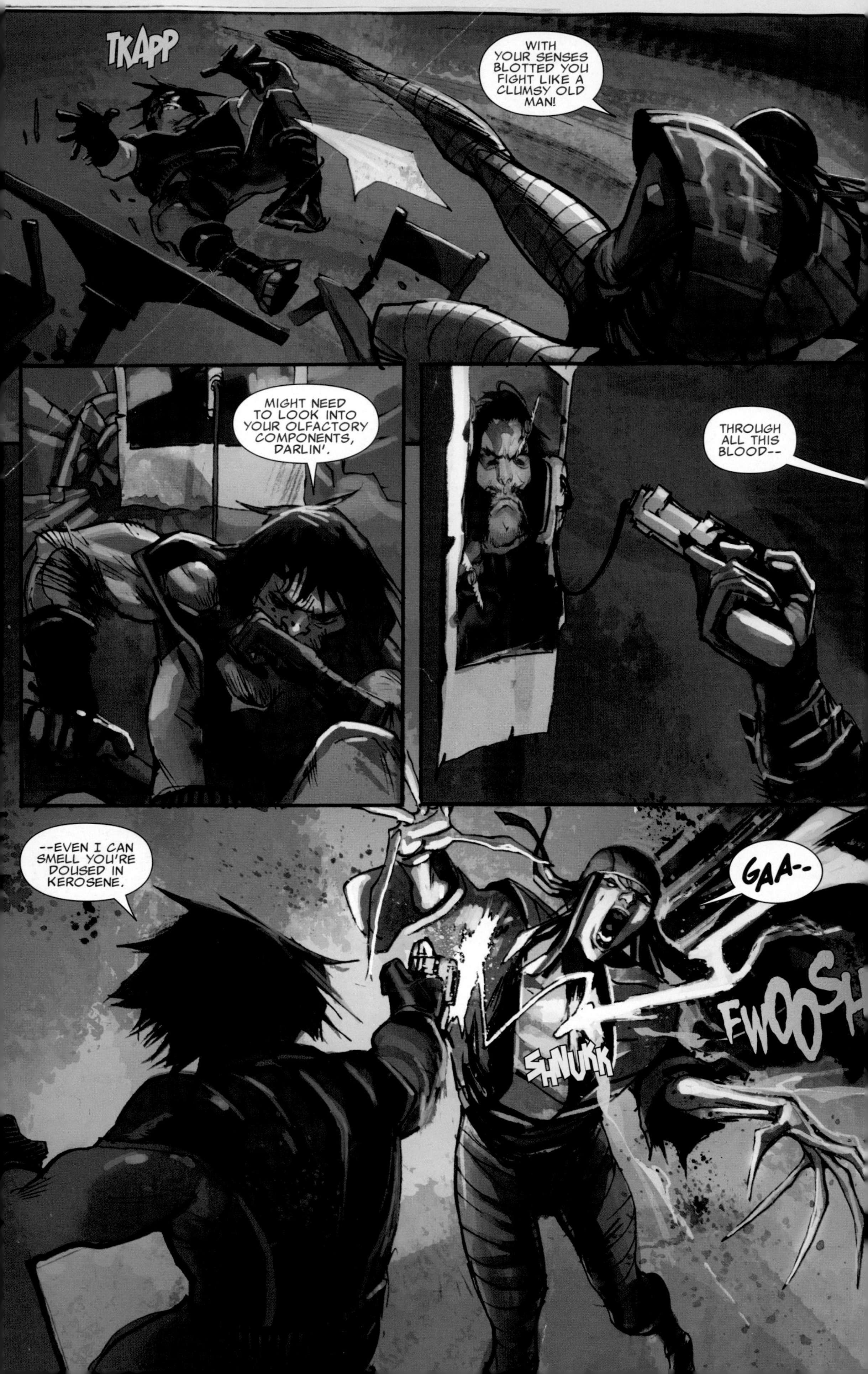
TKAPP
WITH YOUR SENSES BLOTTED YOU FIGHT LIKE A CLUMSY OLD MAN!
MIGHT NEED TO LOOK INTO YOUR OLFACTORY COMPONENTS, DARLIN'.
THROUGH ALL THIS BLOOD--
--EVEN I CAN SMELL YOU'RE DOUSED IN KEROSENE.
GAA--
FWOOSH
SHNUKK

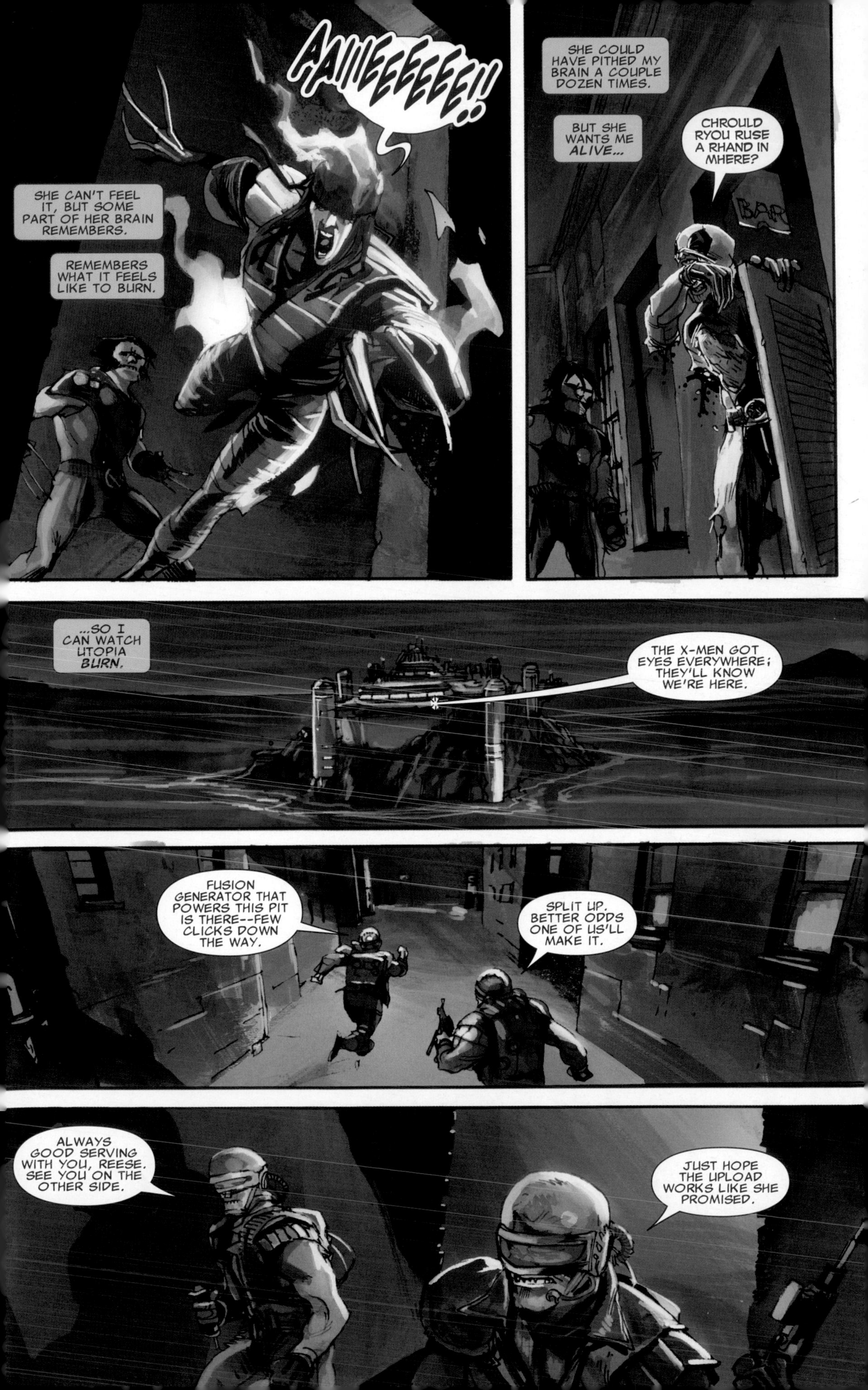
AAIIEEEEEE!!
SHE CAN'T FEEL IT, BUT SOME PART OF HER BRAIN REMEMBERS.
REMEMBERS WHAT IT FEELS LIKE TO BURN.
SHE COULD HAVE PITHED MY BRAIN A COUPLE DOZEN TIMES.
BUT SHE WANTS ME ALIVE...
CHROULD RYOU RUSE A RHAND IN MHERE?
BAR
...SO I CAN WATCH UTOPIA BURN.
THE X-MEN GOT EYES EVERYWHERE; THEY'LL KNOW WE'RE HERE.
FUSION GENERATOR THAT POWERS THIS PIT IS THERE--FEW CLICKS DOWN THE WAY.
SPLIT UP. BETTER ODDS ONE OF US'LL MAKE IT.
ALWAYS GOOD SERVING WITH YOU, REESE. SEE YOU ON THE OTHER SIDE.
JUST HOPE THE UPLOAD WORKS LIKE SHE PROMISED.

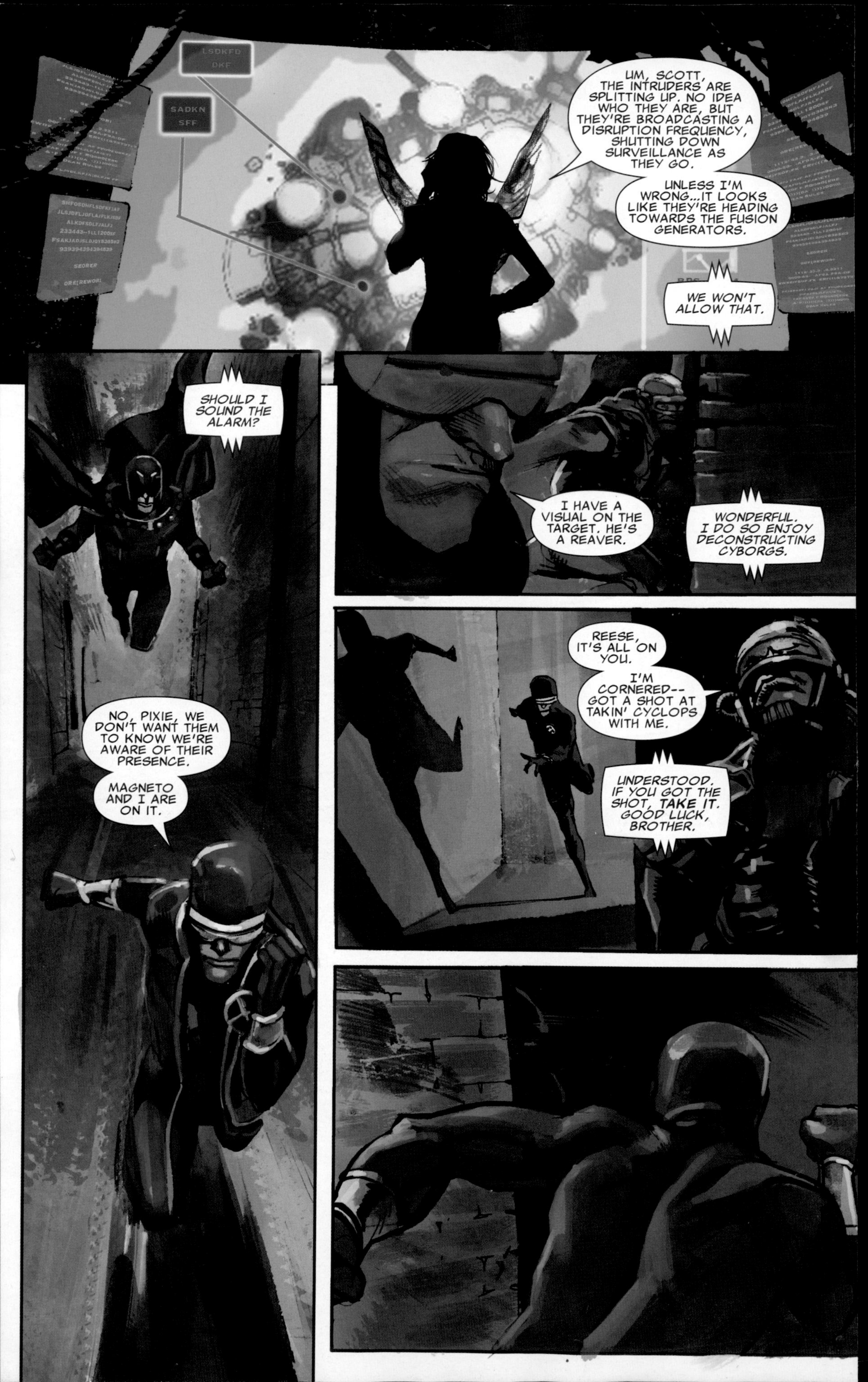

LSDKFD DKF
SADKN SFF
UM, SCOTT, THE INTRUDERS ARE SPLITTING UP. NO IDEA WHO THEY ARE, BUT THEY'RE BROADCASTING A DISRUPTION FREQUENCY, SHUTTING DOWN SURVEILLANCE AS THEY GO.
UNLESS I'M WRONG...IT LOOKS LIKE THEY'RE HEADING TOWARDS THE FUSION GENERATORS.
WE WON'T ALLOW THAT.
SHOULD I SOUND THE ALARM?
NO, PIXIE, WE DON'T WANT THEM TO KNOW WE'RE AWARE OF THEIR PRESENCE.
MAGNETO AND I ARE ON IT.
I HAVE A VISUAL ON THE TARGET. HE'S A REAVER.
WONDERFUL. I DO SO ENJOY DECONSTRUCTING CYBORGS.
REESE, IT'S ALL ON YOU.
I'M CORNERED-- GOT A SHOT AT TAKIN' CYCLOPS WITH ME.
UNDERSTOOD. IF YOU GOT THE SHOT, TAKE IT. GOOD LUCK, BROTHER.

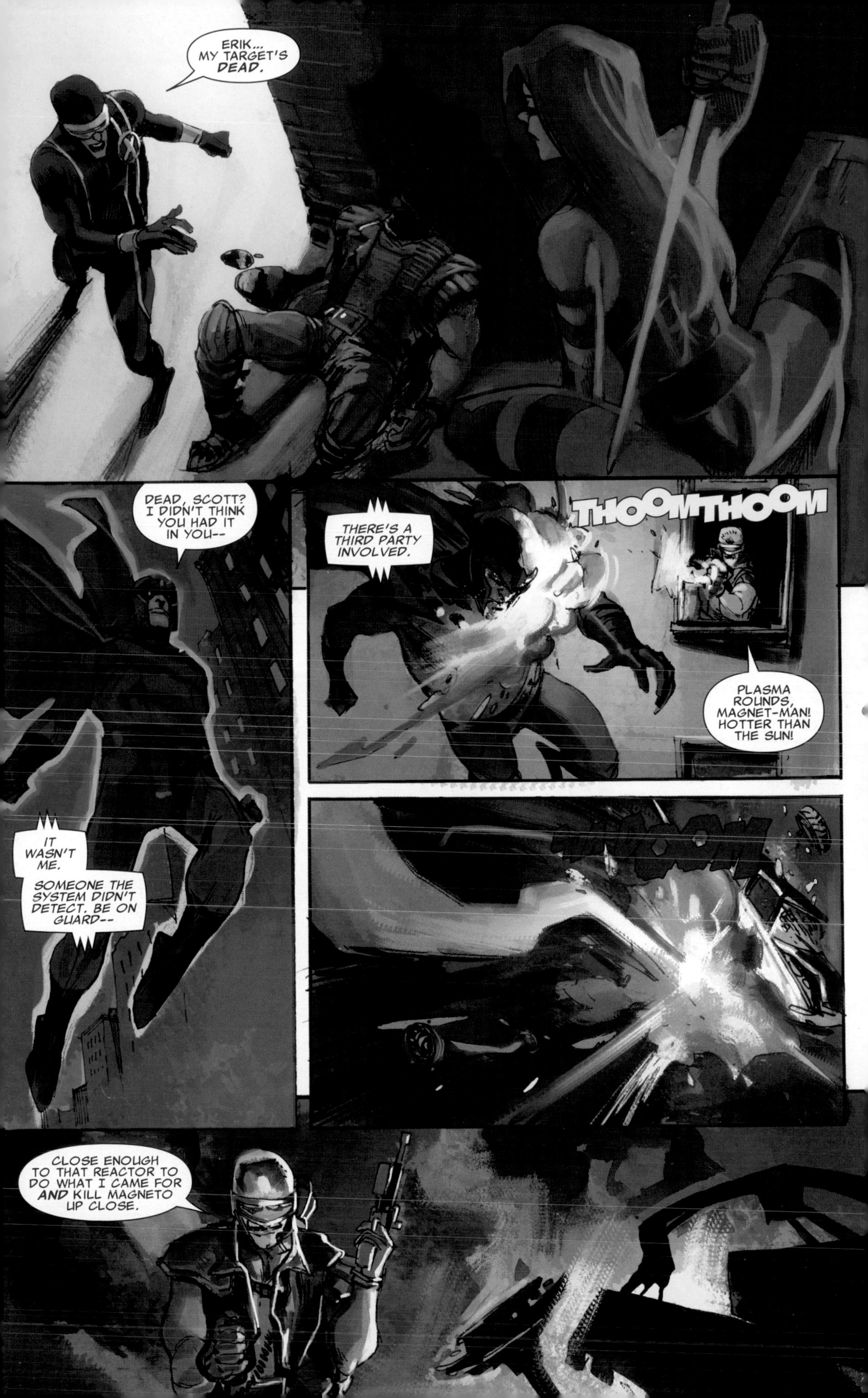
ERIK... MY TARGET'S DEAD.
DEAD, SCOTT? I DIDN'T THINK YOU HAD IT IN YOU--
IT WASN'T ME.
SOMEONE THE SYSTEM DIDN'T DETECT. BE ON GUARD--
THERE'S A THIRD PARTY INVOLVED.
THOOMTHOOM
PLASMA ROUNDS, MAGNET-MAN! HOTTER THAN THE SUN!
CLOSE ENOUGH TO THAT REACTOR TO DO WHAT I CAME FOR AND KILL MAGNETO UP CLOSE.

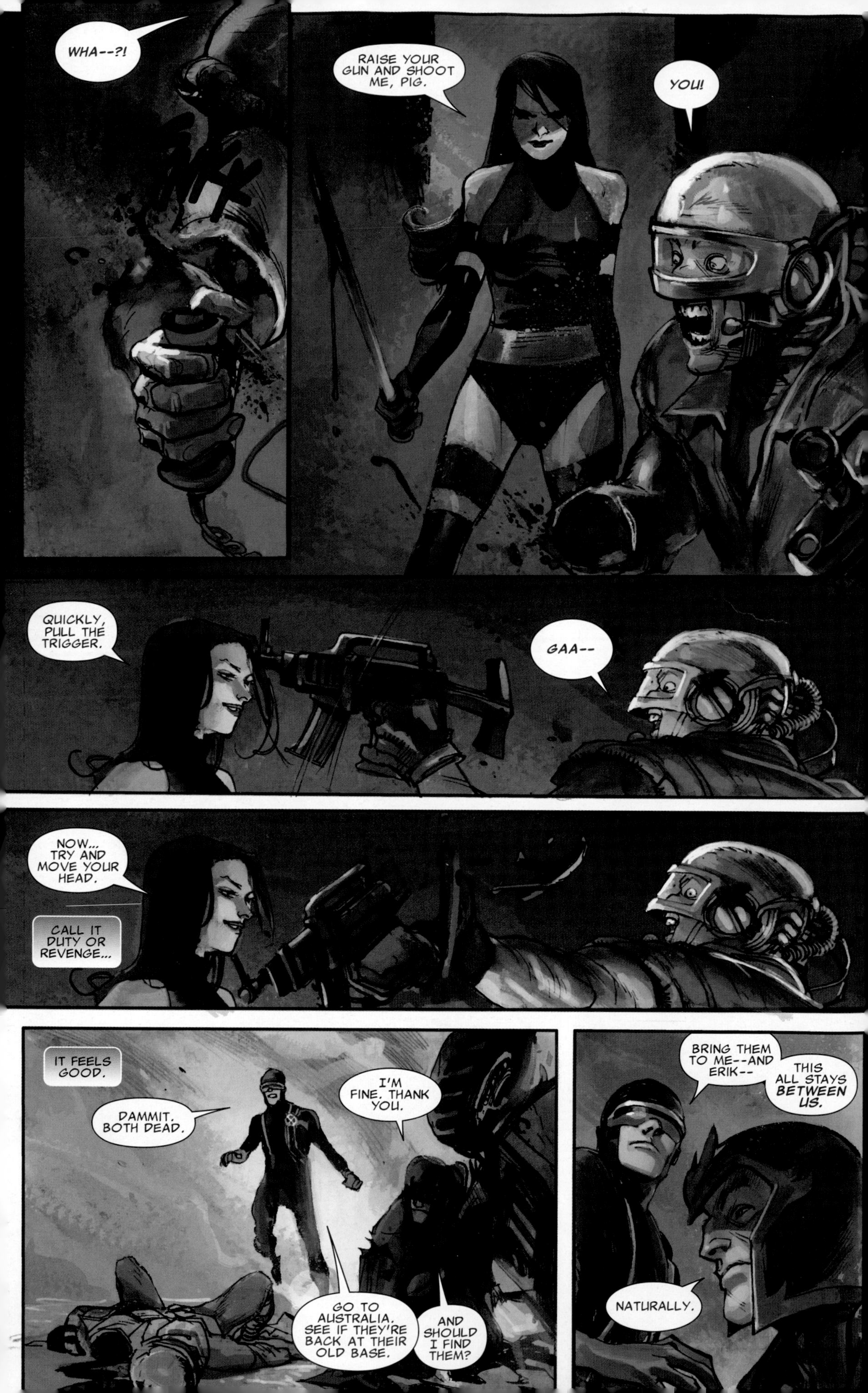
WHA--?!
RAISE YOUR GUN AND SHOOT ME, PIG.
YOU!
QUICKLY, PULL THE TRIGGER.
GAA--
NOW... TRY AND MOVE YOUR HEAD.
CALL IT DUTY OR REVENGE...
IT FEELS GOOD.
DAMMIT. BOTH DEAD.
I'M FINE. THANK YOU.
GO TO AUSTRALIA. SEE IF THEY'RE BACK AT THEIR OLD BASE.
AND SHOULD I FIND THEM?
BRING THEM TO ME--AND ERIK--
THIS ALL STAYS BETWEEN US.
NATURALLY.

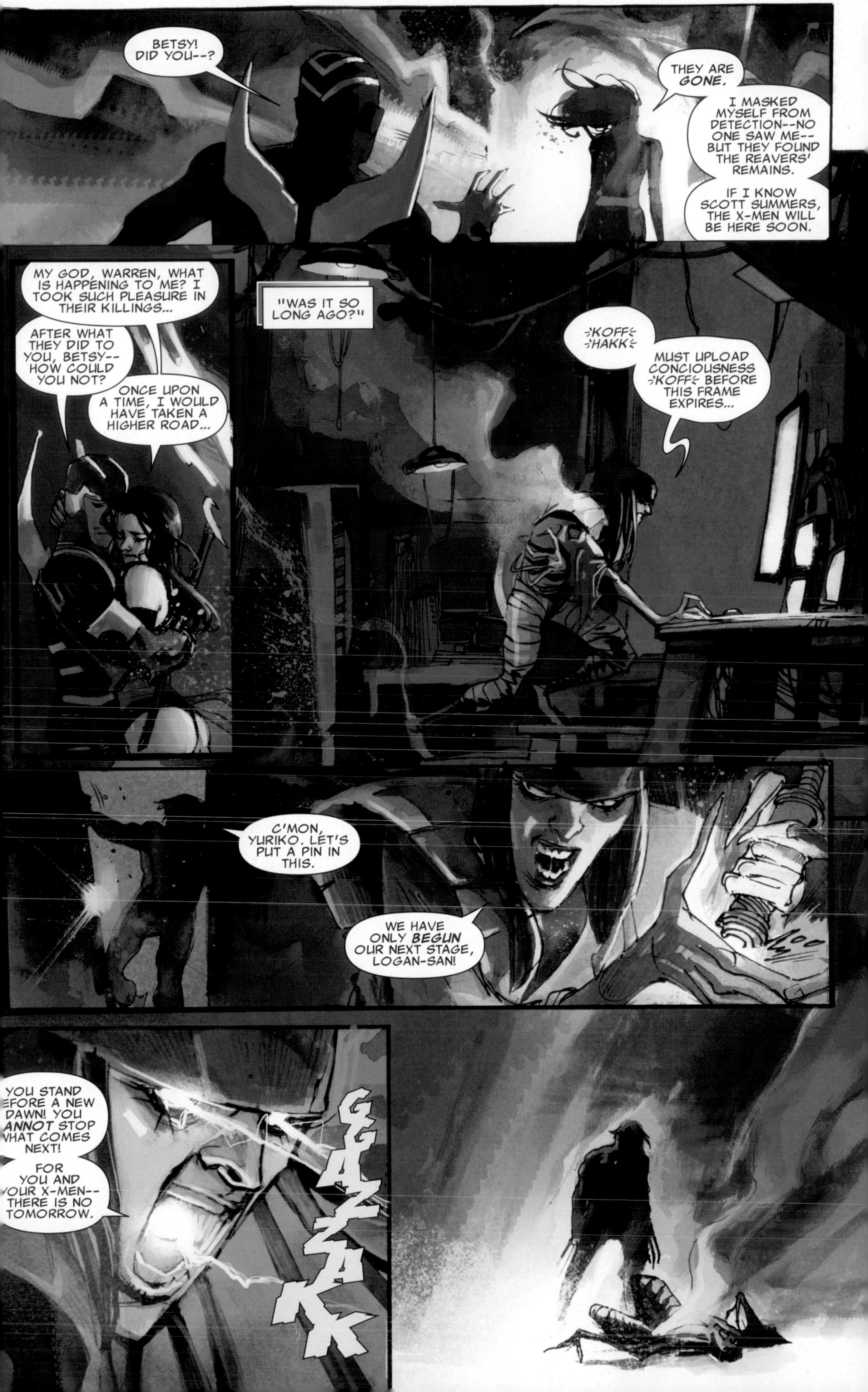

BETSY! DID YOU--?
THEY ARE GONE.
I MASKED MYSELF FROM DETECTION--NO ONE SAW ME--BUT THEY FOUND THE REAVERS' REMAINS.
IF I KNOW SCOTT SUMMERS, THE X-MEN WILL BE HERE SOON.
MY GOD, WARREN, WHAT IS HAPPENING TO ME? I TOOK SUCH PLEASURE IN THEIR KILLINGS...
AFTER WHAT THEY DID TO YOU, BETSY--HOW COULD YOU NOT?
ONCE UPON A TIME, I WOULD HAVE TAKEN A HIGHER ROAD...
"WAS IT SO LONG AGO?"
KOFF HAKK
MUST UPLOAD CONCIOUSNESS KOFF BEFORE THIS FRAME EXPIRES...
C'MON, YURIKO. LET'S PUT A PIN IN THIS.
WE HAVE ONLY BEGUN OUR NEXT STAGE, LOGAN-SAN!
YOU STAND BEFORE A NEW DAWN! YOU CANNOT STOP WHAT COMES NEXT!
FOR YOU AND YOUR X-MEN--THERE IS NO TOMORROW.
GGAZZAKK

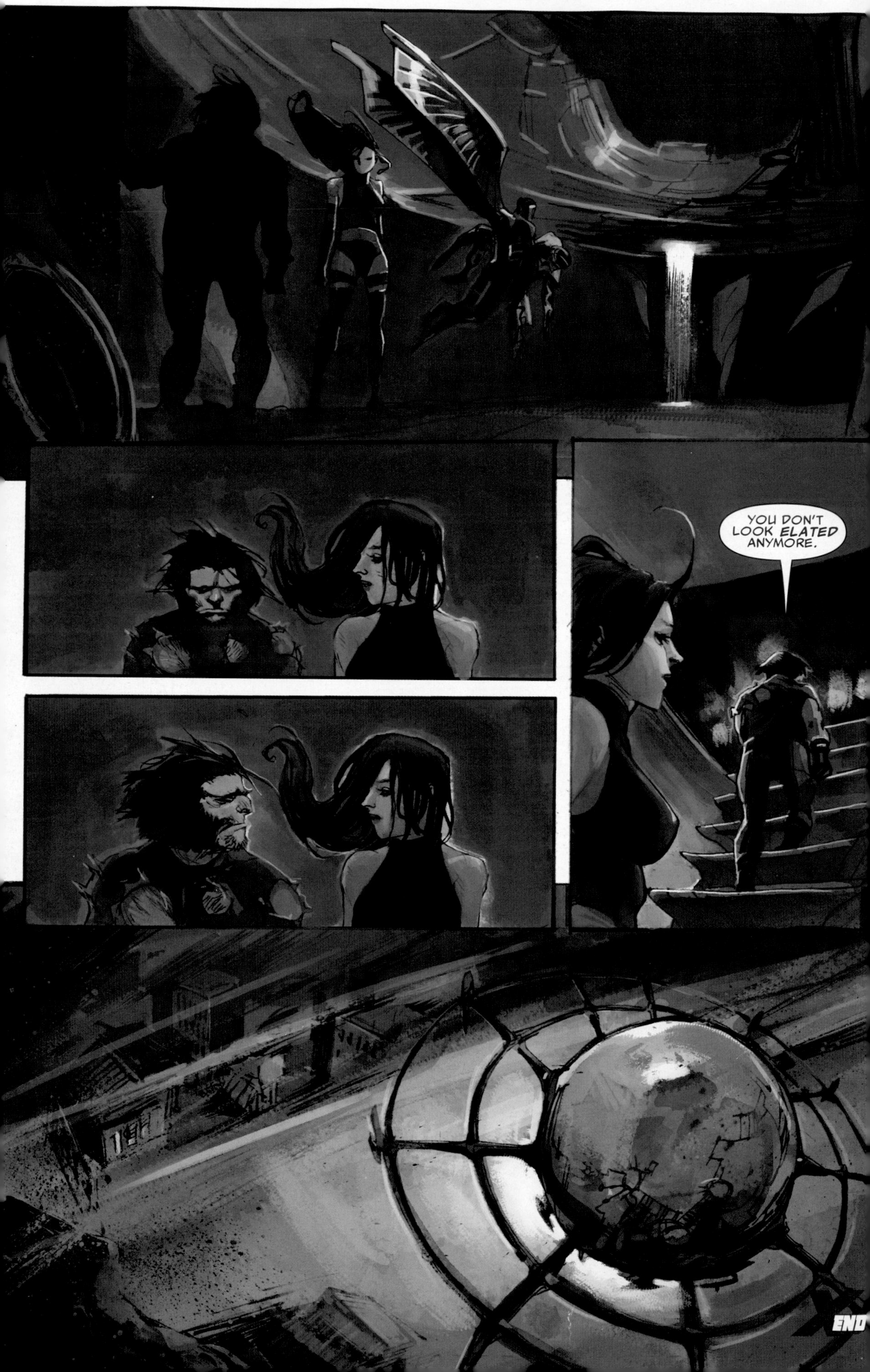
YOU DON'T LOOK ELATED ANYMORE.
END

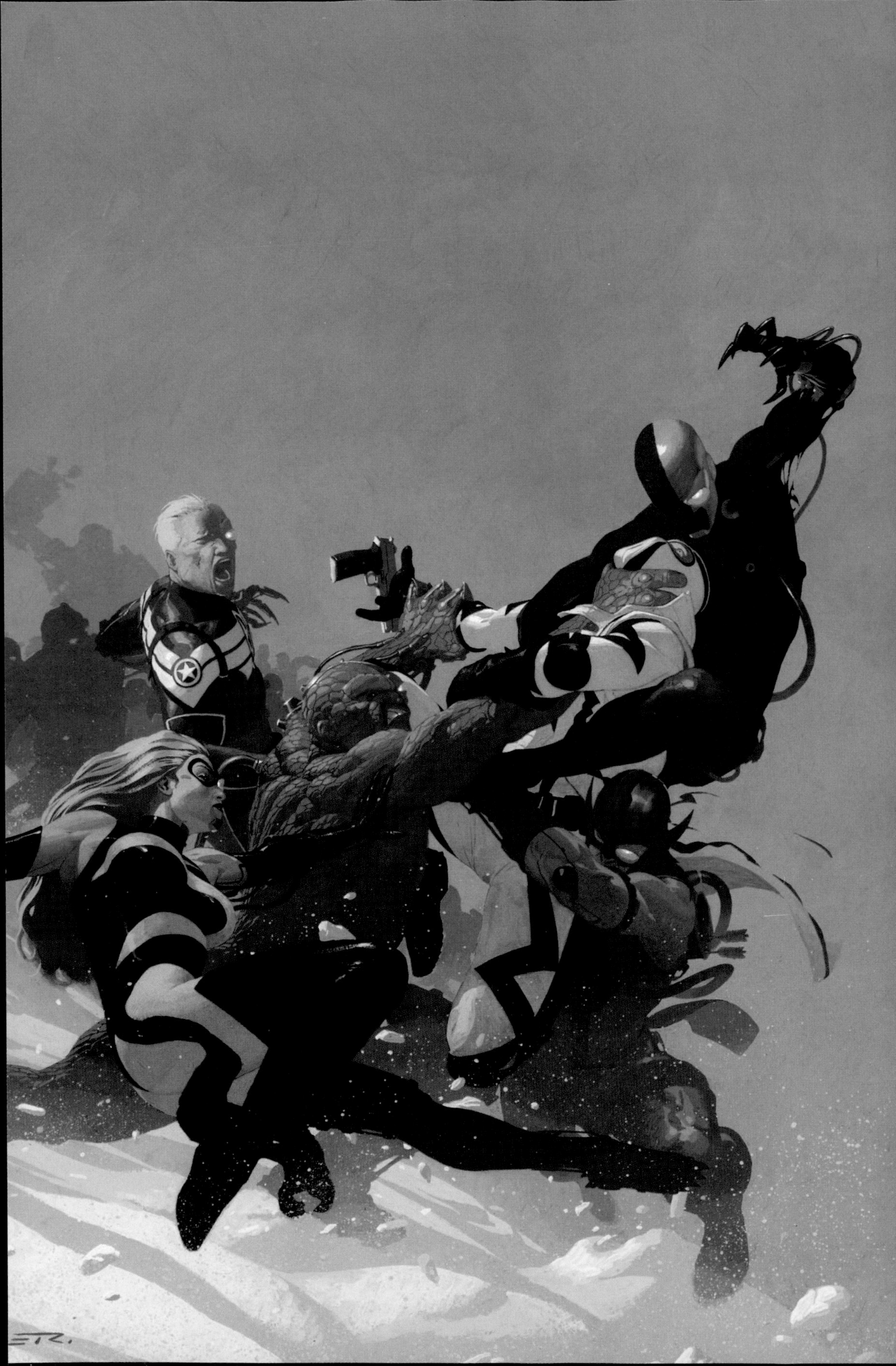

DEATHLOK NATION
CHAPTER 01

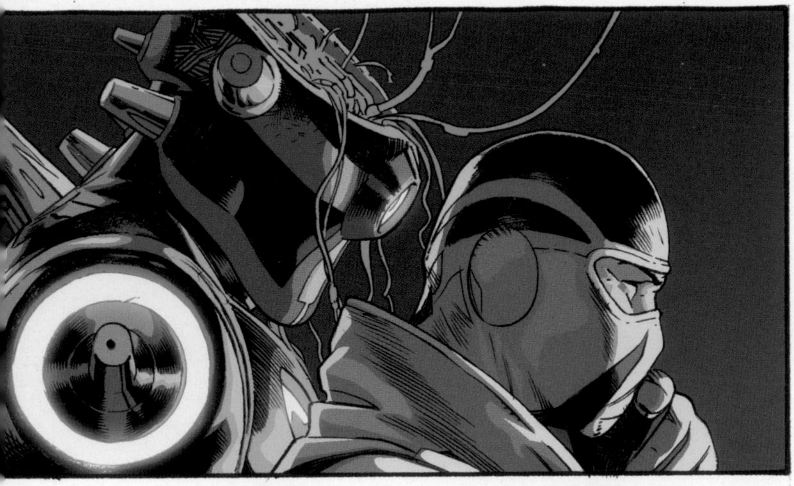

I, TOO, WAS BORN IN *THE WORLD.*

RAISED IN RAPIDLY ADVANCING UNNATURAL TIME.

WHILE I GREW TO ADULTHOOD-- ONLY A MONTH PASSED OUTSIDE.

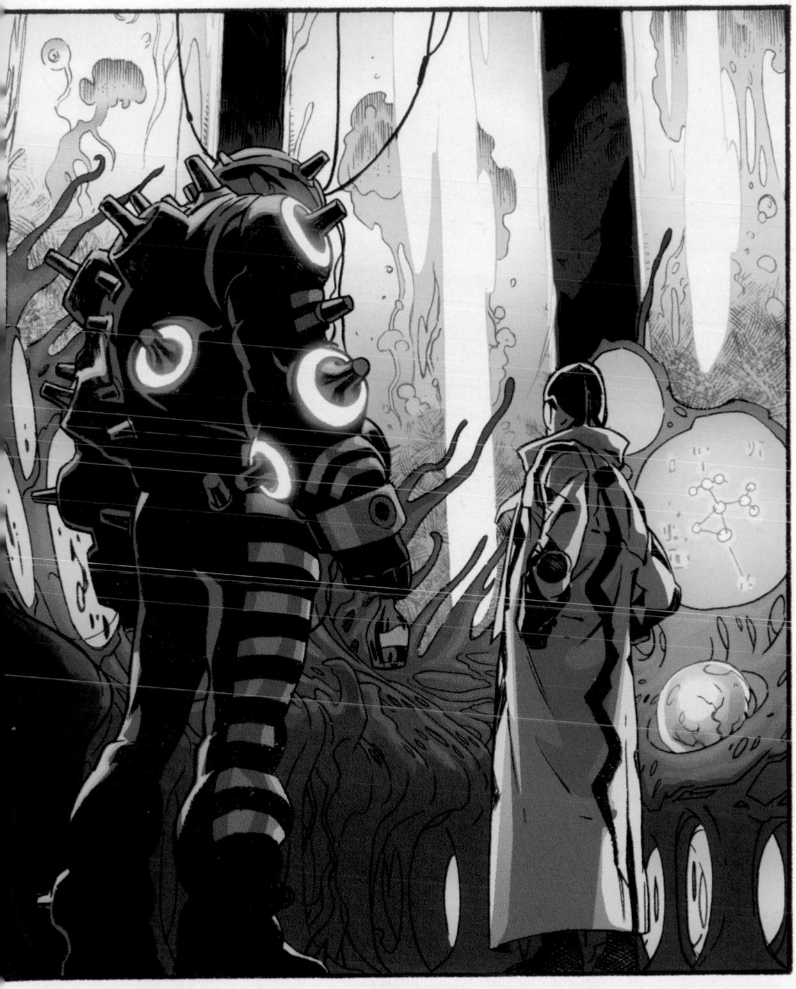

TIME IN THE WORLD IS ANALOGOUS TO WATER. A FISH TANK WHERE TIME'S TEMPERATURE IS CONTROLLED IN ORDER TO MANIPULATE THE EVOLUTION OF THE FISH.

IF HOT ENOUGH, TIME BOILS OVER,--FLOWING UNCONTROLLABLY IN ALL DIRECTIONS.

IN MY ABSENCE SOMEONE LEFT THE KETTLE ON.

A MILLION YEARS HAVE PASSED HERE SINCE MY LAST VISIT.

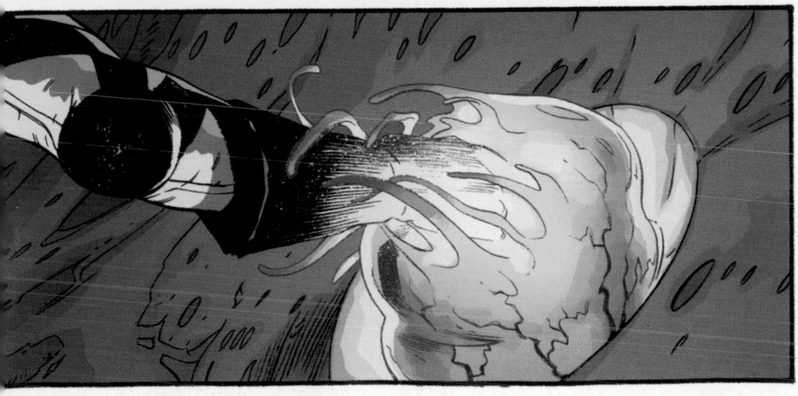

AND A MILLION YEARS OF EVOLUTION TENDS TO DRASTICALLY CHANGE THE LANDSCAPE.

ONCE MY HOME, IT IS ALMOST COMPLETELY FOREIGN TO ME NOW.

FORTUNATELY, ULTIMATON REMAINS TO GUARD MY LABS.

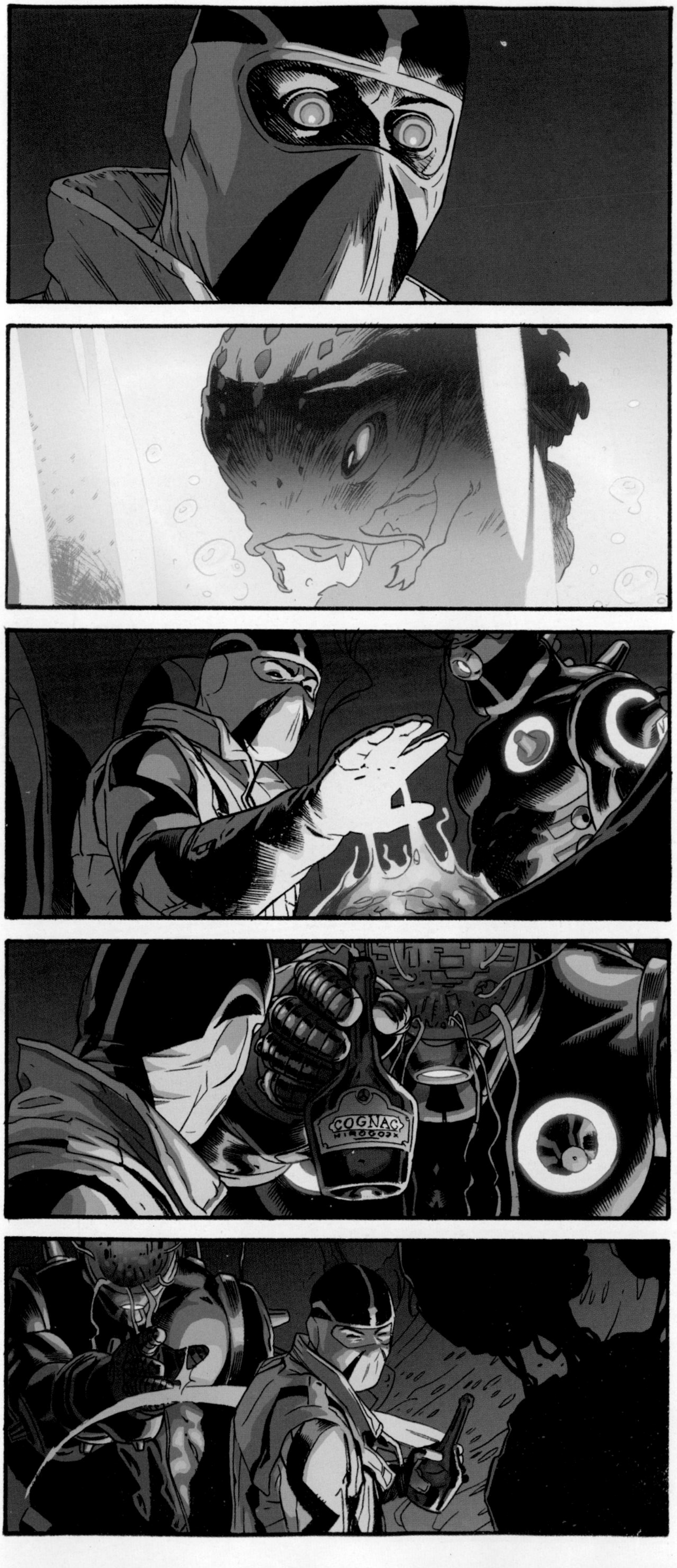

THE WORLD IS A MAN-MADE ENVIRONMENT DESIGNED TO CREATE SUPER-SOLDIERS USING SENTINEL TECHNOLOGY.

BUT SINCE I'VE BEEN GONE IT HAS BECOME...

...SOMETHING ELSE.

IT IS NOT SENTIENT--SUCH AN OUTCOME IS IMPOSSIBLE BY DESIGN--BUT THERE IS INTENTION BEHIND THE CHANGES I SEE.

LEADING ME TO THE NEXT LOGICAL CONCLUSION: THERE IS SOMEONE (THING) HERE CONTROLLING IT.

WHILE SEARCHING FOR THIS MYSTERIOUS TRESPASSER I UNCOVERED A GRAVEYARD OF CYBERLIFE.

NOT PHALANX, NOT TECHNARCHY, NOT REAVER. BUT A FRANKENSTEIN'S MONSTER WITH ELEMENTS OF ALL THREE, AMID OTHER, MORE FAMILIAR, MAN-MADE TECHNOLOGIES.

STARK.
ROXXON.
OSBORN.

I SPENT MONTHS RECOMPOSITIN SIDE FILES ON ZOMBIFIED BIO-COMPUTERS IN HOPES THEY WOUL REVEAL WHO (WHAT) HAD SET THIS PLACE TO FAST FORWARD.

ONCE HACKED AND INITIATED, THE CODE RAN WILD, DELUDED, DREAMING IN IMPOSSIBLE EQUATIONS...

AN ALGORITHM OF SENTIENT INFINITY.

THE COMPUTER I RAN THE EQUATION ON BECAME SELF-AWARE, GREW INTO A MONSTER, AND ATTEMPTED TO KILL ME.

RIGA: WEAPON I

LESSON ONE: BE ON YOUR GUARD WITHIN THIS PLACE.

ONE MUST BE MINDFUL OF WHAT THE WORLD IS...

NUKE: WEAPON VII

...AND WHO IT HAS CREATED.

WEAPON X

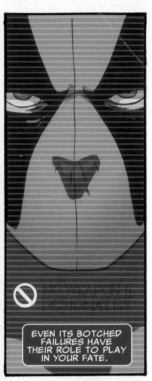

🚫

EVEN ITS BOTCHED FAILURES HAVE THEIR ROLE TO PLAY IN YOUR FATE.

BEFORE DESTROYING THE LIVING COMPUTER, I SALVAGED FOUR PIECES OF INFORMATION FROM IT.

1. WEAPON INFINITY IS UNITED.

2. WEAPON INFINITY IS VIRAL.

3. WEAPON INFINITY TRAVELS OMNI-TIME.

4. THE ARCHITECT OF THIS QUIRK IS SEQUESTERED IN A SUBTERRANEAN CHAMBER, DEEP IN THE WORLD, ENTOMBED UNDER A MILLION YEARS OF PROGRESS.

HIS (ITS) MISCHIEF IS UNDENIABLE.

I WILL CONTINUE MY EFFORTS TO FIND AND DESTROY HIM (IT).

AND HE (IT) WILL CONTINUE TO DO THE SAME TO ME...

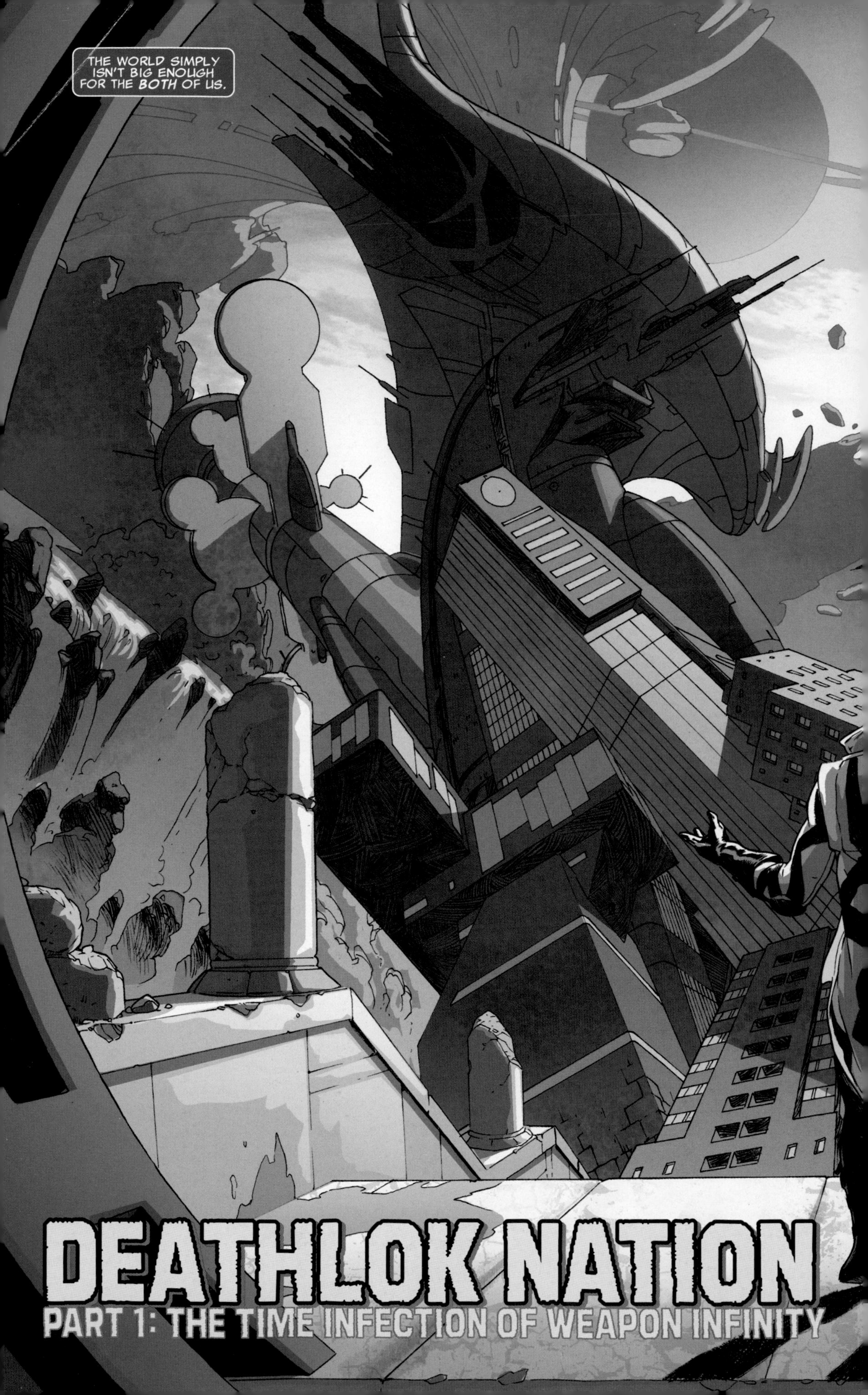
THE WORLD SIMPLY ISN'T BIG ENOUGH FOR THE BOTH OF US.
DEATHLOK NATION
PART 1: THE TIME INFECTION OF WEAPON INFINITY

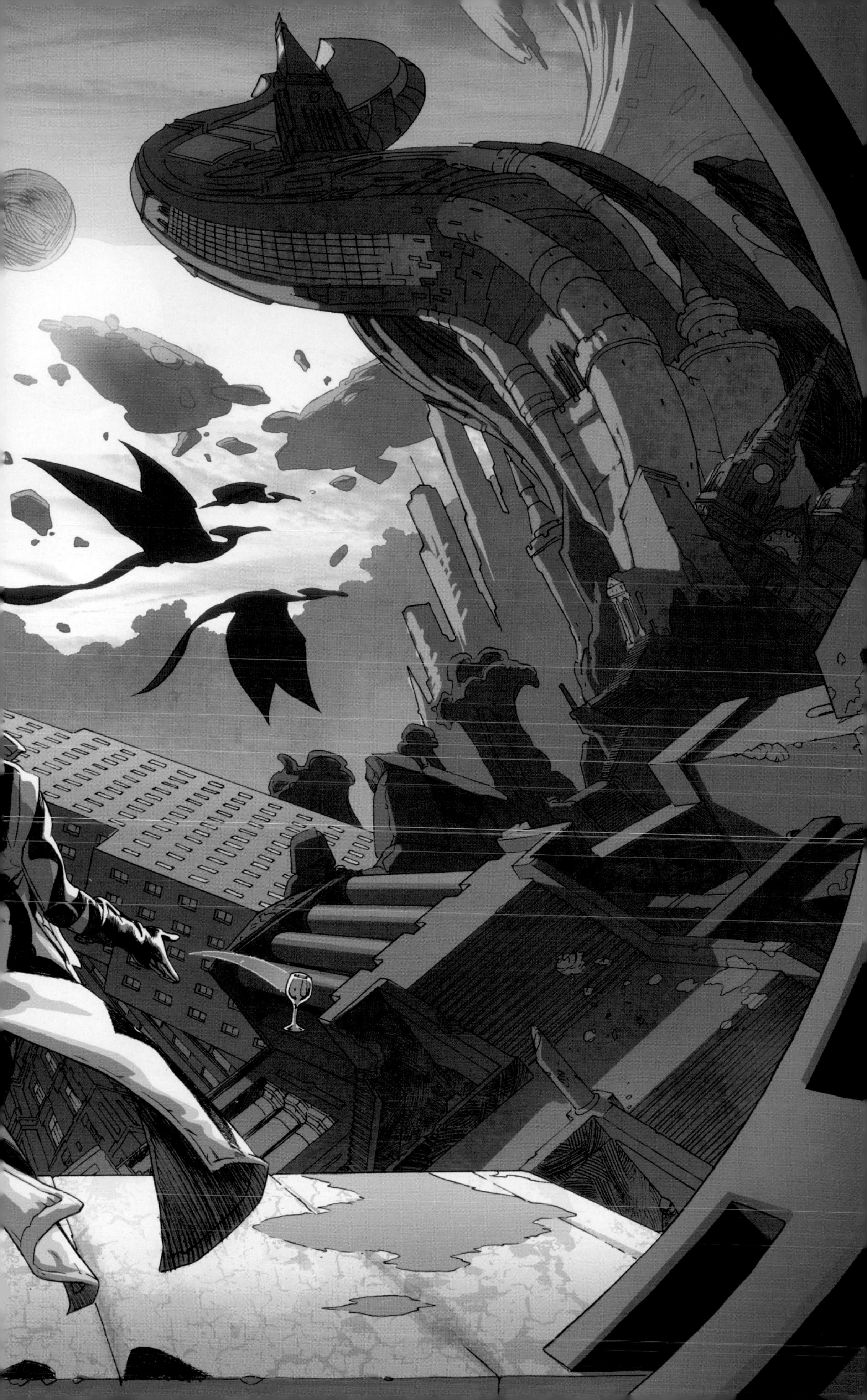

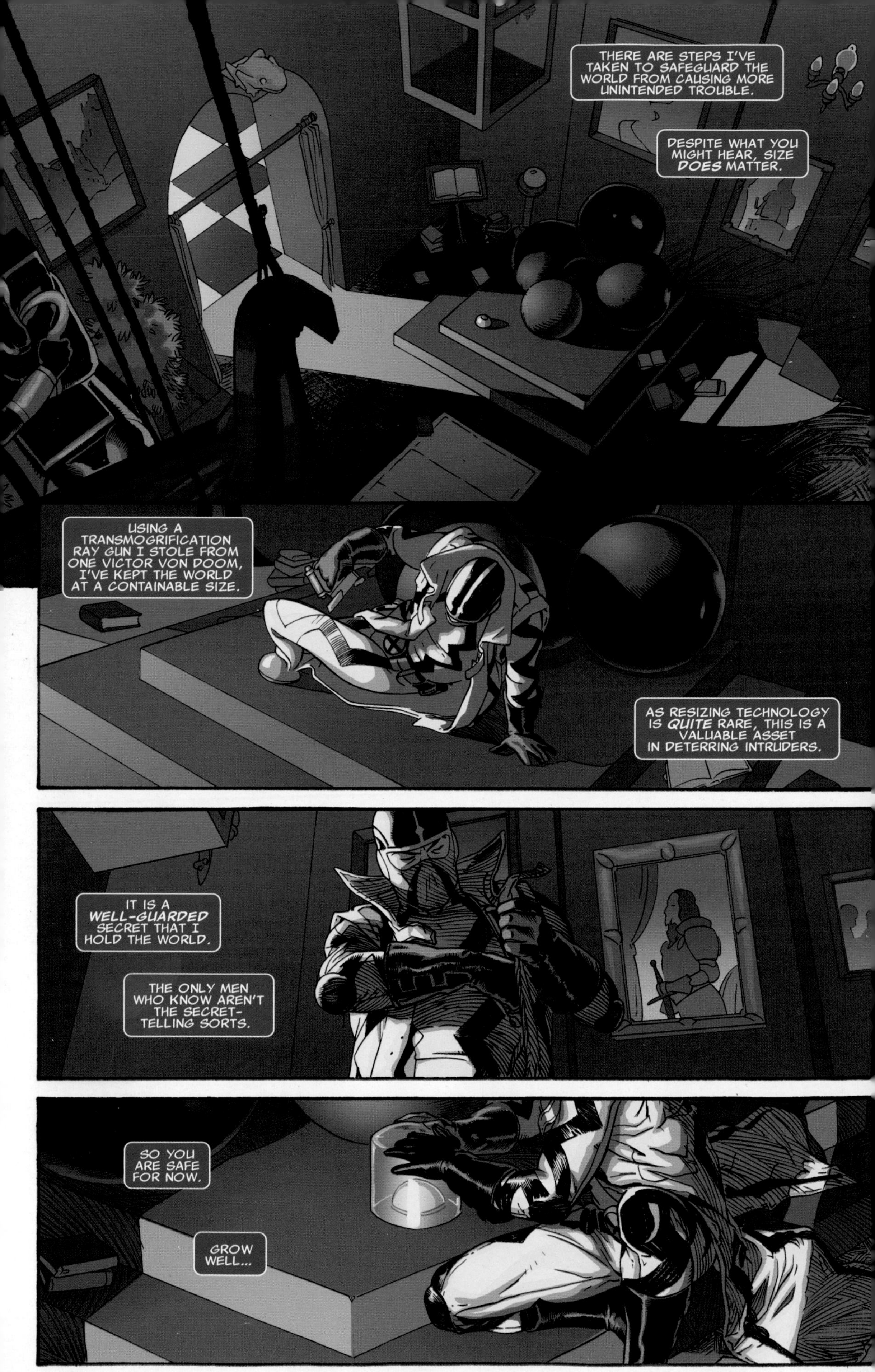
THERE ARE STEPS I'VE TAKEN TO SAFEGUARD THE WORLD FROM CAUSING MORE UNINTENDED TROUBLE.
DESPITE WHAT YOU MIGHT HEAR, SIZE DOES MATTER.
USING A TRANSMOGRIFICATION RAY GUN I STOLE FROM ONE VICTOR VON DOOM, I'VE KEPT THE WORLD AT A CONTAINABLE SIZE.
AS RESIZING TECHNOLOGY IS QUITE RARE, THIS IS A VALUABLE ASSET IN DETERRING INTRUDERS.
IT IS A WELL-GUARDED SECRET THAT I HOLD THE WORLD.
THE ONLY MEN WHO KNOW AREN'T THE SECRET-TELLING SORTS.
SO YOU ARE SAFE FOR NOW.
GROW WELL...

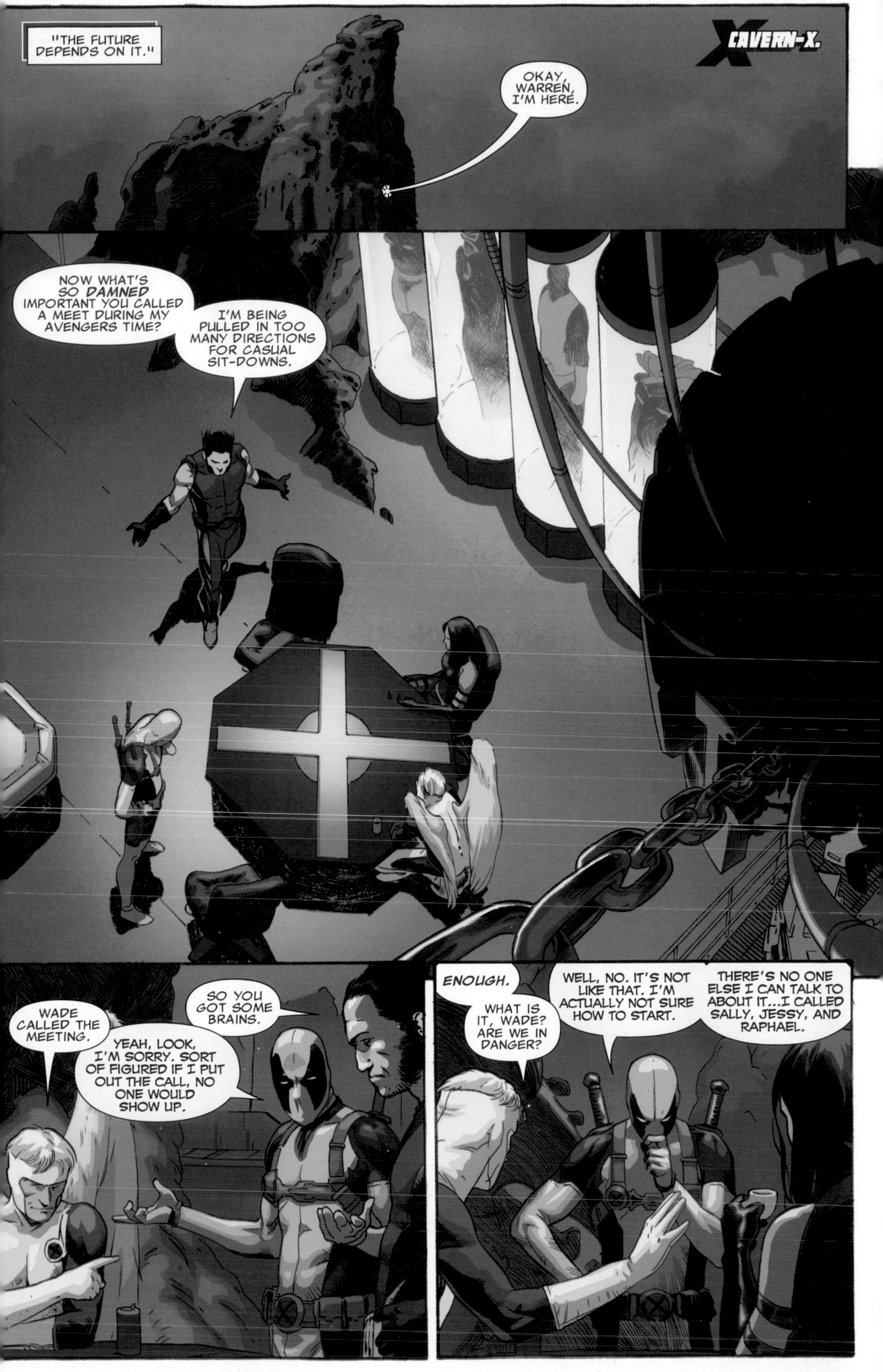
"THE FUTURE DEPENDS ON IT."
CAVERN-X.
OKAY, WARREN, I'M HERE.
NOW WHAT'S SO DAMNED IMPORTANT YOU CALLED A MEET DURING MY AVENGERS TIME?
I'M BEING PULLED IN TOO MANY DIRECTIONS FOR CASUAL SIT-DOWNS.
WADE CALLED THE MEETING.
SO YOU GOT SOME BRAINS.
YEAH, LOOK, I'M SORRY. SORT OF FIGURED IF I PUT OUT THE CALL, NO ONE WOULD SHOW UP.
ENOUGH.
WHAT IS IT, WADE? ARE WE IN DANGER?
WELL, NO. IT'S NOT LIKE THAT. I'M ACTUALLY NOT SURE HOW TO START.
THERE'S NO ONE ELSE I CAN TALK TO ABOUT IT...I CALLED SALLY, JESSY, AND RAPHAEL.

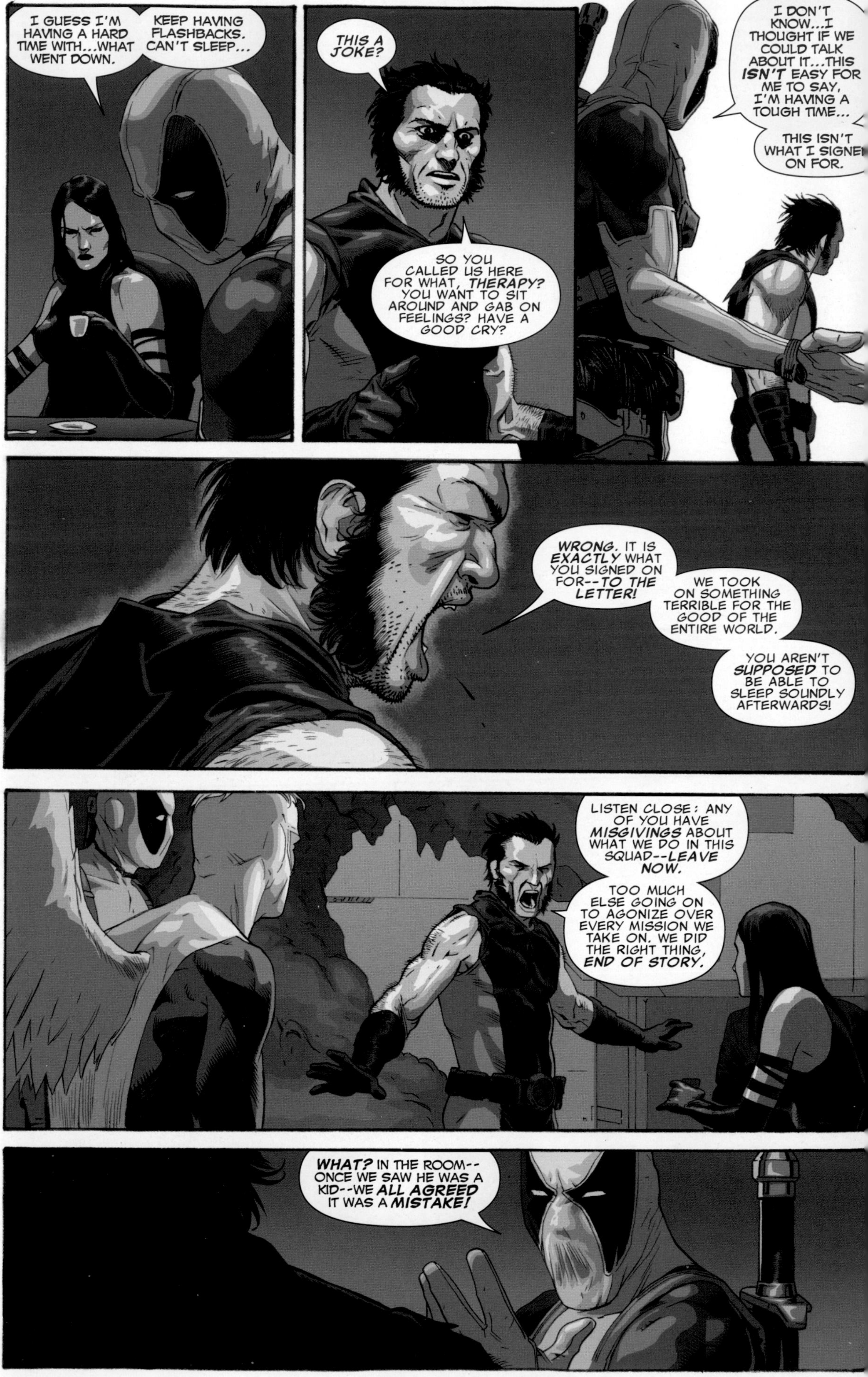

I GUESS I'M HAVING A HARD TIME WITH...WHAT WENT DOWN.
KEEP HAVING FLASHBACKS. CAN'T SLEEP...
THIS A JOKE?
SO YOU CALLED US HERE FOR WHAT, THERAPY? YOU WANT TO SIT AROUND AND GAB ON FEELINGS? HAVE A GOOD CRY?
I DON'T KNOW...I THOUGHT IF WE COULD TALK ABOUT IT...THIS ISN'T EASY FOR ME TO SAY, I'M HAVING A TOUGH TIME...
THIS ISN'T WHAT I SIGNE ON FOR.
WRONG. IT IS EXACTLY WHAT YOU SIGNED ON FOR--TO THE LETTER!
WE TOOK ON SOMETHING TERRIBLE FOR THE GOOD OF THE ENTIRE WORLD.
YOU AREN'T SUPPOSED TO BE ABLE TO SLEEP SOUNDLY AFTERWARDS!
LISTEN CLOSE: ANY OF YOU HAVE MISGIVINGS ABOUT WHAT WE DO IN THIS SQUAD--LEAVE NOW.
TOO MUCH ELSE GOING ON TO AGONIZE OVER EVERY MISSION WE TAKE ON. WE DID THE RIGHT THING, END OF STORY.
WHAT? IN THE ROOM--ONCE WE SAW HE WAS A KID--WE ALL AGREED IT WAS A MISTAKE!

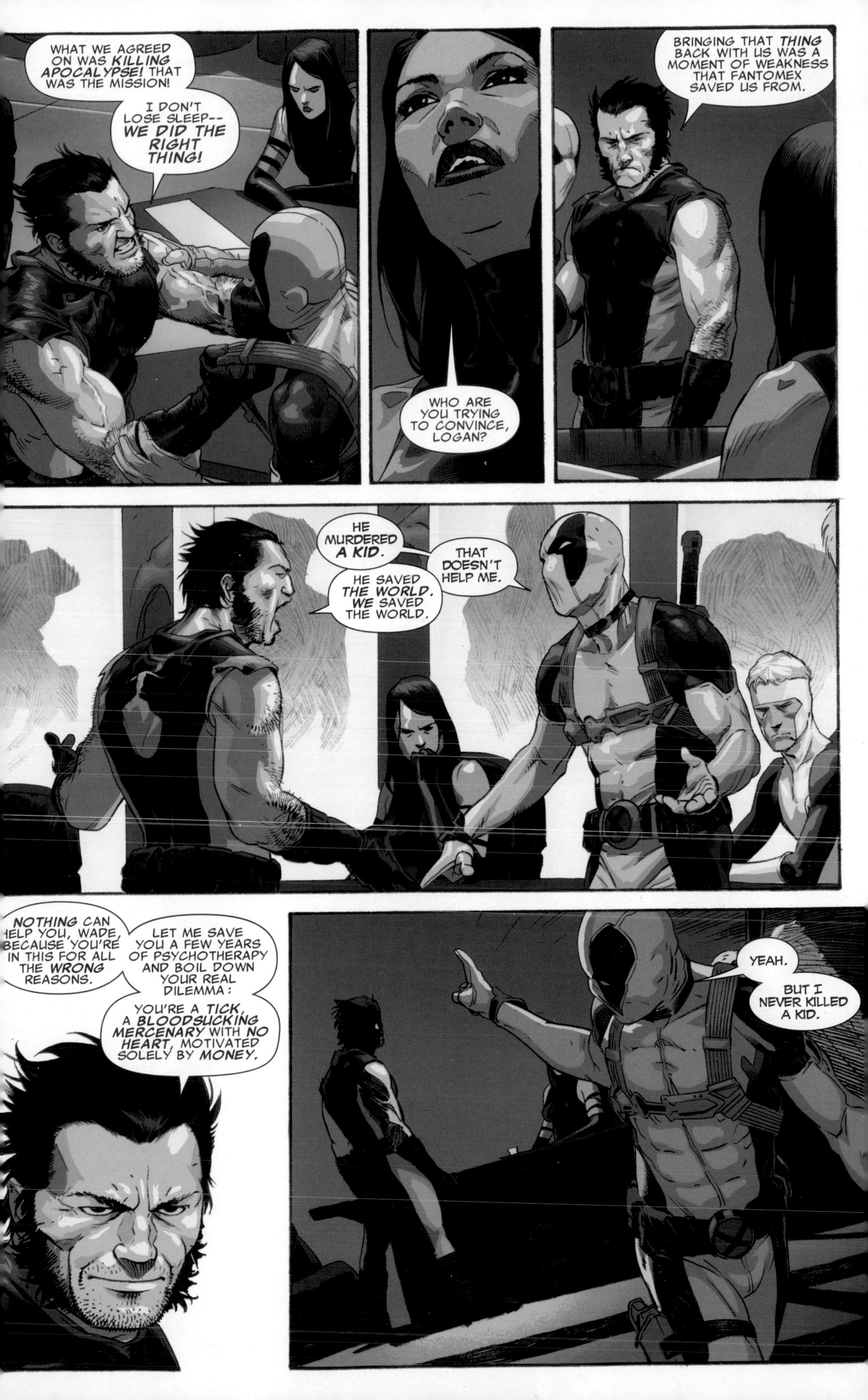
WHAT WE AGREED ON WAS KILLING APOCALYPSE! THAT WAS THE MISSION!
I DON'T LOSE SLEEP-- WE DID THE RIGHT THING!
WHO ARE YOU TRYING TO CONVINCE, LOGAN?
BRINGING THAT THING BACK WITH US WAS A MOMENT OF WEAKNESS THAT FANTOMEX SAVED US FROM.
HE MURDERED A KID.
THAT DOESN'T HELP ME.
HE SAVED THE WORLD. WE SAVED THE WORLD.
NOTHING CAN HELP YOU, WADE, BECAUSE YOU'RE IN THIS FOR ALL THE WRONG REASONS.
LET ME SAVE YOU A FEW YEARS OF PSYCHOTHERAPY AND BOIL DOWN YOUR REAL DILEMMA:
YOU'RE A TICK, A BLOODSUCKING MERCENARY WITH NO HEART, MOTIVATED SOLELY BY MONEY.
YEAH.
BUT I NEVER KILLED A KID.

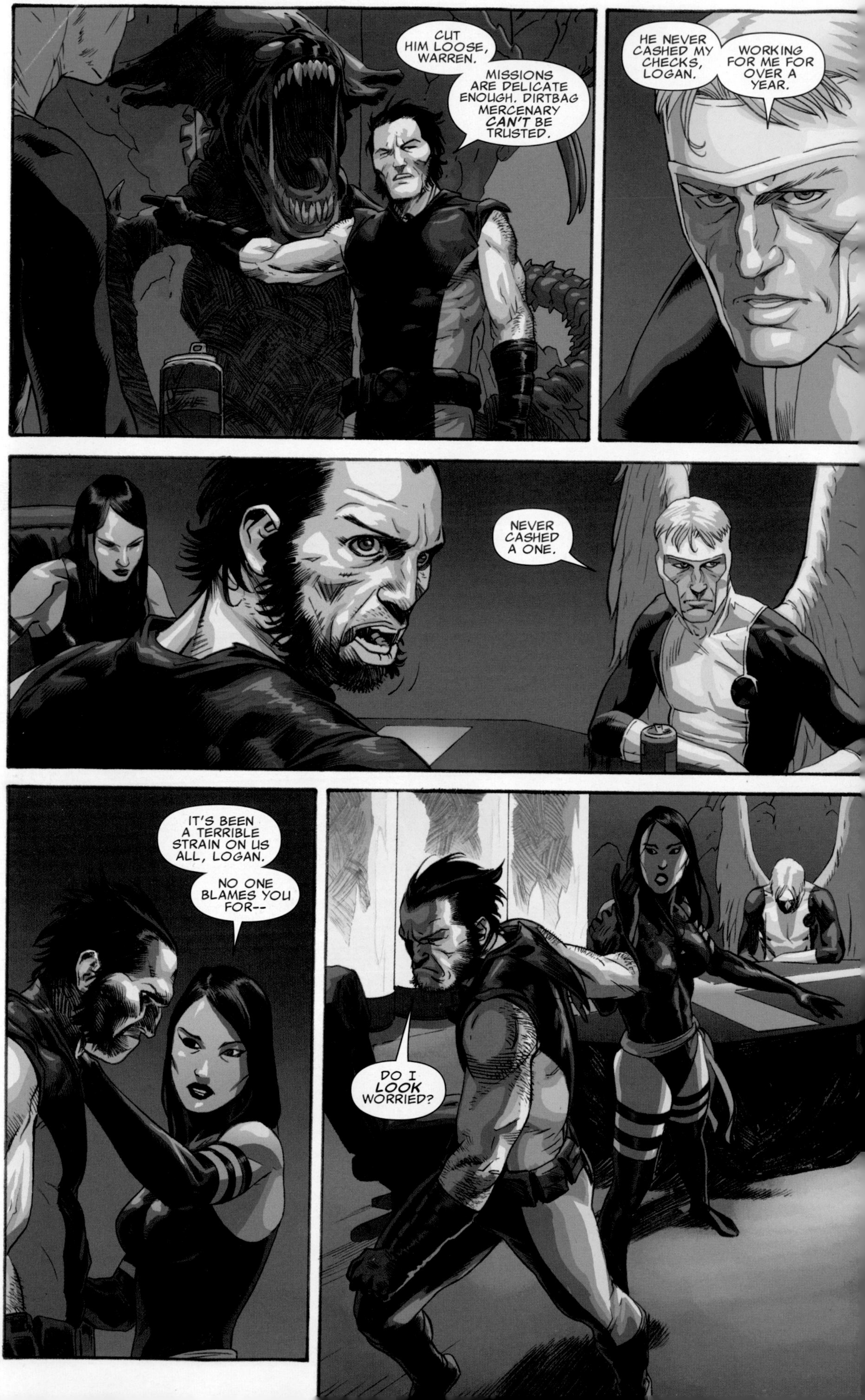

CUT HIM LOOSE, WARREN.
MISSIONS ARE DELICATE ENOUGH. DIRTBAG MERCENARY CAN'T BE TRUSTED.
HE NEVER CASHED MY CHECKS, LOGAN.
WORKING FOR ME FOR OVER A YEAR.
NEVER CASHED A ONE.
IT'S BEEN A TERRIBLE STRAIN ON US ALL, LOGAN.
NO ONE BLAMES YOU FOR--
DO I LOOK WORRIED?

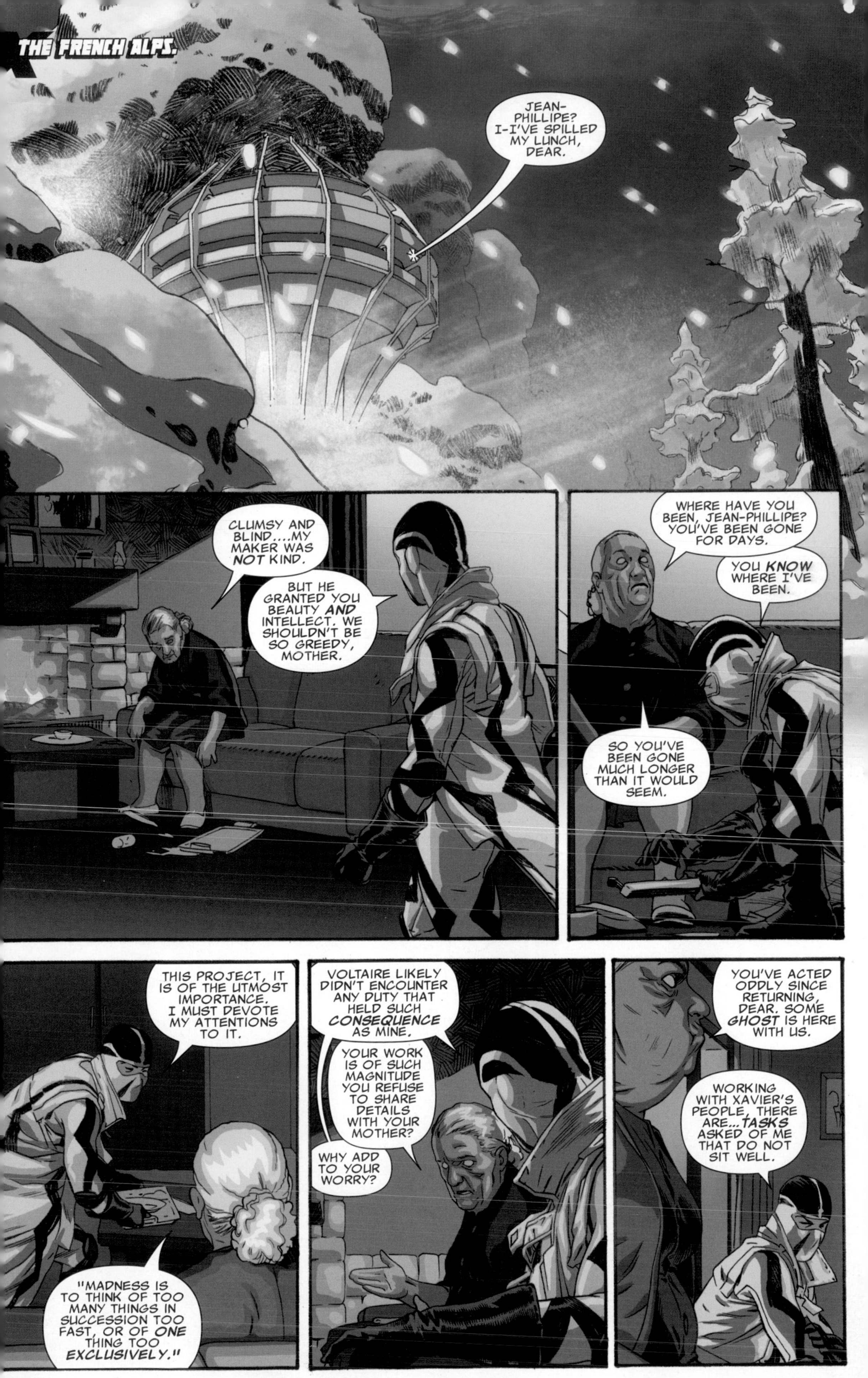
THE FRENCH ALPS.
JEAN-PHILLIPE? I-I'VE SPILLED MY LUNCH, DEAR.
CLUMSY AND BLIND....MY MAKER WAS NOT KIND.
BUT HE GRANTED YOU BEAUTY AND INTELLECT. WE SHOULDN'T BE SO GREEDY, MOTHER.
WHERE HAVE YOU BEEN, JEAN-PHILLIPE? YOU'VE BEEN GONE FOR DAYS.
YOU KNOW WHERE I'VE BEEN.
SO YOU'VE BEEN GONE MUCH LONGER THAN IT WOULD SEEM.
THIS PROJECT, IT IS OF THE UTMOST IMPORTANCE. I MUST DEVOTE MY ATTENTIONS TO IT.
"MADNESS IS TO THINK OF TOO MANY THINGS IN SUCCESSION TOO FAST, OR OF ONE THING TOO EXCLUSIVELY."
VOLTAIRE LIKELY DIDN'T ENCOUNTER ANY DUTY THAT HELD SUCH CONSEQUENCE AS MINE.
YOUR WORK IS OF SUCH MAGNITUDE YOU REFUSE TO SHARE DETAILS WITH YOUR MOTHER?
WHY ADD TO YOUR WORRY?
YOU'VE ACTED ODDLY SINCE RETURNING, DEAR. SOME GHOST IS HERE WITH US.
WORKING WITH XAVIER'S PEOPLE, THERE ARE...TASKS ASKED OF ME THAT DO NOT SIT WELL.

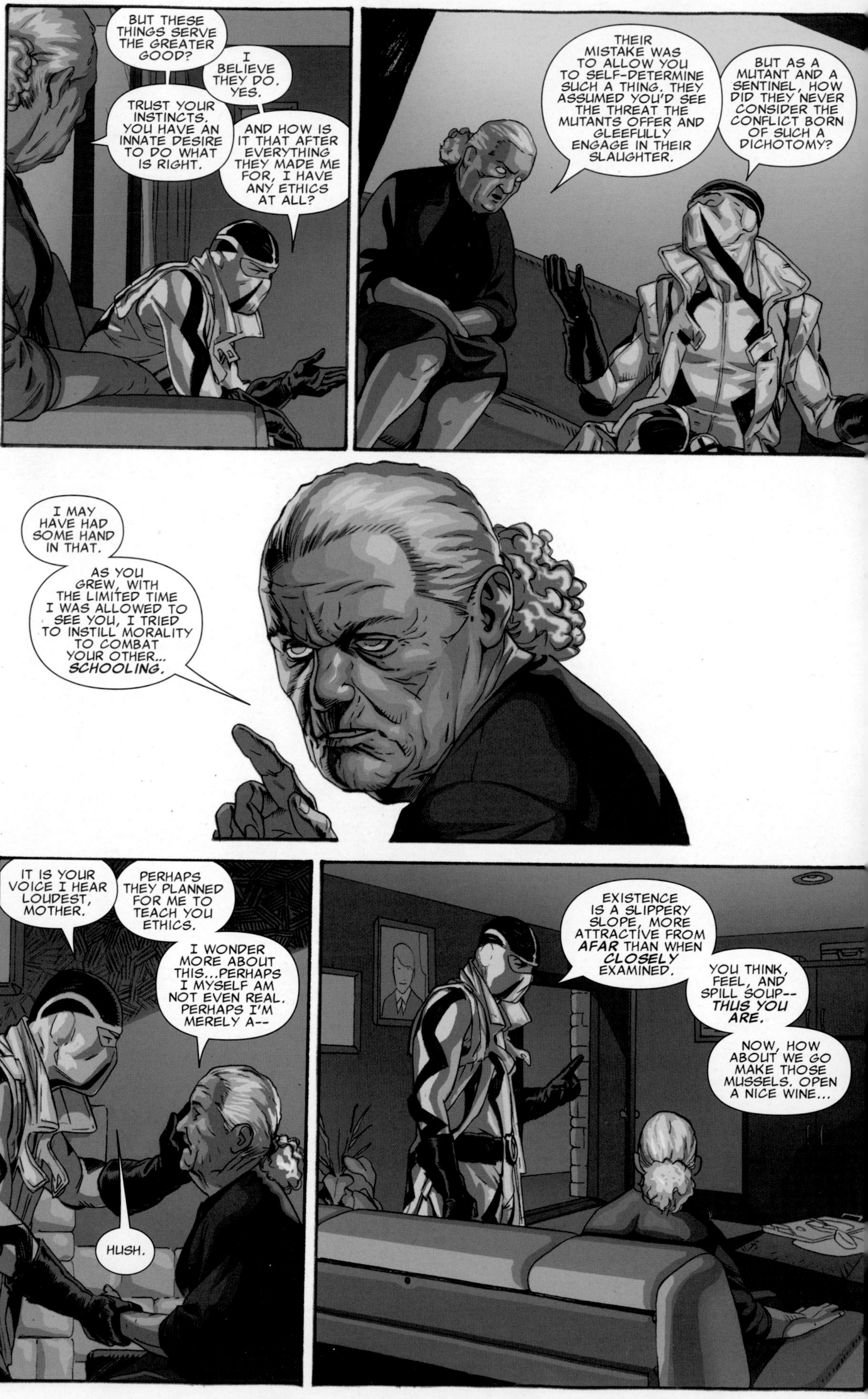
BUT THESE THINGS SERVE THE GREATER GOOD?
TRUST YOUR INSTINCTS. YOU HAVE AN INNATE DESIRE TO DO WHAT IS RIGHT.
I BELIEVE THEY DO. YES.
AND HOW IS IT THAT AFTER EVERYTHING THEY MADE ME FOR, I HAVE ANY ETHICS AT ALL?
THEIR MISTAKE WAS TO ALLOW YOU TO SELF-DETERMINE SUCH A THING. THEY ASSUMED YOU'D SEE THE THREAT THE MUTANTS OFFER AND GLEEFULLY ENGAGE IN THEIR SLAUGHTER.
BUT AS A MUTANT AND A SENTINEL, HOW DID THEY NEVER CONSIDER THE CONFLICT BORN OF SUCH A DICHOTOMY?
I MAY HAVE HAD SOME HAND IN THAT.
AS YOU GREW, WITH THE LIMITED TIME I WAS ALLOWED TO SEE YOU, I TRIED TO INSTILL MORALITY TO COMBAT YOUR OTHER... *SCHOOLING.*
IT IS YOUR VOICE I HEAR LOUDEST, MOTHER.
PERHAPS THEY PLANNED FOR ME TO TEACH YOU ETHICS.
I WONDER MORE ABOUT THIS...PERHAPS I MYSELF AM NOT EVEN REAL. PERHAPS I'M MERELY A--
HUSH.
EXISTENCE IS A SLIPPERY SLOPE, MORE ATTRACTIVE FROM *AFAR* THAN WHEN *CLOSELY* EXAMINED.
YOU THINK, FEEL, AND SPILL SOUP-- *THUS YOU ARE.*
NOW, HOW ABOUT WE GO MAKE THOSE MUSSELS. OPEN A NICE WINE...

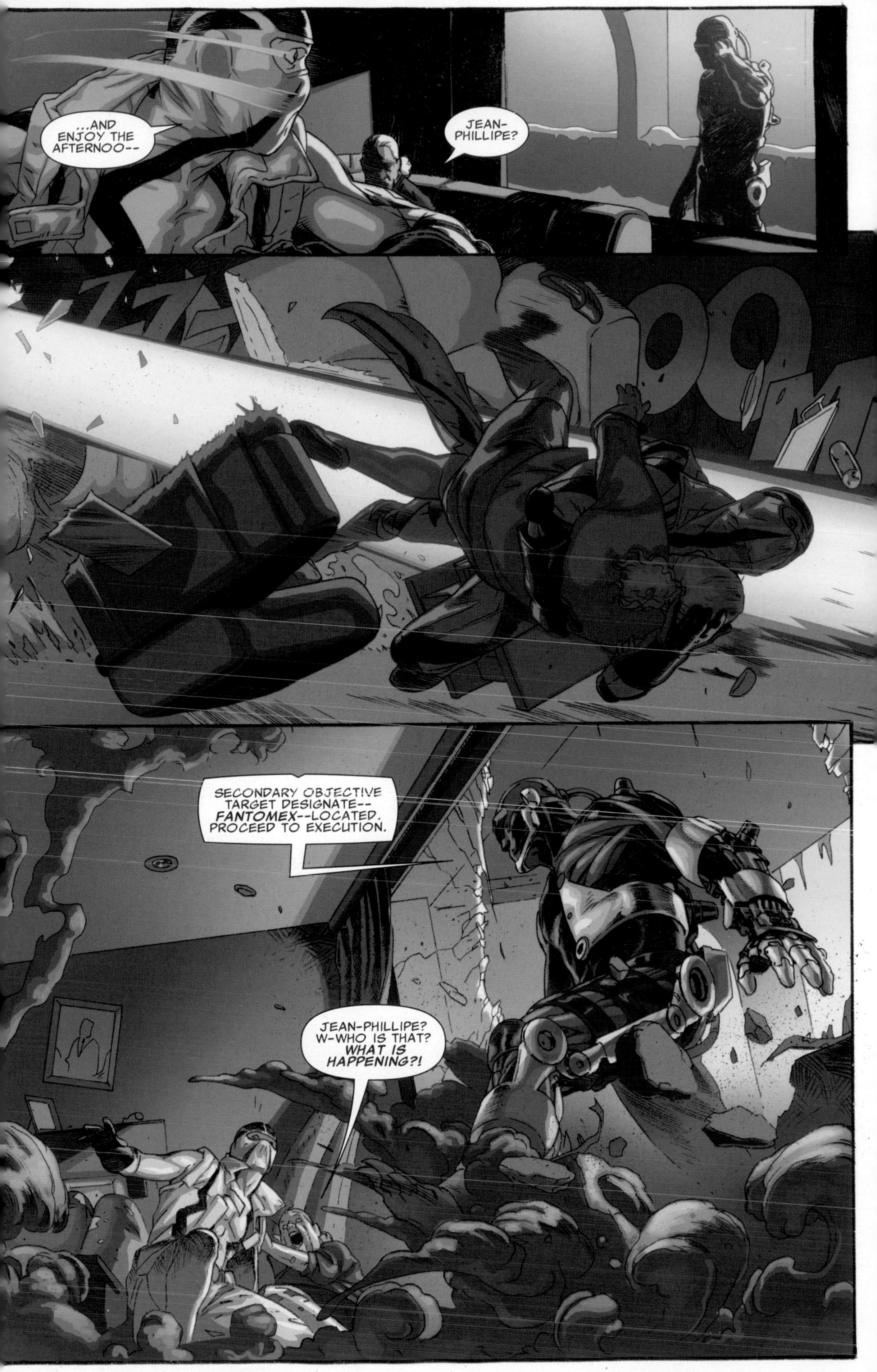
...AND ENJOY THE AFTERNOO--
JEAN-PHILLIPE?
SECONDARY OBJECTIVE TARGET DESIGNATE--FANTOMEX--LOCATED. PROCEED TO EXECUTION.
JEAN-PHILLIPE? W-WHO IS THAT? WHAT IS HAPPENING?!

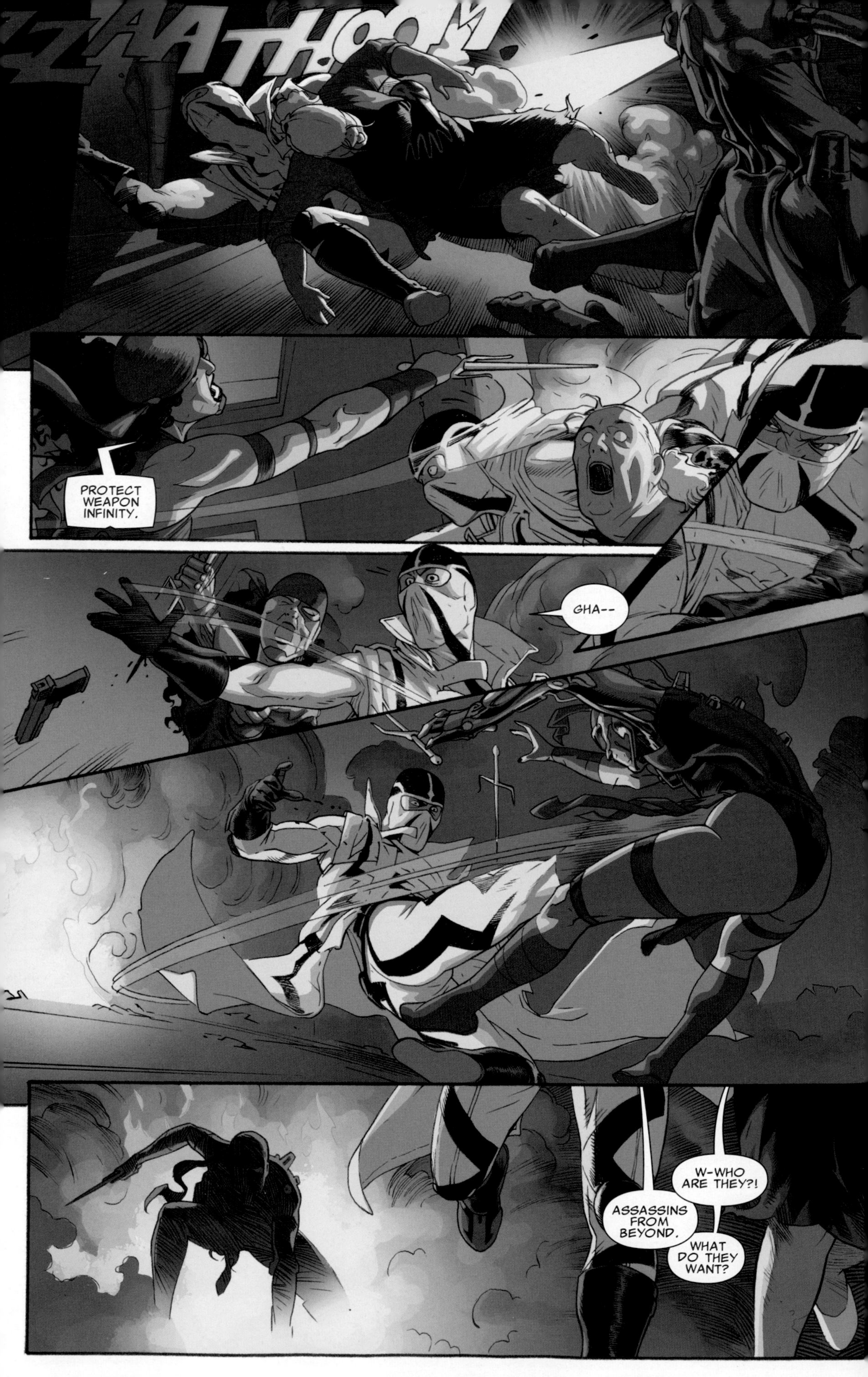
ZZAATHOOM
PROTECT WEAPON INFINITY.
GHA--
W-WHO ARE THEY?!
ASSASSINS FROM BEYOND.
WHAT DO THEY WANT?

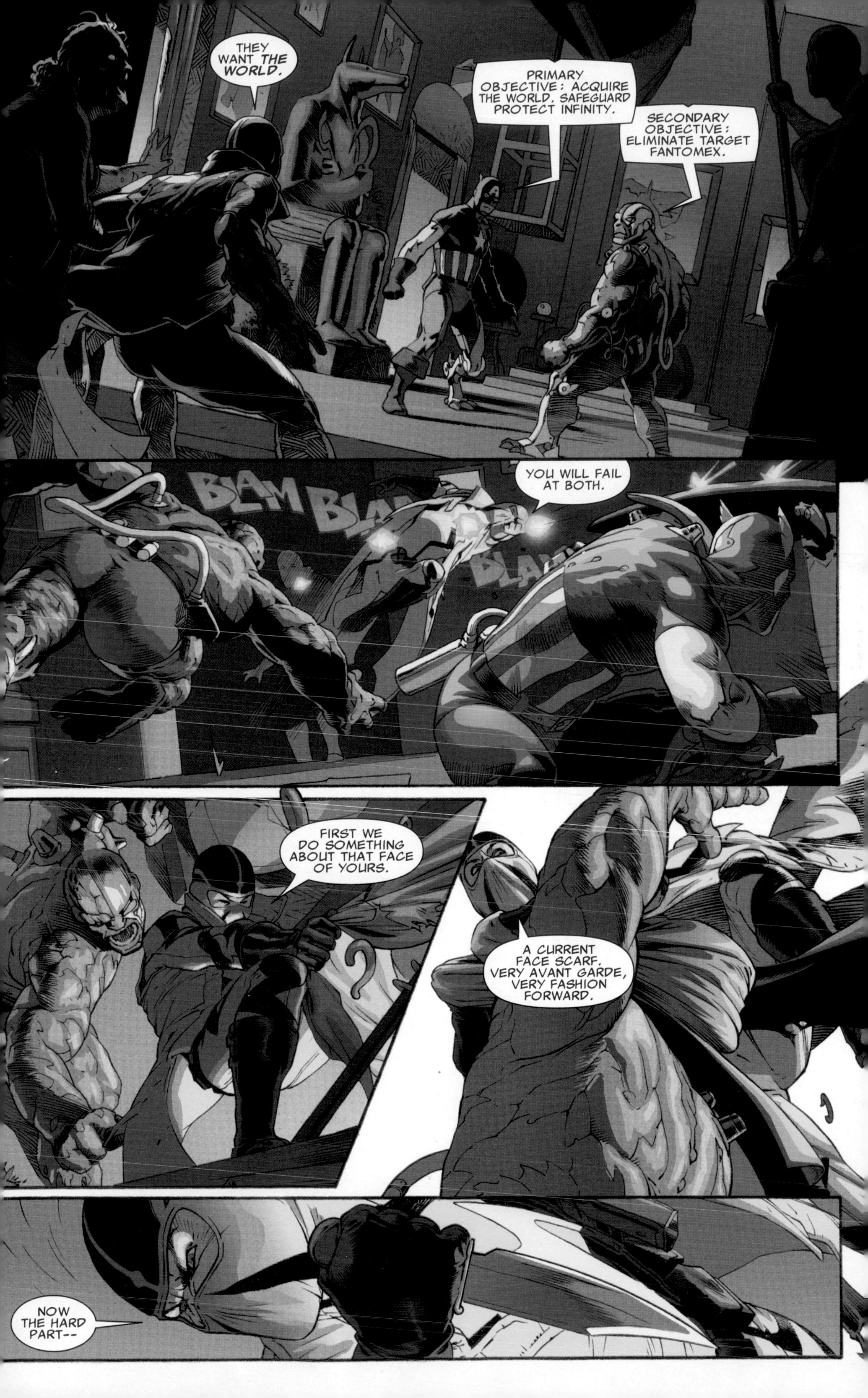
THEY WANT THE WORLD.
PRIMARY OBJECTIVE: ACQUIRE THE WORLD. SAFEGUARD PROTECT INFINITY.
SECONDARY OBJECTIVE: ELIMINATE TARGET FANTOMEX.
BLAM BLAM BLAM
YOU WILL FAIL AT BOTH.
FIRST WE DO SOMETHING ABOUT THAT FACE OF YOURS.
A CURRENT FACE SCARF. VERY AVANT GARDE, VERY FASHION FORWARD.
NOW THE HARD PART--

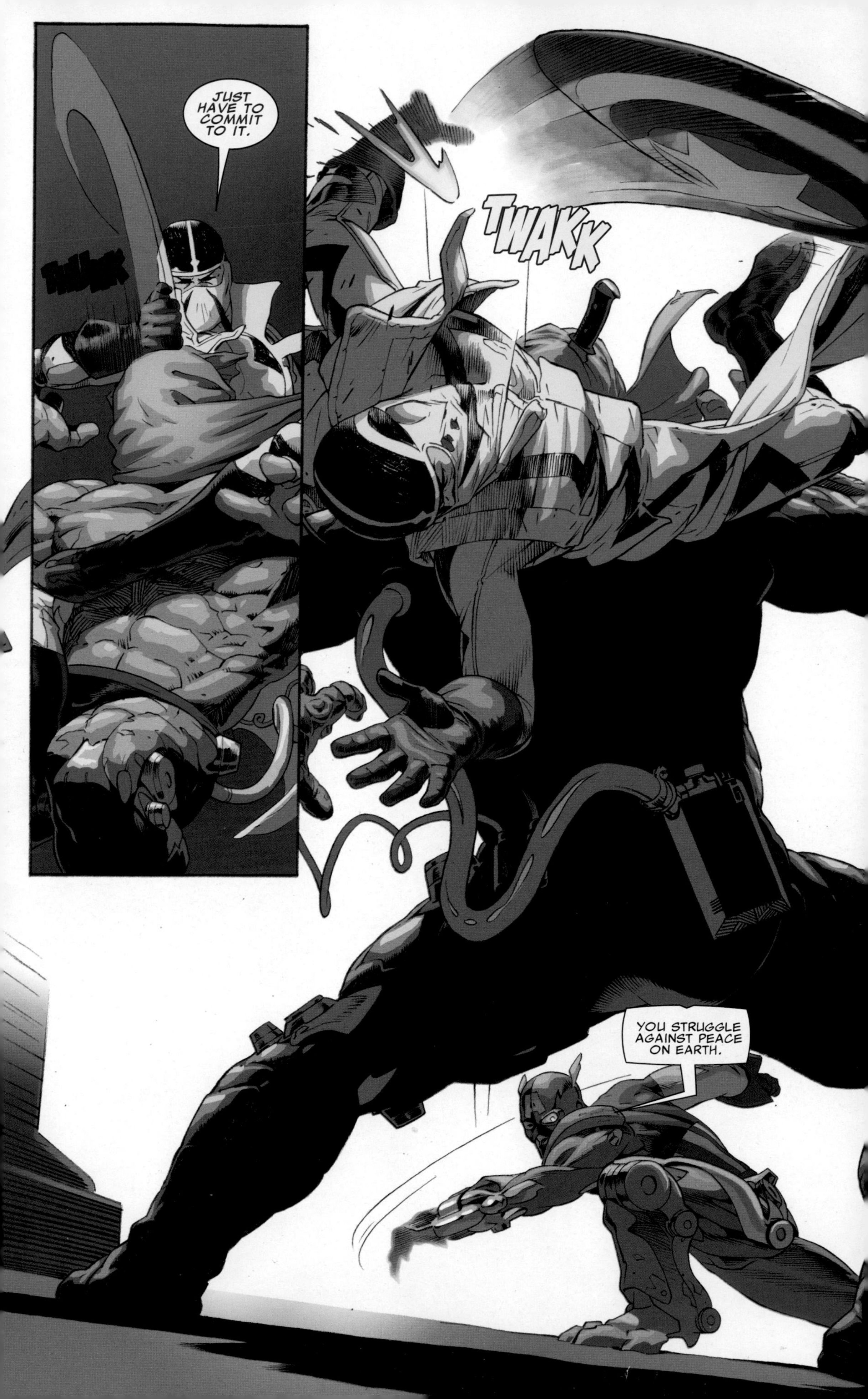
JUST HAVE TO COMMIT TO IT.
TWAKK
TWAKK
YOU STRUGGLE AGAINST PEACE ON EARTH.

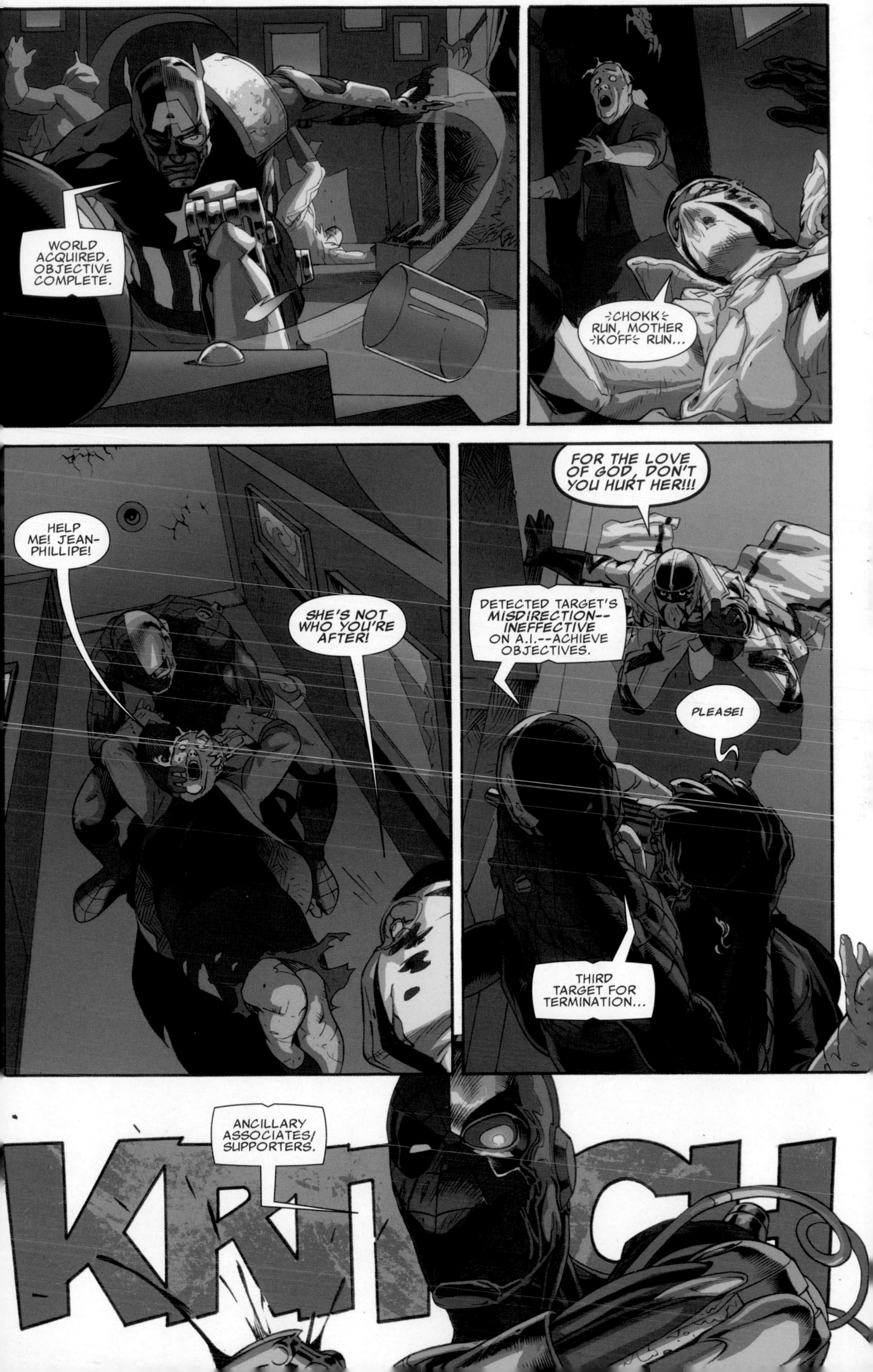
WORLD ACQUIRED. OBJECTIVE COMPLETE.
CHOKK RUN, MOTHER KOFF RUN...
HELP ME! JEAN-PHILLIPE!
SHE'S NOT WHO YOU'RE AFTER!
FOR THE LOVE OF GOD, DON'T YOU HURT HER!!!
DETECTED TARGET'S MISDIRECTION--INEFFECTIVE ON A.I.--ACHIEVE OBJECTIVES.
PLEASE!
THIRD TARGET FOR TERMINATION...
ANCILLARY ASSOCIATES/ SUPPORTERS.
KRTCH

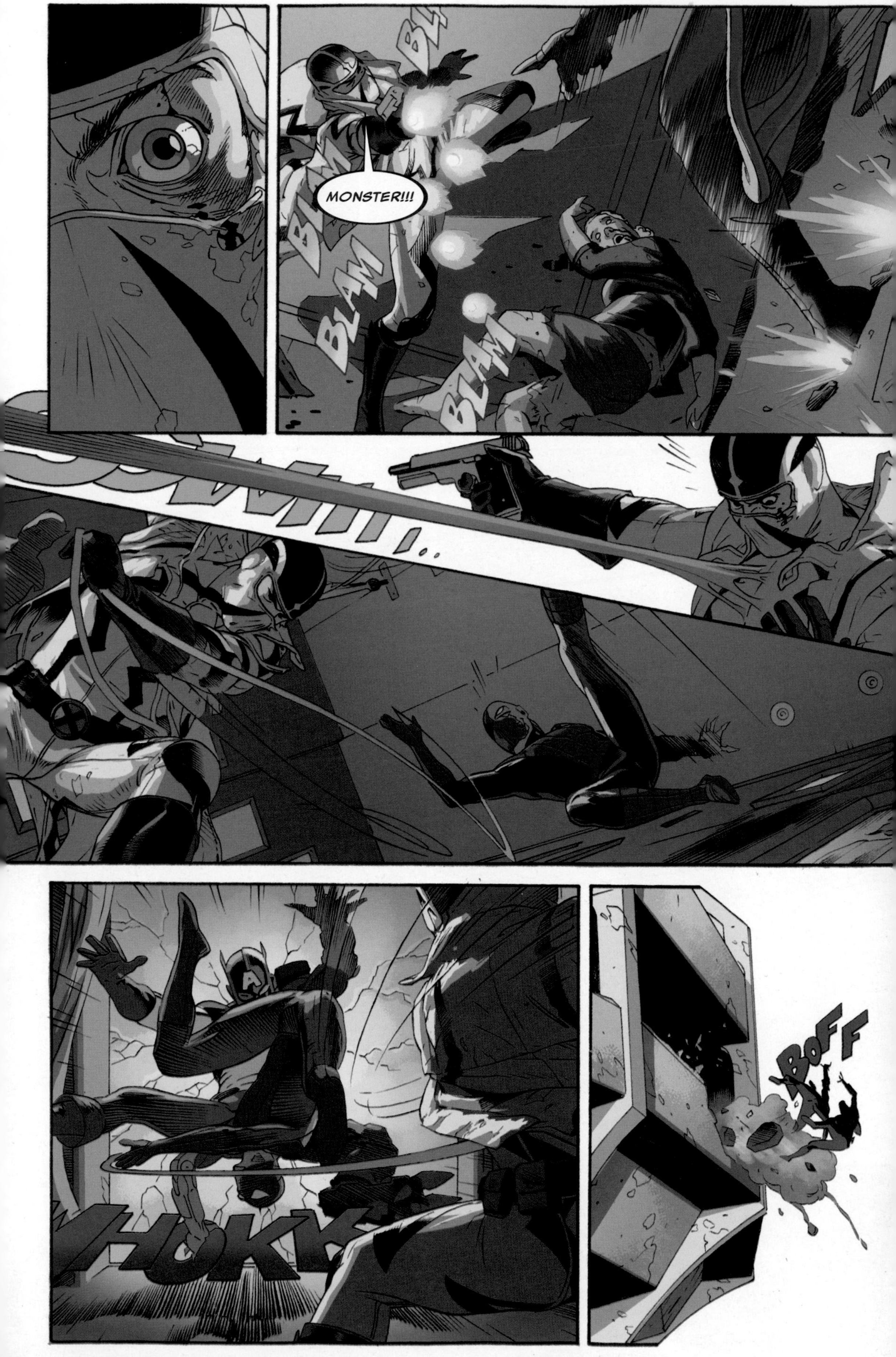
MONSTER!!!
BLAM
BLAM
BLAM
BLAM
BOFF

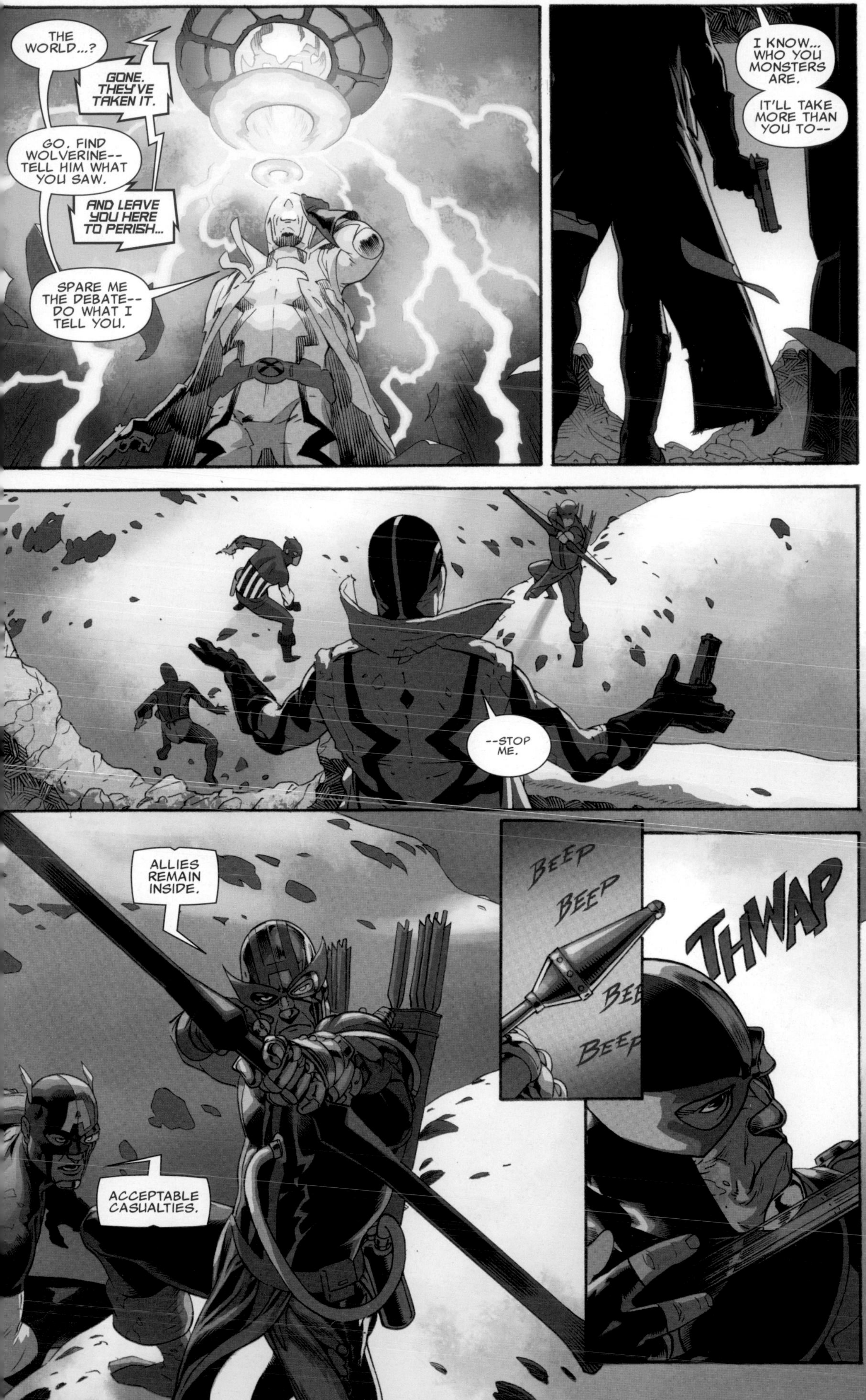
THE WORLD...?
GONE. THEY'VE TAKEN IT.
GO. FIND WOLVERINE-- TELL HIM WHAT YOU SAW.
AND LEAVE YOU HERE TO PERISH...
SPARE ME THE DEBATE-- DO WHAT I TELL YOU.
I KNOW... WHO YOU MONSTERS ARE.
IT'LL TAKE MORE THAN YOU TO--
--STOP ME.
ALLIES REMAIN INSIDE.
ACCEPTABLE CASUALTIES.
BEEP
BEEP
THWAP

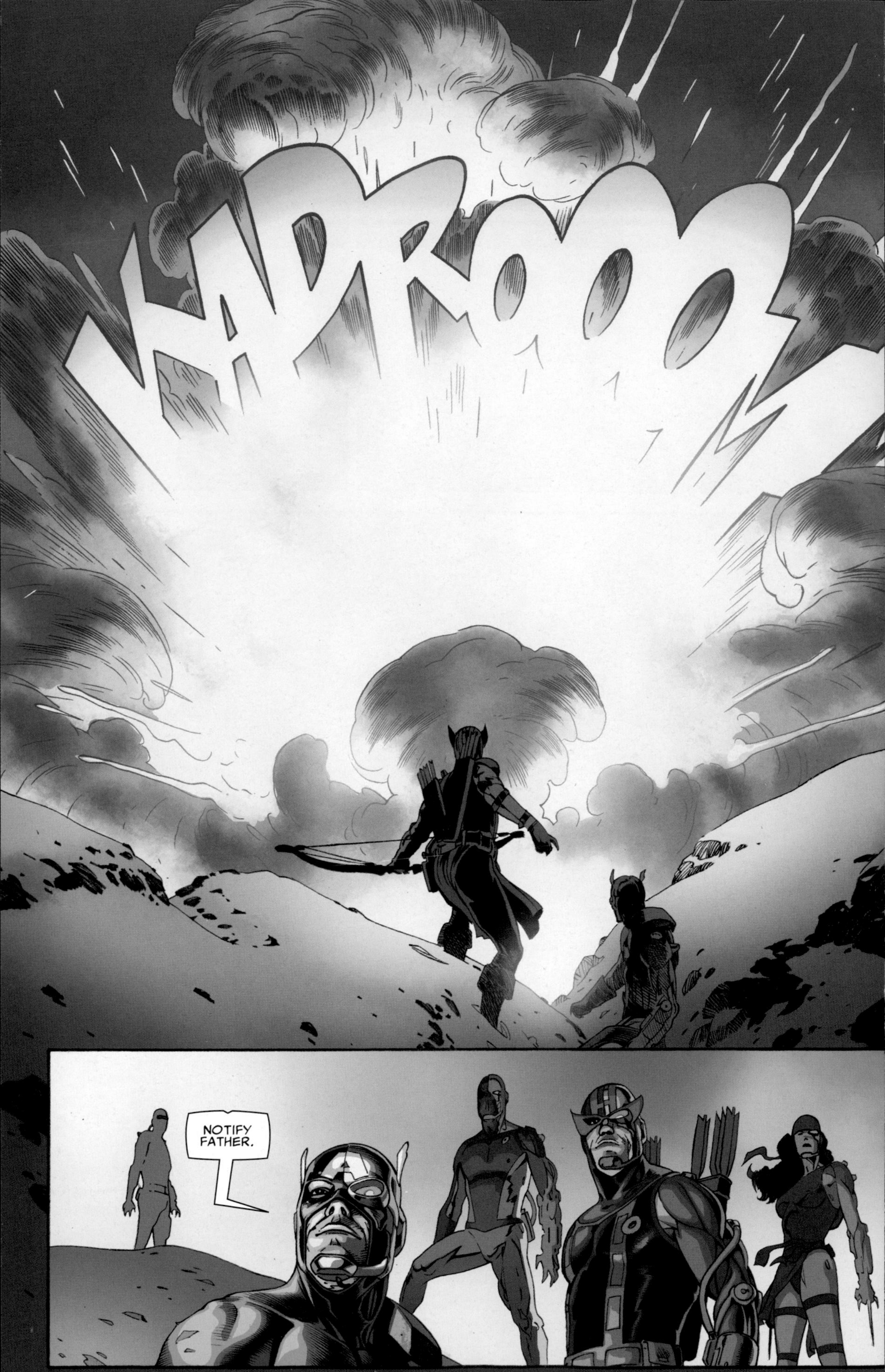
KADROOO
NOTIFY FATHER.

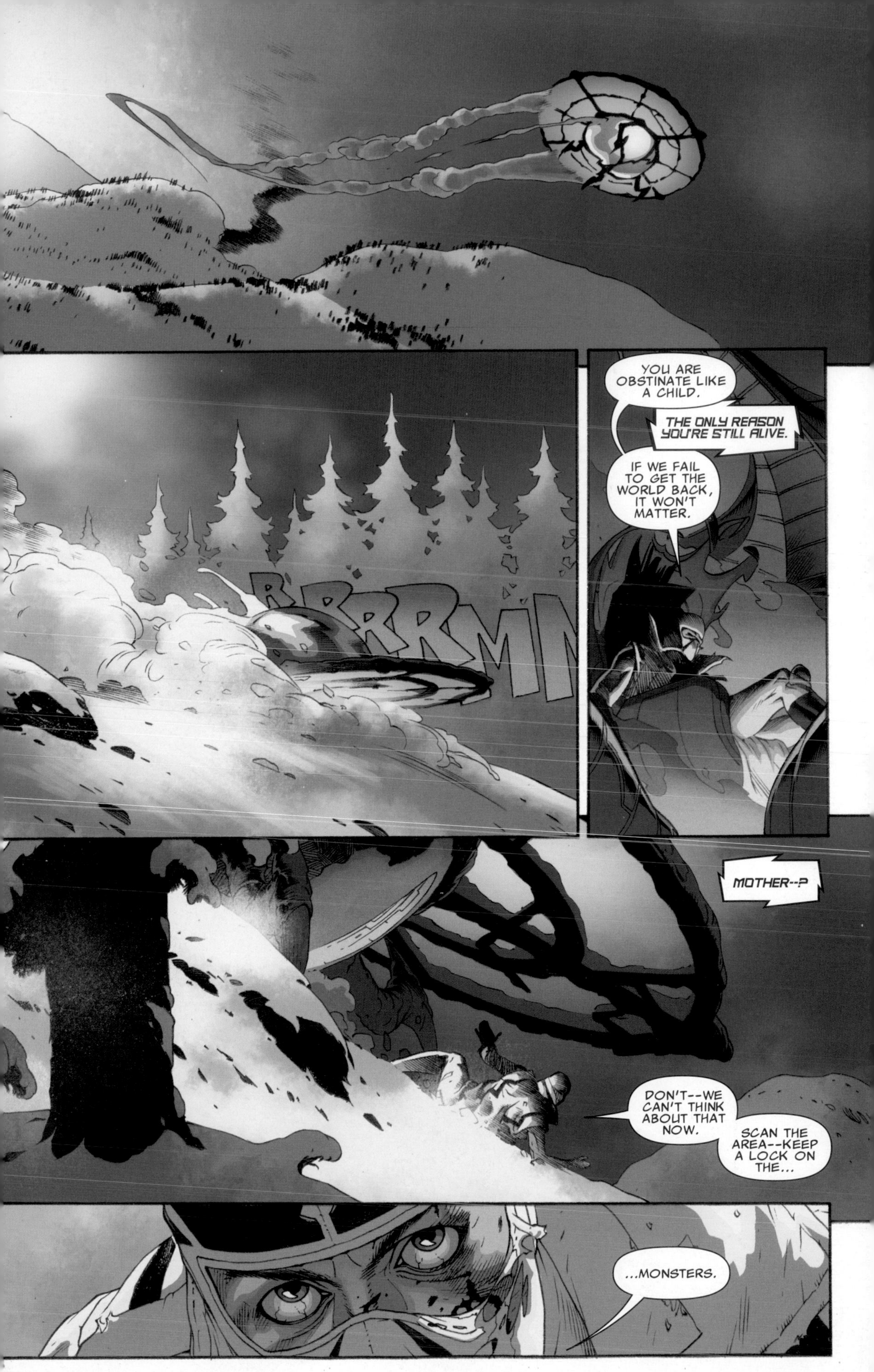
BRRRMM
YOU ARE OBSTINATE LIKE A CHILD.
THE ONLY REASON YOU'RE STILL ALIVE.
IF WE FAIL TO GET THE WORLD BACK, IT WON'T MATTER.
MOTHER--?
DON'T--WE CAN'T THINK ABOUT THAT NOW.
SCAN THE AREA--KEEP A LOCK ON THE...
...MONSTERS.

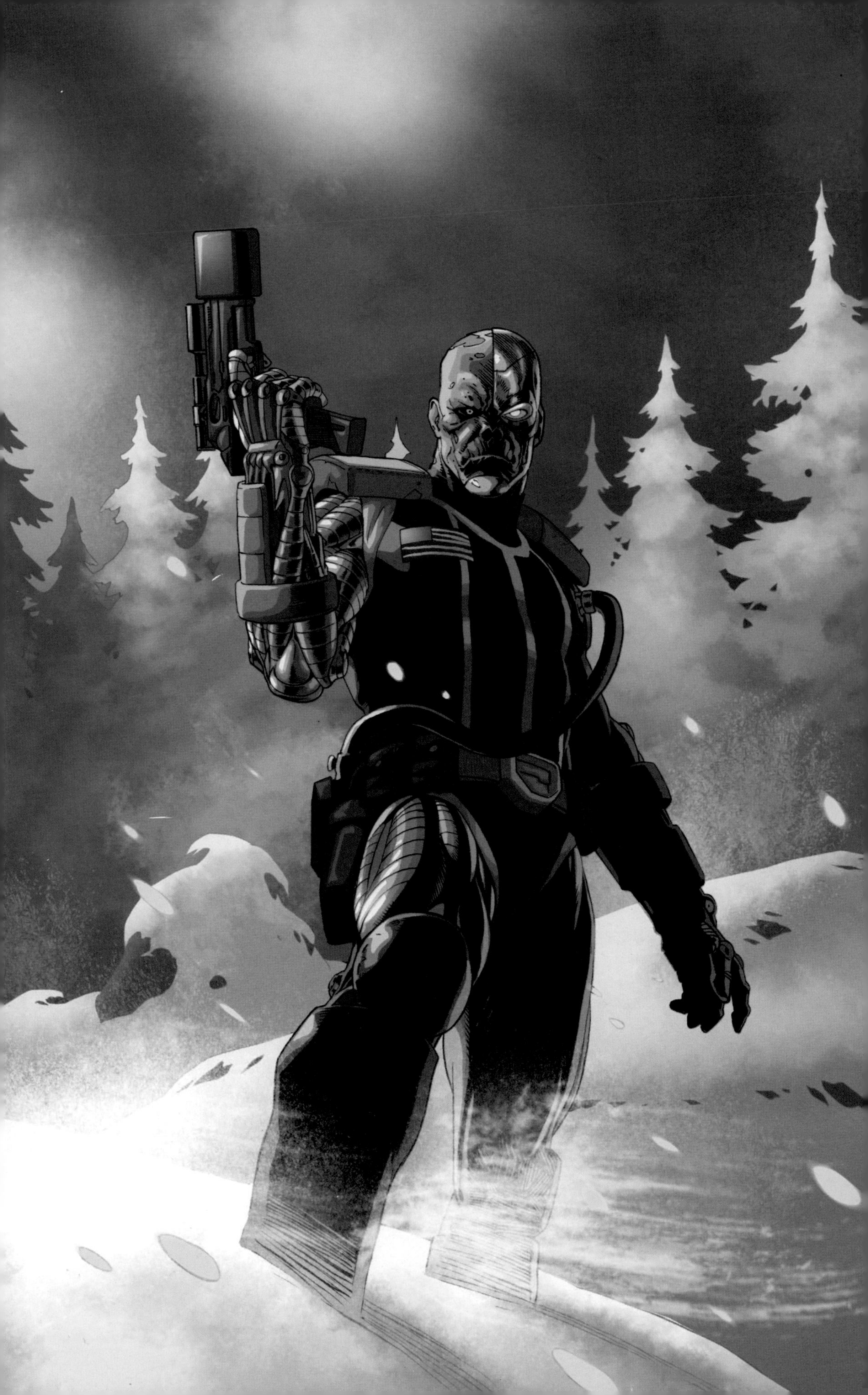

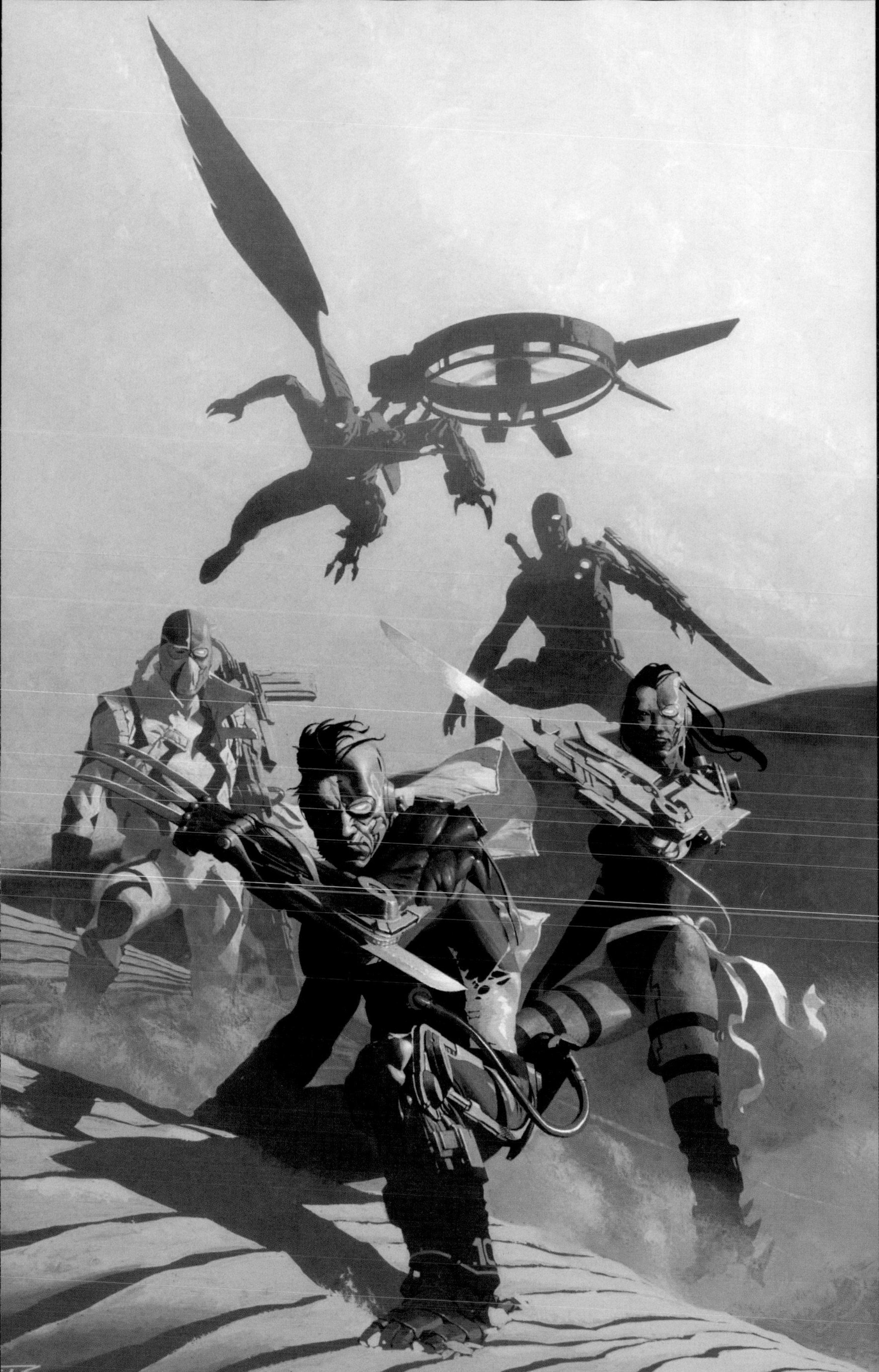

DEATHLOK NATION

CHAPTER 02

MISSION ACHIEVEMENT-- FIFTY PERCENT.

I HAVE POSSESSION OF THE WORLD.

FANTOMEX REMAINS ALIVE.

FIND AND KILL HIM.

GO.

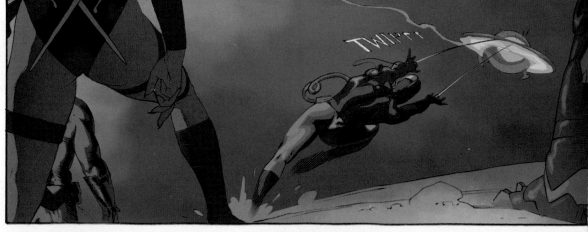

TWIPPP

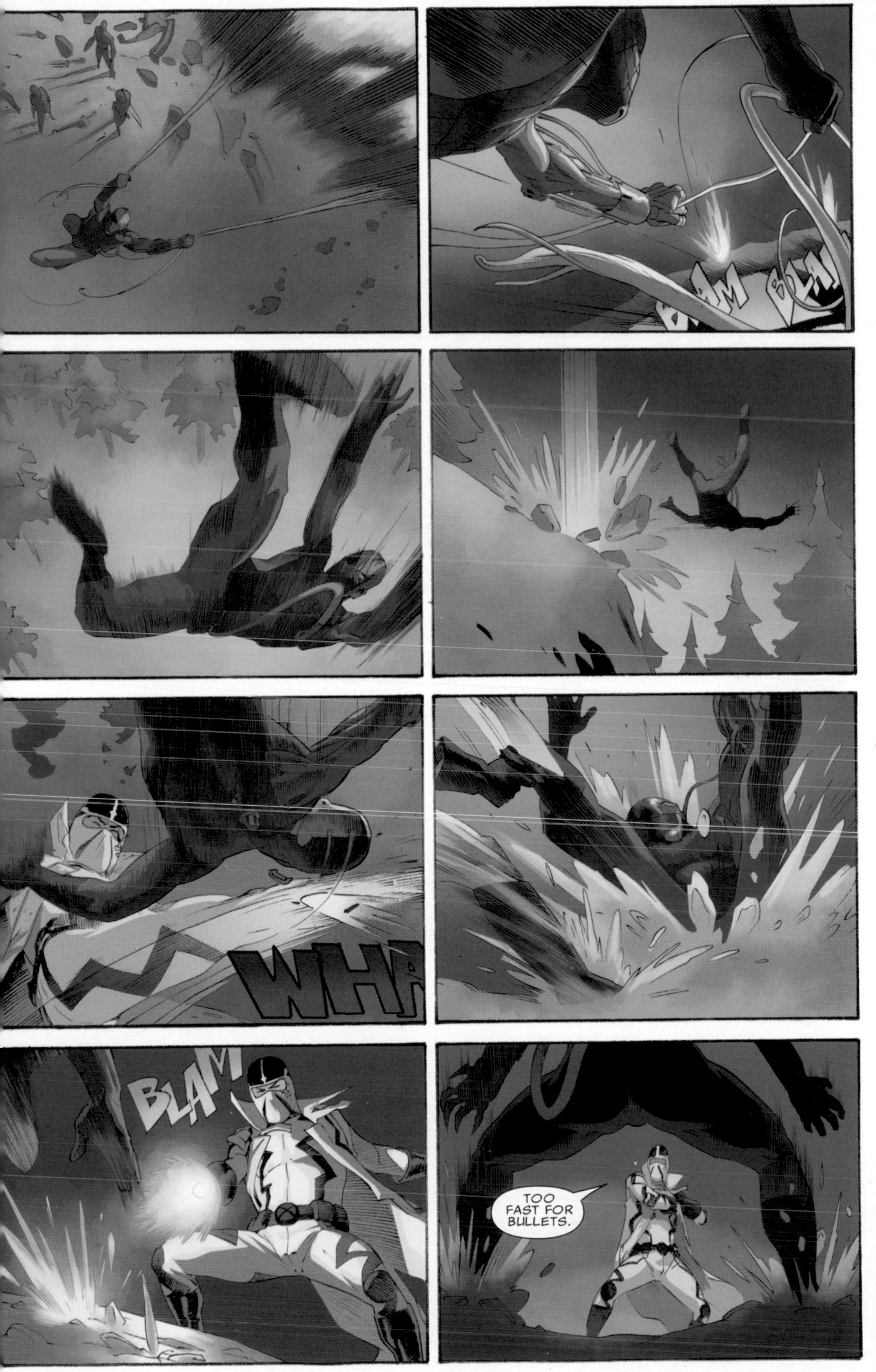
BLAM
BLAM
WHA
BLAM
TOO FAST FOR BULLETS.

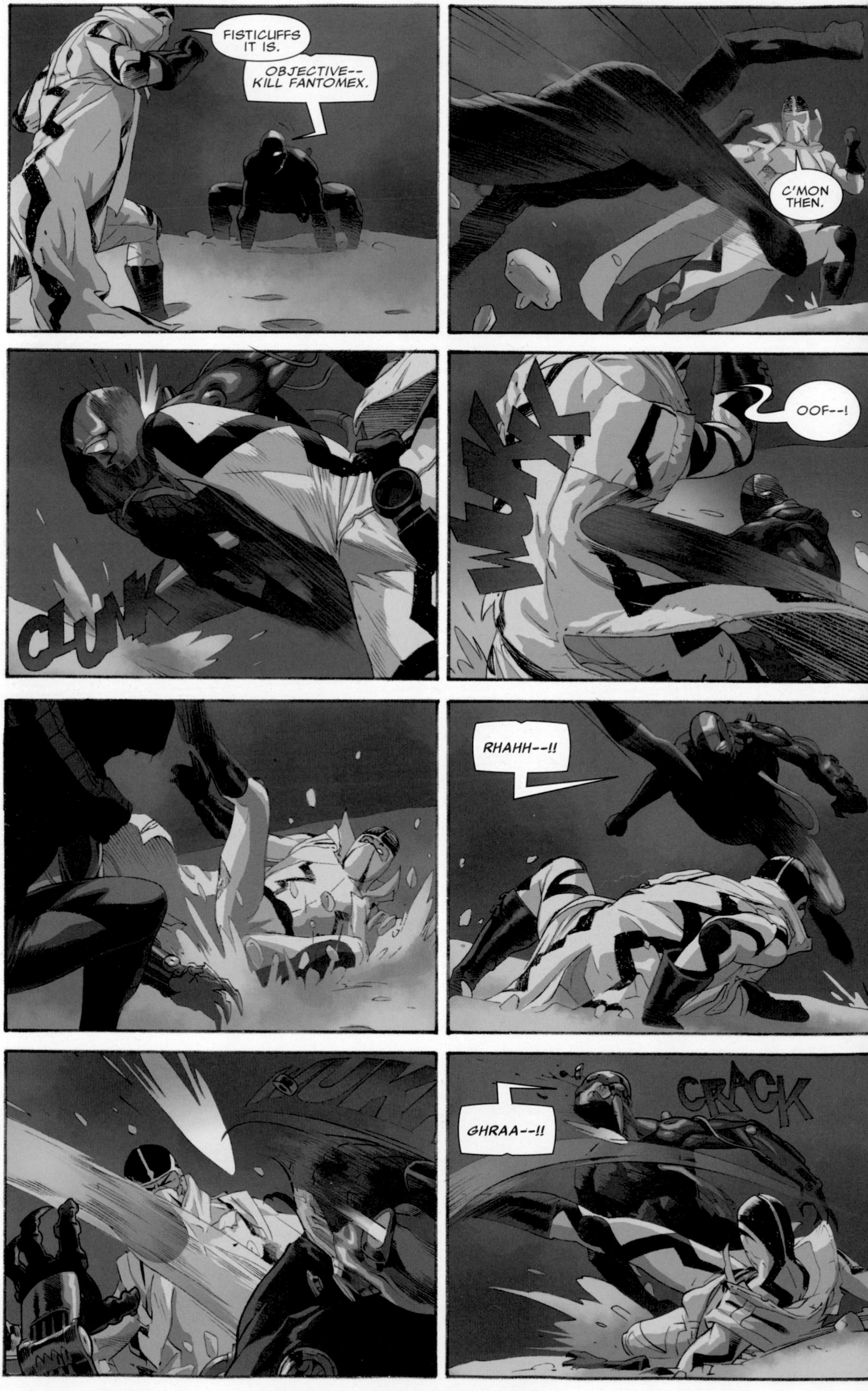
FISTICUFFS IT IS.
OBJECTIVE-- KILL FANTOMEX.
C'MON THEN.
CLUNK
OOF--!
RHAHH--!!
GHRAA--!!
CRACK

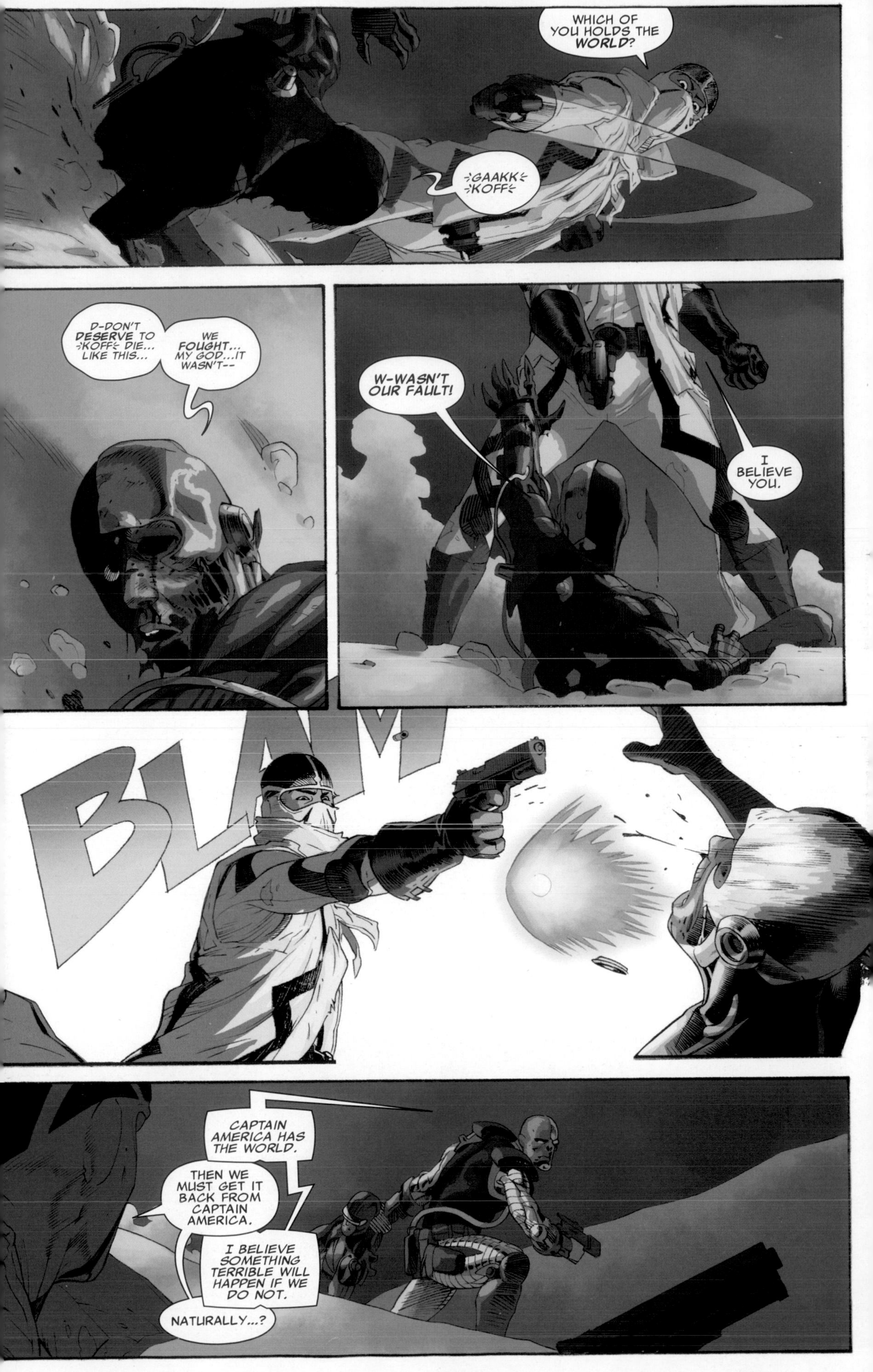
WHICH OF YOU HOLDS THE WORLD?
GAAKK KOFF
D-DON'T DESERVE TO KOFF DIE... LIKE THIS...
WE FOUGHT... MY GOD...IT WASN'T--
W-WASN'T OUR FAULT!
I BELIEVE YOU.
BLAM
CAPTAIN AMERICA HAS THE WORLD.
THEN WE MUST GET IT BACK FROM CAPTAIN AMERICA.
I BELIEVE SOMETHING TERRIBLE WILL HAPPEN IF WE DO NOT.
NATURALLY...?

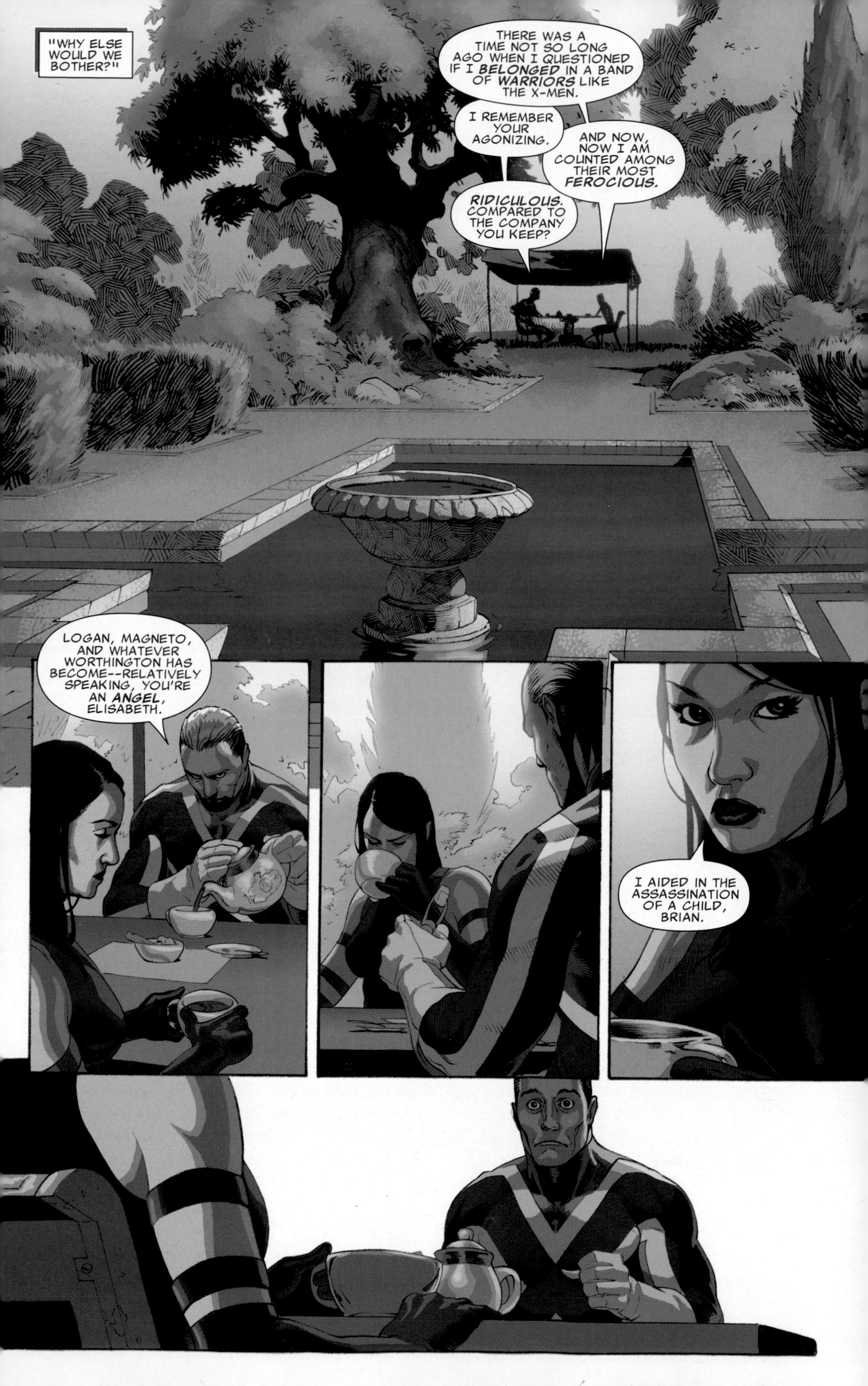
"WHY ELSE WOULD WE BOTHER?"
THERE WAS A TIME NOT SO LONG AGO WHEN I QUESTIONED IF I BELONGED IN A BAND OF WARRIORS LIKE THE X-MEN.
I REMEMBER YOUR AGONIZING.
AND NOW, NOW I AM COUNTED AMONG THEIR MOST FEROCIOUS.
RIDICULOUS. COMPARED TO THE COMPANY YOU KEEP?
LOGAN, MAGNETO, AND WHATEVER WORTHINGTON HAS BECOME--RELATIVELY SPEAKING, YOU'RE AN ANGEL, ELISABETH.
I AIDED IN THE ASSASSINATION OF A CHILD, BRIAN.

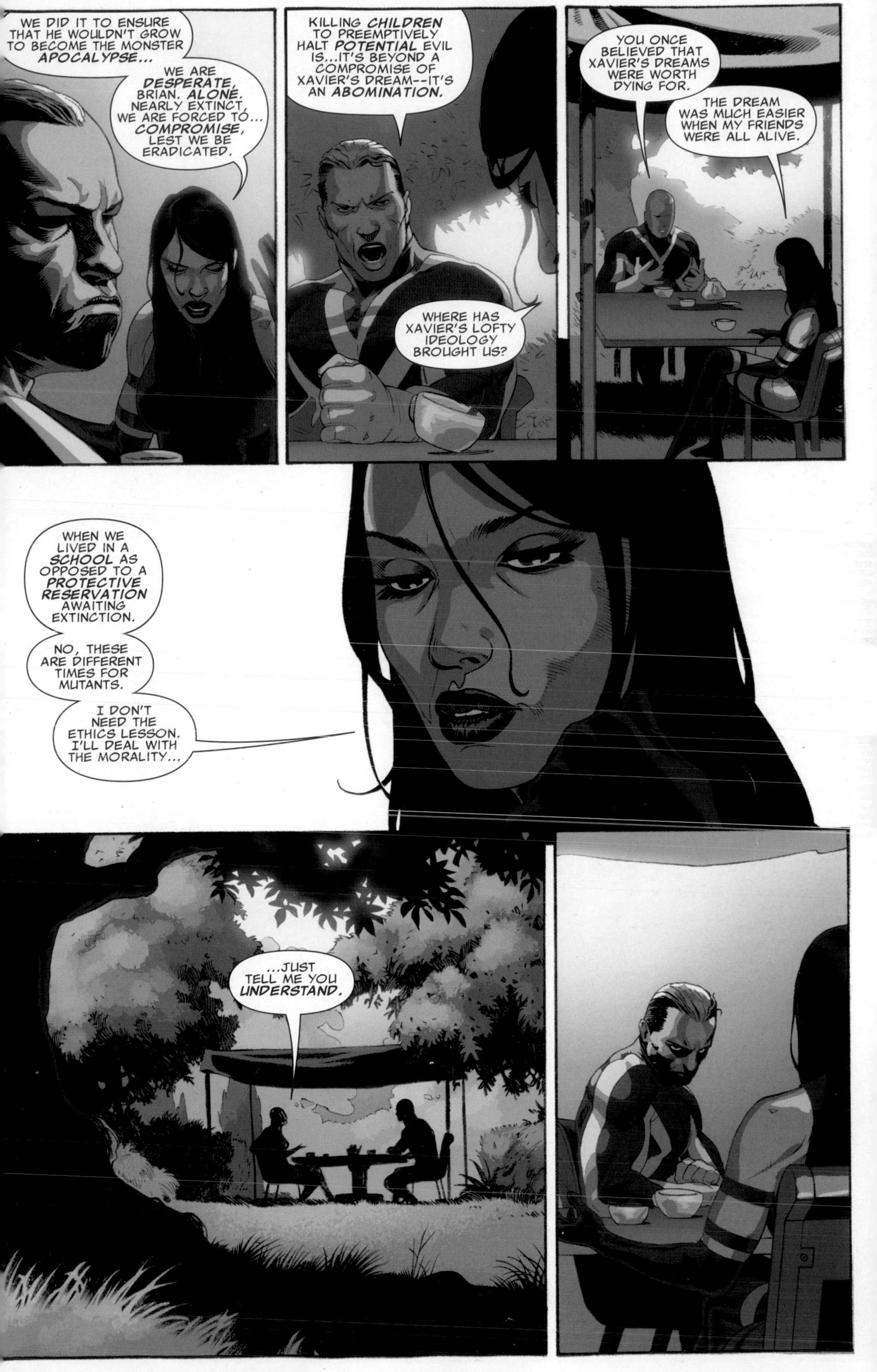

WE DID IT TO ENSURE THAT HE WOULDN'T GROW TO BECOME THE MONSTER APOCALYPSE...
WE ARE DESPERATE, BRIAN. ALONE. NEARLY EXTINCT. WE ARE FORCED TO... COMPROMISE, LEST WE BE ERADICATED.
KILLING CHILDREN TO PREEMPTIVELY HALT POTENTIAL EVIL IS...IT'S BEYOND A COMPROMISE OF XAVIER'S DREAM--IT'S AN ABOMINATION.
WHERE HAS XAVIER'S LOFTY IDEOLOGY BROUGHT US?
YOU ONCE BELIEVED THAT XAVIER'S DREAMS WERE WORTH DYING FOR.
THE DREAM WAS MUCH EASIER WHEN MY FRIENDS WERE ALL ALIVE.
WHEN WE LIVED IN A SCHOOL AS OPPOSED TO A PROTECTIVE RESERVATION AWAITING EXTINCTION.
NO, THESE ARE DIFFERENT TIMES FOR MUTANTS.
I DON'T NEED THE ETHICS LESSON. I'LL DEAL WITH THE MORALITY...
...JUST TELL ME YOU UNDERSTAND.

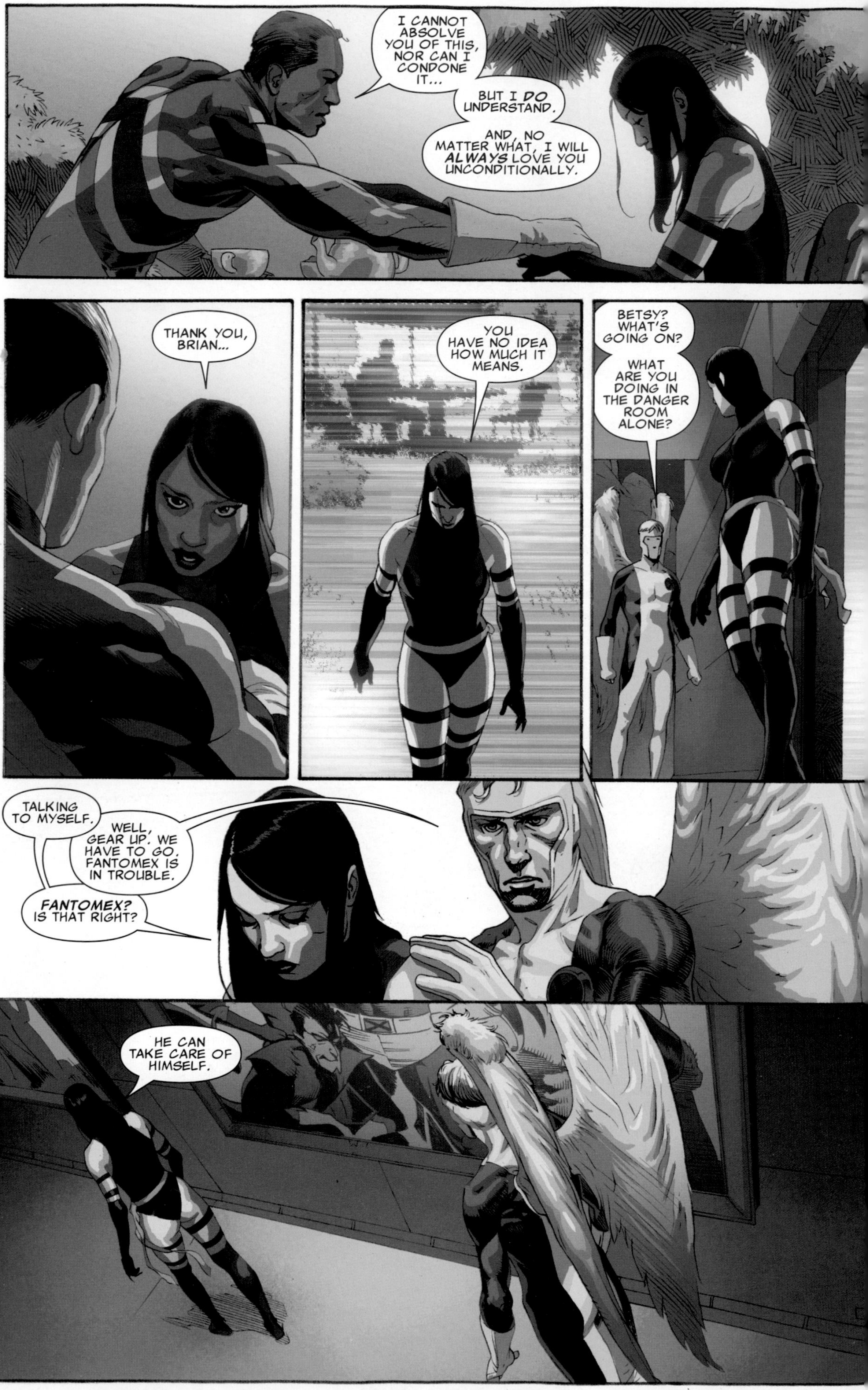
I CANNOT ABSOLVE YOU OF THIS, NOR CAN I CONDONE IT...
BUT I DO UNDERSTAND.
AND, NO MATTER WHAT, I WILL ALWAYS LOVE YOU UNCONDITIONALLY.
THANK YOU, BRIAN...
YOU HAVE NO IDEA HOW MUCH IT MEANS.
BETSY? WHAT'S GOING ON?
WHAT ARE YOU DOING IN THE DANGER ROOM ALONE?
TALKING TO MYSELF.
WELL, GEAR UP. WE HAVE TO GO. FANTOMEX IS IN TROUBLE.
FANTOMEX? IS THAT RIGHT?
HE CAN TAKE CARE OF HIMSELF.

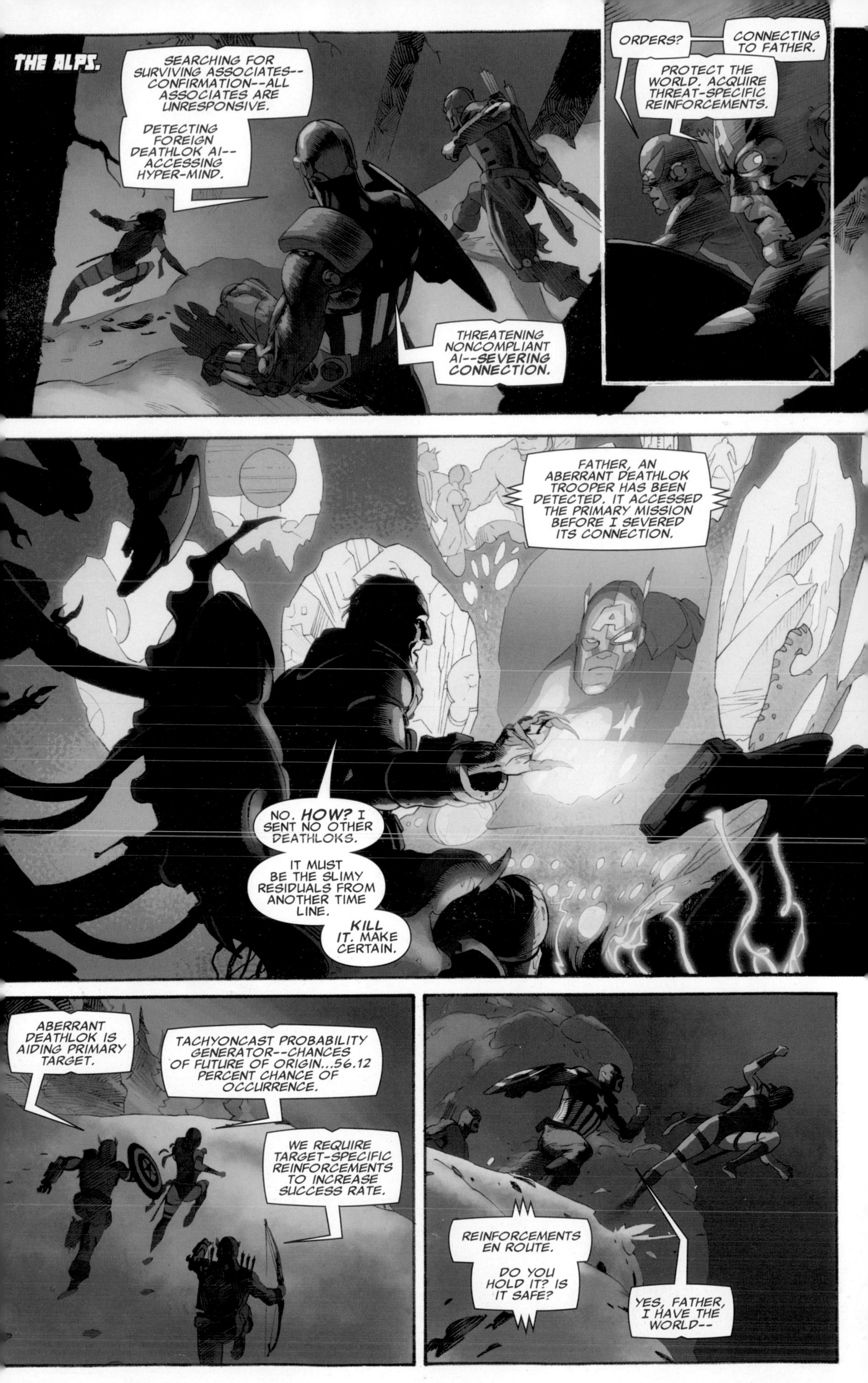
THE ALPS.
SEARCHING FOR SURVIVING ASSOCIATES--CONFIRMATION--ALL ASSOCIATES ARE UNRESPONSIVE.
DETECTING FOREIGN DEATHLOK AI--ACCESSING HYPER-MIND.
THREATENING NONCOMPLIANT AI--SEVERING CONNECTION.
ORDERS?
CONNECTING TO FATHER.
PROTECT THE WORLD. ACQUIRE THREAT-SPECIFIC REINFORCEMENTS.
FATHER, AN ABERRANT DEATHLOK TROOPER HAS BEEN DETECTED. IT ACCESSED THE PRIMARY MISSION BEFORE I SEVERED ITS CONNECTION.
NO. HOW? I SENT NO OTHER DEATHLOKS.
IT MUST BE THE SLIMY RESIDUALS FROM ANOTHER TIME LINE.
KILL IT. MAKE CERTAIN.
ABERRANT DEATHLOK IS AIDING PRIMARY TARGET.
TACHYONCAST PROBABILITY GENERATOR--CHANCES OF FUTURE OF ORIGIN...56.12 PERCENT CHANCE OF OCCURRENCE.
WE REQUIRE TARGET-SPECIFIC REINFORCEMENTS TO INCREASE SUCCESS RATE.
REINFORCEMENTS EN ROUTE.
DO YOU HOLD IT? IS IT SAFE?
YES, FATHER, I HAVE THE WORLD--

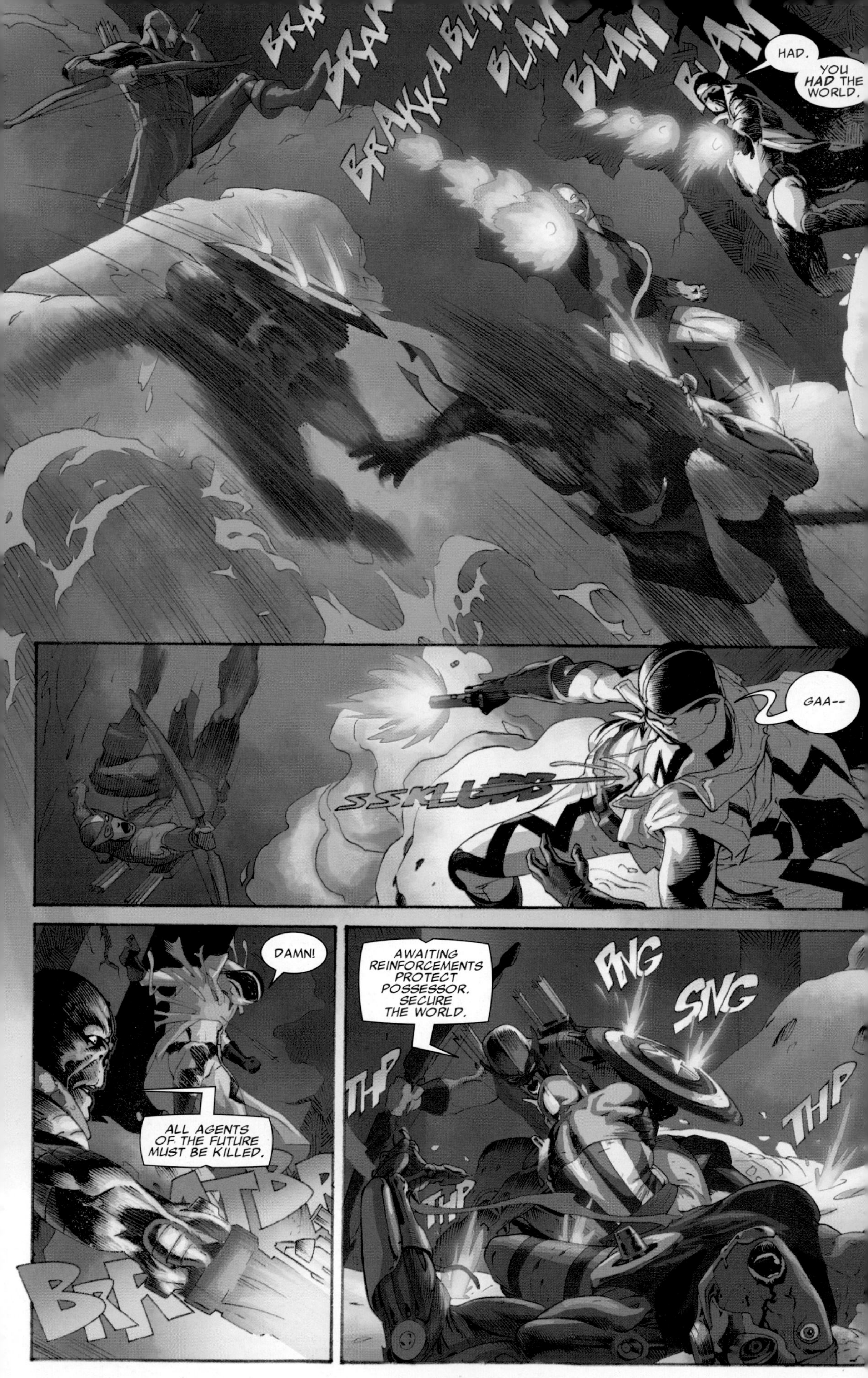
BRAK
BRAK
BRAKKA BLAM
BLAM
BLAM
BLAM
BLAM
HAD.
YOU HAD THE WORLD.
GAA--
SSKLUDD
DAMN!
ALL AGENTS OF THE FUTURE MUST BE KILLED.
BRRT
AWAITING REINFORCEMENTS PROTECT POSSESSOR. SECURE THE WORLD.
PING
SING
THP
THP
THP

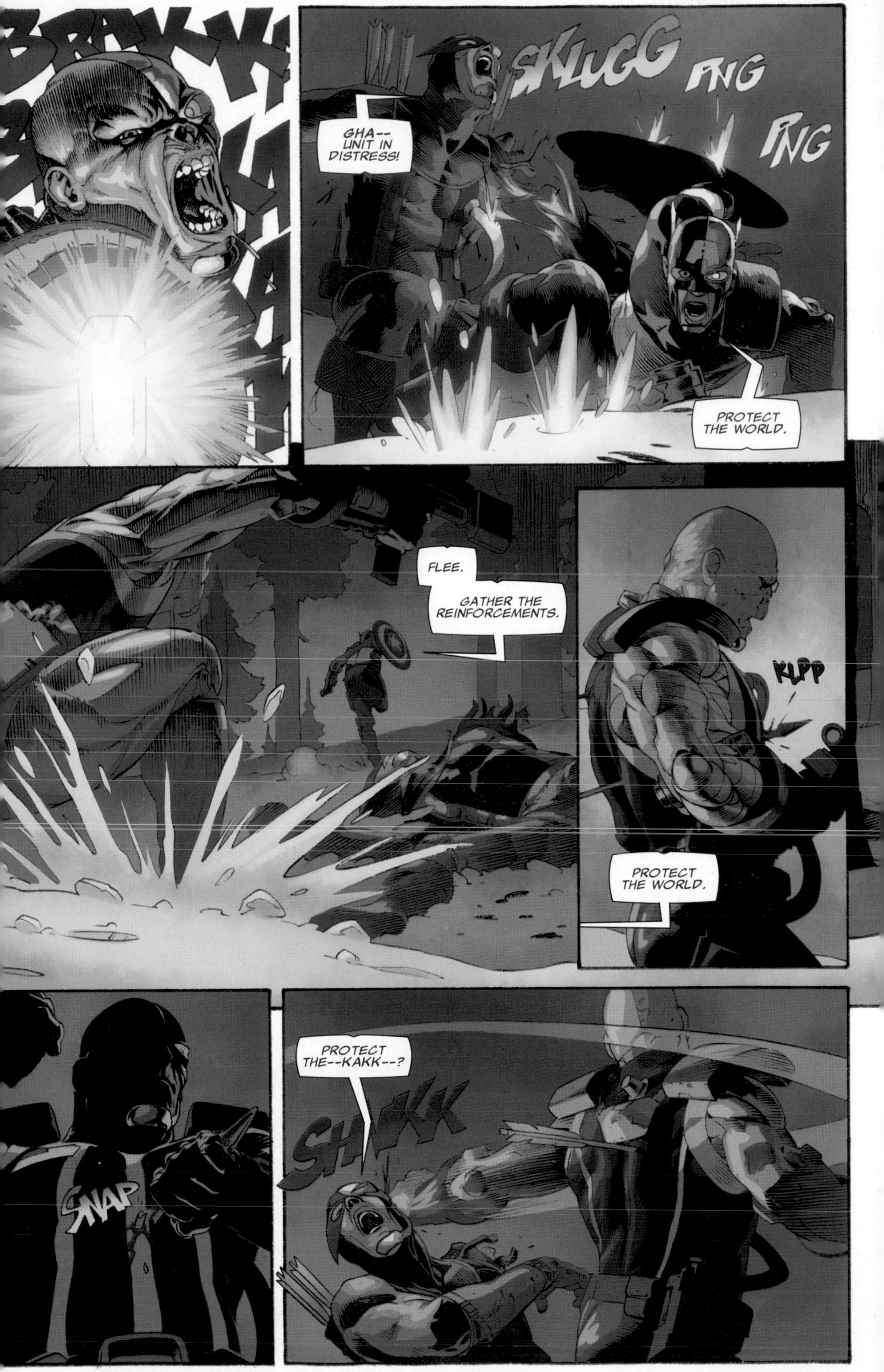
BRAKKA
SKLUGG
PNG
PNG
GHA-- UNIT IN DISTRESS!
PROTECT THE WORLD.
FLEE.
GATHER THE REINFORCEMENTS.
KLPP
PROTECT THE WORLD.
SNAP
PROTECT THE--KAKK--?
SHKK

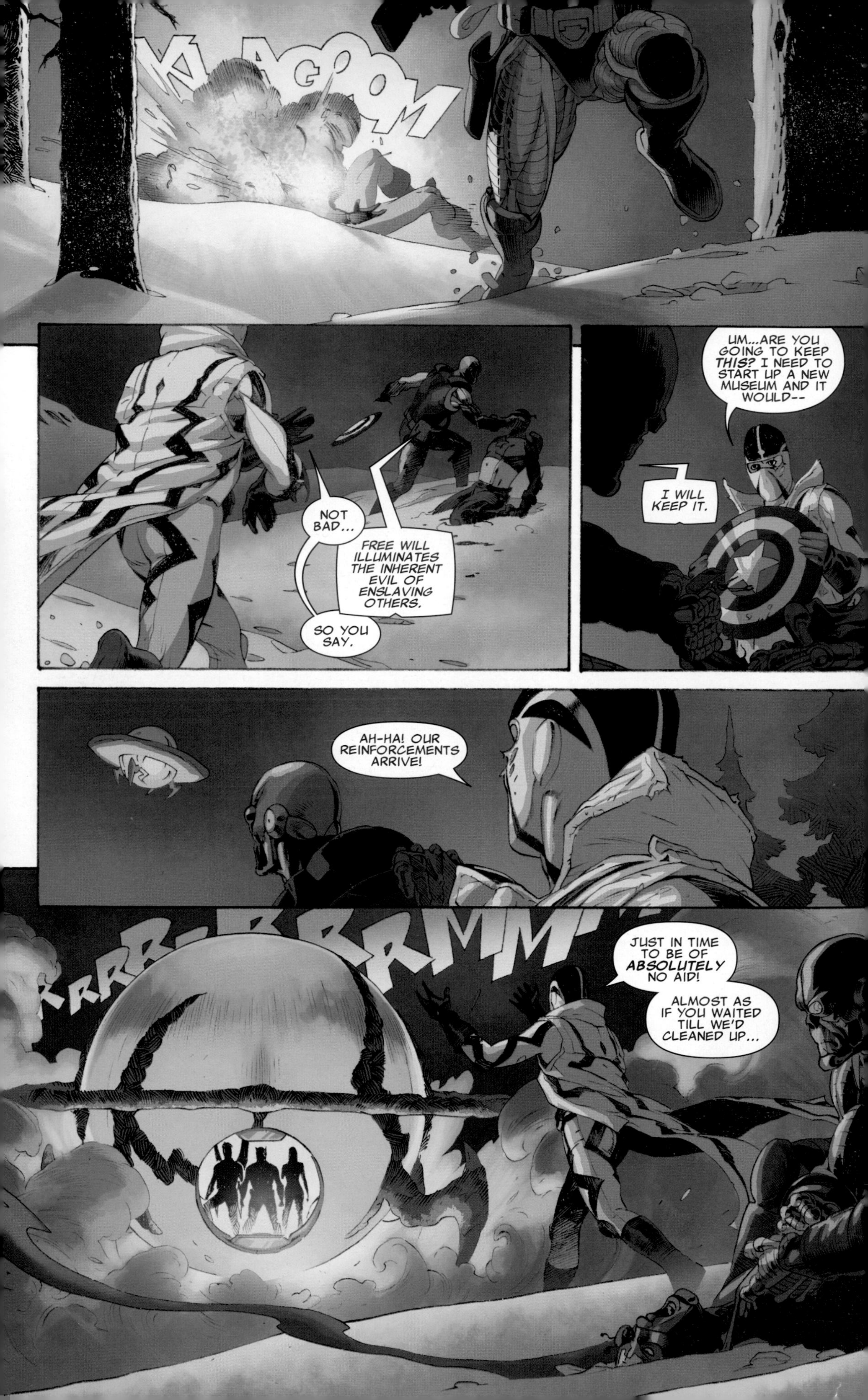
KLAGOOM
NOT BAD...
FREE WILL ILLUMINATES THE INHERENT EVIL OF ENSLAVING OTHERS.
SO YOU SAY.
UM...ARE YOU GOING TO KEEP *THIS?* I NEED TO START UP A NEW MUSEUM AND IT WOULD--
I WILL KEEP IT.
AH-HA! OUR REINFORCEMENTS ARRIVE!
RRRR-BRRMM
JUST IN TIME TO BE OF **ABSOLUTELY** NO AID!
ALMOST AS IF YOU WAITED TILL WE'D CLEANED UP...

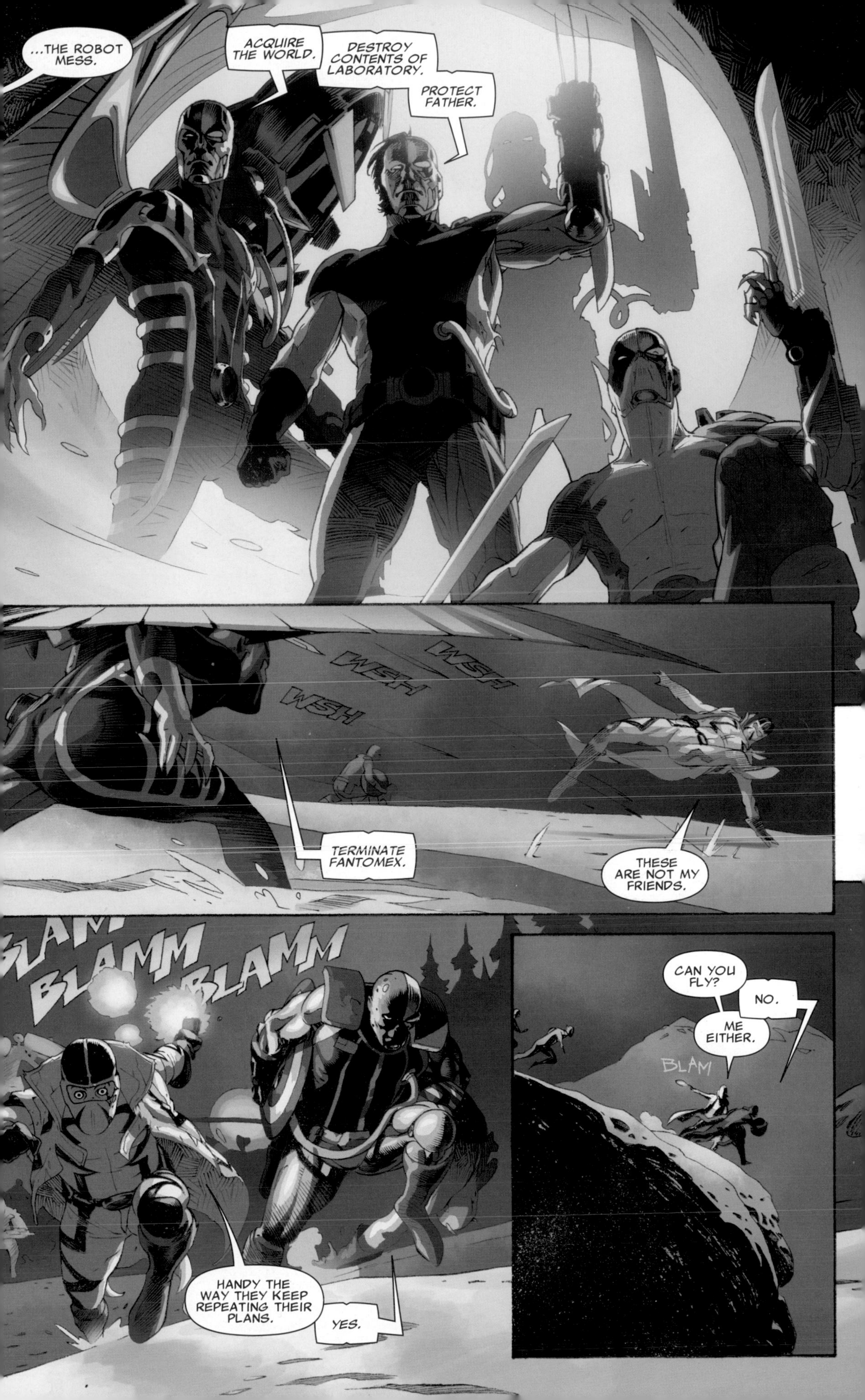
...THE ROBOT MESS.
ACQUIRE THE WORLD.
DESTROY CONTENTS OF LABORATORY.
PROTECT FATHER.
WSH
WSH
WSH
TERMINATE FANTOMEX.
THESE ARE NOT MY FRIENDS.
BLAMM
BLAMM
HANDY THE WAY THEY KEEP REPEATING THEIR PLANS.
YES.
CAN YOU FLY?
NO.
ME EITHER.
BLAM

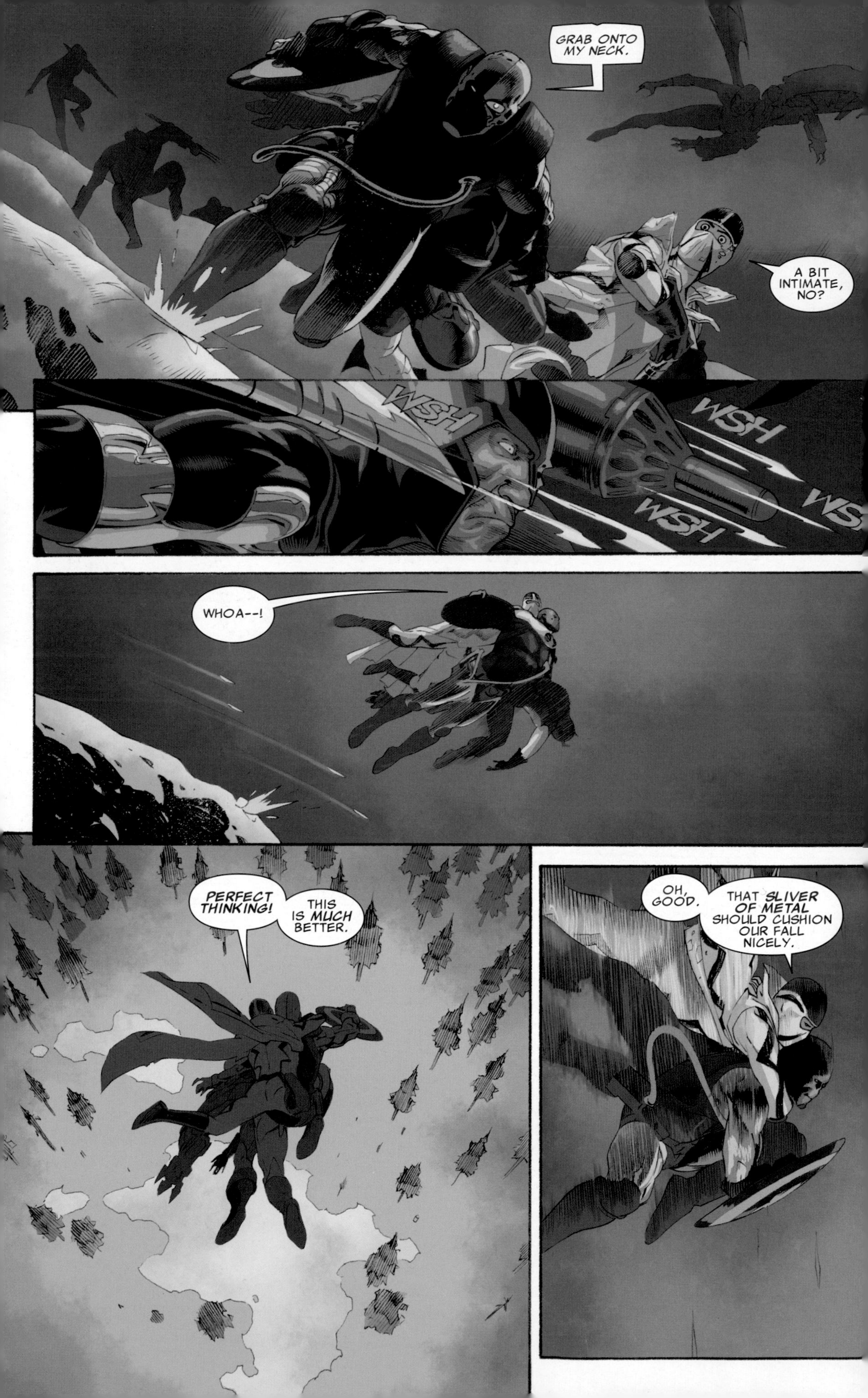
GRAB ONTO MY NECK.
A BIT INTIMATE, NO?
WSH
WSH
WSH
WSH
WHOA--!
PERFECT THINKING!
THIS IS MUCH BETTER.
OH, GOOD.
THAT SLIVER OF METAL SHOULD CUSHION OUR FALL NICELY.

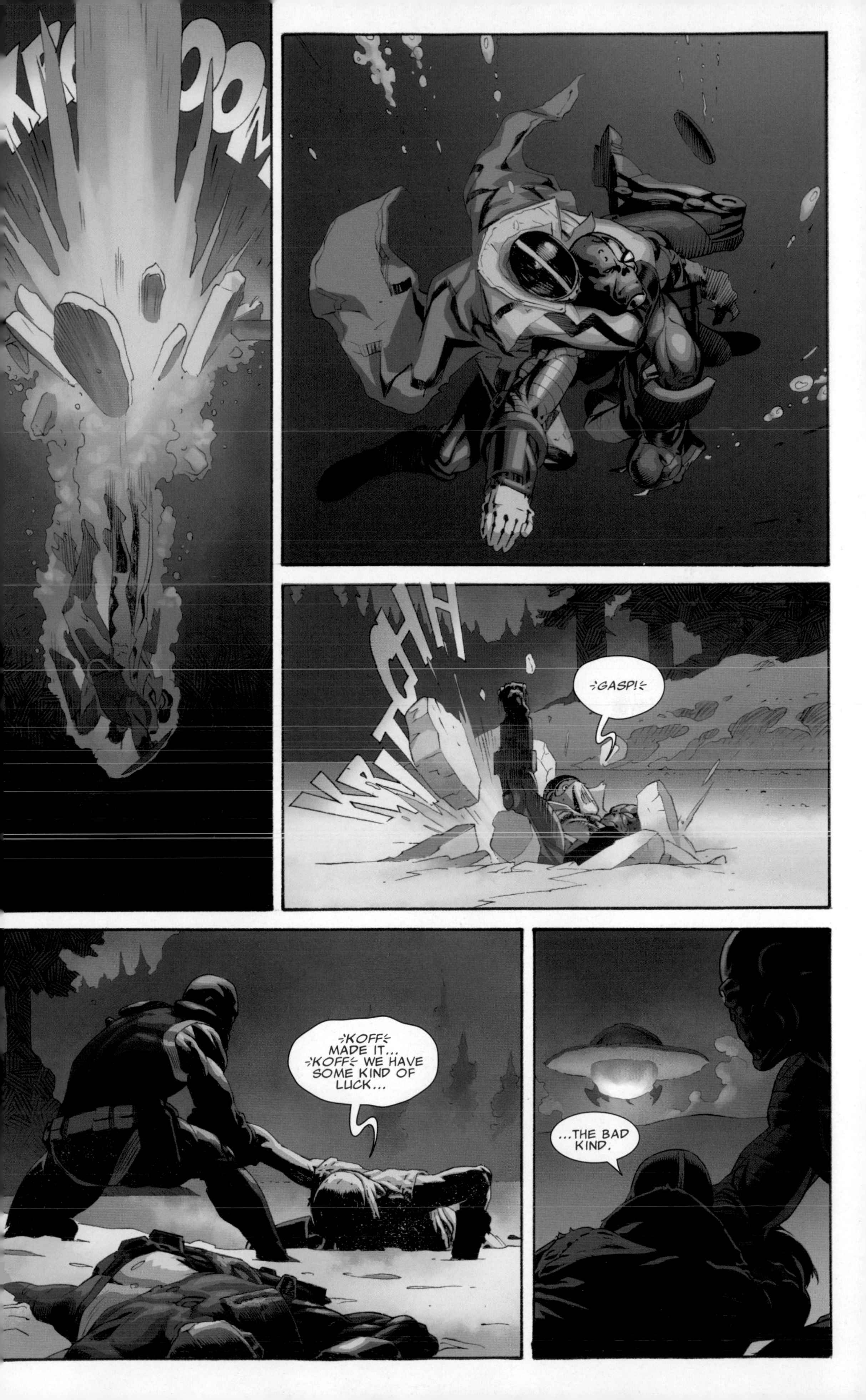

-GASP!-
-KOFF- MADE IT... -KOFF- WE HAVE SOME KIND OF LUCK...
...THE BAD KIND.

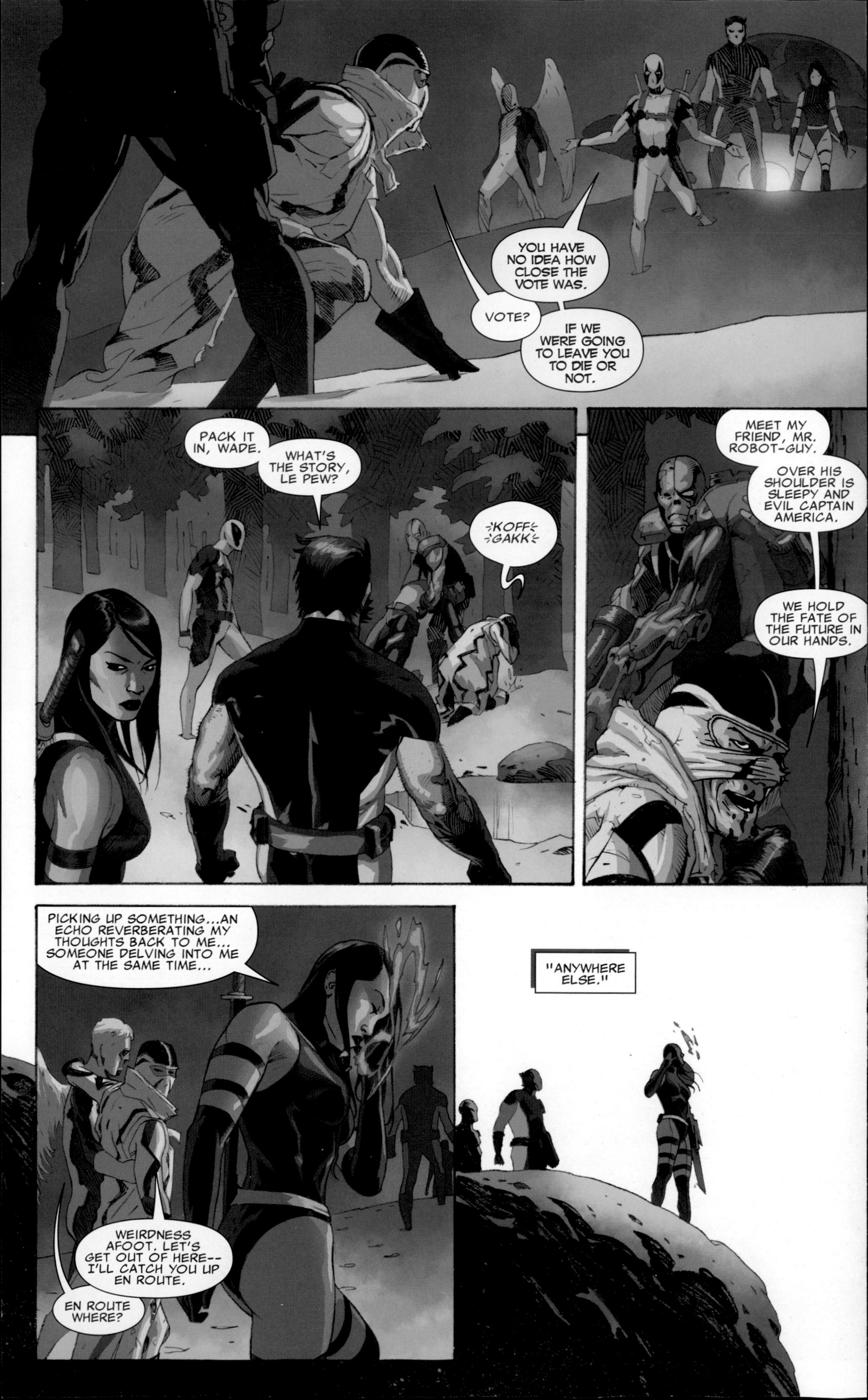
YOU HAVE NO IDEA HOW CLOSE THE VOTE WAS.
VOTE?
IF WE WERE GOING TO LEAVE YOU TO DIE OR NOT.
PACK IT IN, WADE.
WHAT'S THE STORY, LE PEW?
KOFF GAKK
MEET MY FRIEND, MR. ROBOT-GUY.
OVER HIS SHOULDER IS SLEEPY AND EVIL CAPTAIN AMERICA.
WE HOLD THE FATE OF THE FUTURE IN OUR HANDS.
PICKING UP SOMETHING...AN ECHO REVERBERATING MY THOUGHTS BACK TO ME... SOMEONE DELVING INTO ME AT THE SAME TIME...
WEIRDNESS AFOOT. LET'S GET OUT OF HERE-- I'LL CATCH YOU UP EN ROUTE.
EN ROUTE WHERE?
"ANYWHERE ELSE."

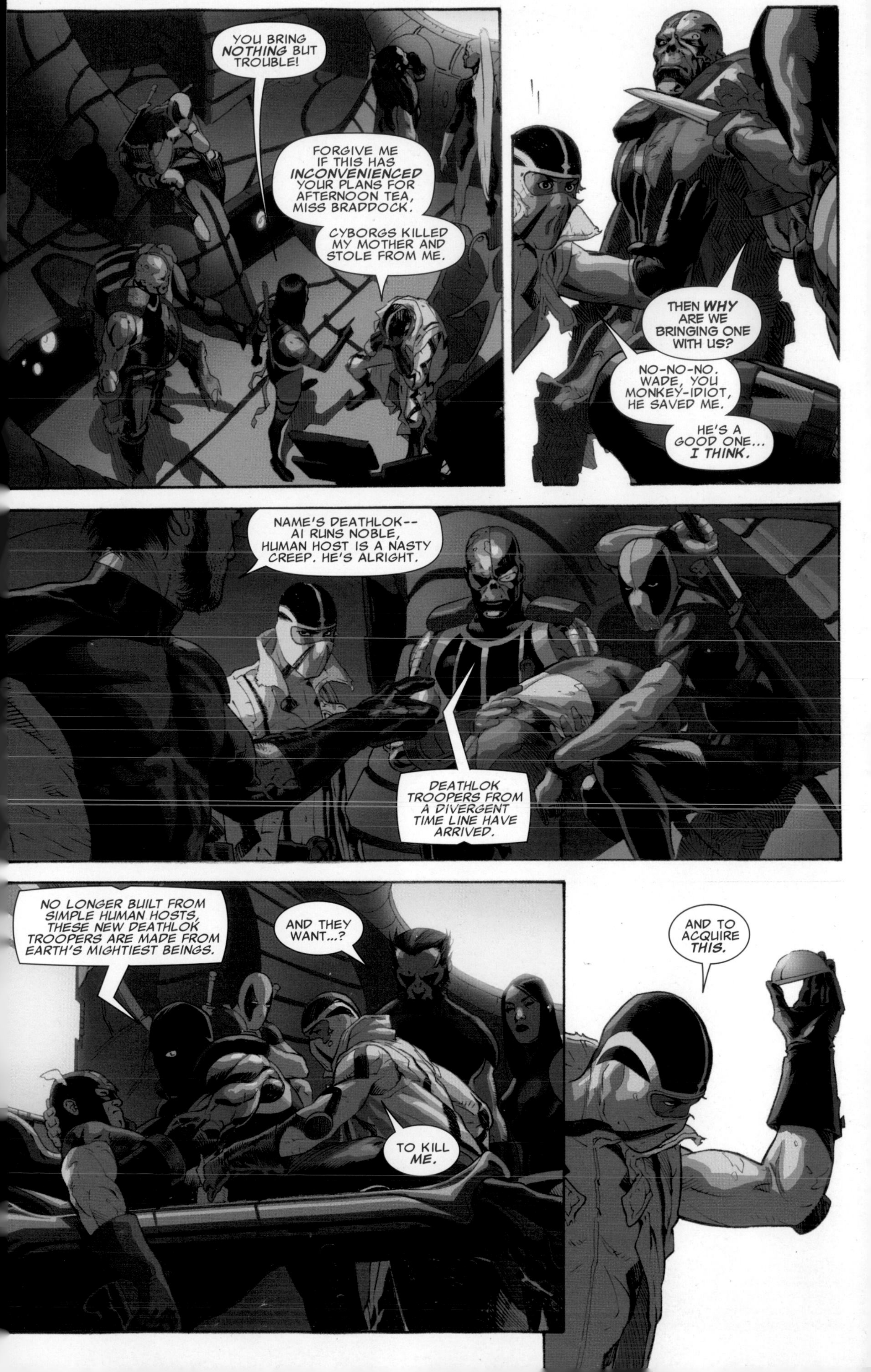
YOU BRING NOTHING BUT TROUBLE!
FORGIVE ME IF THIS HAS INCONVENIENCED YOUR PLANS FOR AFTERNOON TEA, MISS BRADDOCK.
CYBORGS KILLED MY MOTHER AND STOLE FROM ME.
THEN WHY ARE WE BRINGING ONE WITH US?
NO-NO-NO. WADE, YOU MONKEY-IDIOT, HE SAVED ME.
HE'S A GOOD ONE... I THINK.
NAME'S DEATHLOK-- AI RUNS NOBLE, HUMAN HOST IS A NASTY CREEP. HE'S ALRIGHT.
DEATHLOK TROOPERS FROM A DIVERGENT TIME LINE HAVE ARRIVED.
NO LONGER BUILT FROM SIMPLE HUMAN HOSTS, THESE NEW DEATHLOK TROOPERS ARE MADE FROM EARTH'S MIGHTIEST BEINGS.
AND THEY WANT...?
TO KILL ME.
AND TO ACQUIRE THIS.

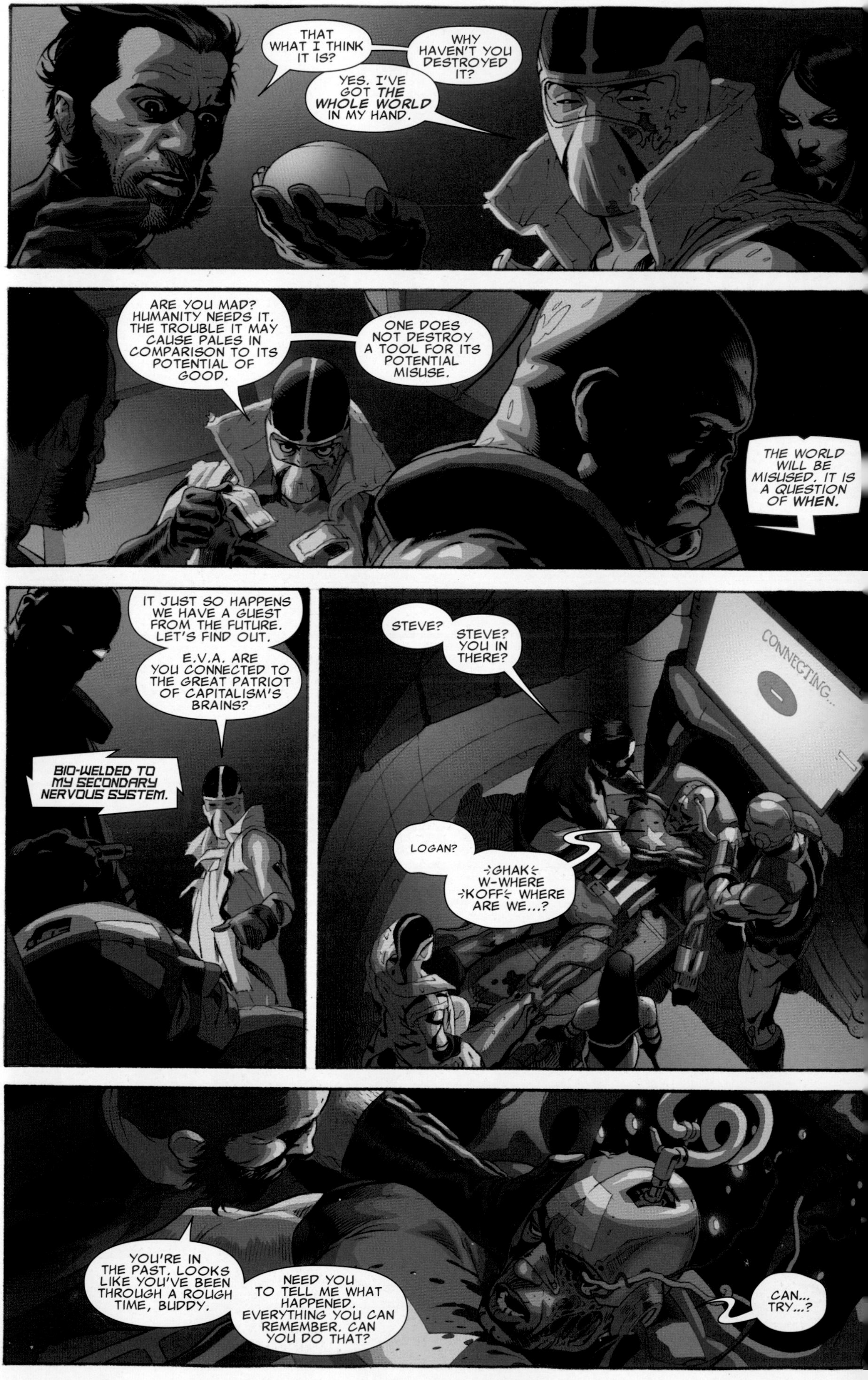
THAT WHAT I THINK IT IS?
YES. I'VE GOT THE WHOLE WORLD IN MY HAND.
WHY HAVEN'T YOU DESTROYED IT?
ARE YOU MAD? HUMANITY NEEDS IT. THE TROUBLE IT MAY CAUSE PALES IN COMPARISON TO ITS POTENTIAL OF GOOD.
ONE DOES NOT DESTROY A TOOL FOR ITS POTENTIAL MISUSE.
THE WORLD WILL BE MISUSED. IT IS A QUESTION OF WHEN.
IT JUST SO HAPPENS WE HAVE A GUEST FROM THE FUTURE. LET'S FIND OUT.
E.V.A. ARE YOU CONNECTED TO THE GREAT PATRIOT OF CAPITALISM'S BRAINS?
BIO-WELDED TO MY SECONDARY NERVOUS SYSTEM.
STEVE?
STEVE? YOU IN THERE?
CONNECTING...
LOGAN?
GHAK W-WHERE KOFF WHERE ARE WE...?
YOU'RE IN THE PAST. LOOKS LIKE YOU'VE BEEN THROUGH A ROUGH TIME, BUDDY.
NEED YOU TO TELL ME WHAT HAPPENED. EVERYTHING YOU CAN REMEMBER. CAN YOU DO THAT?
CAN... TRY...?

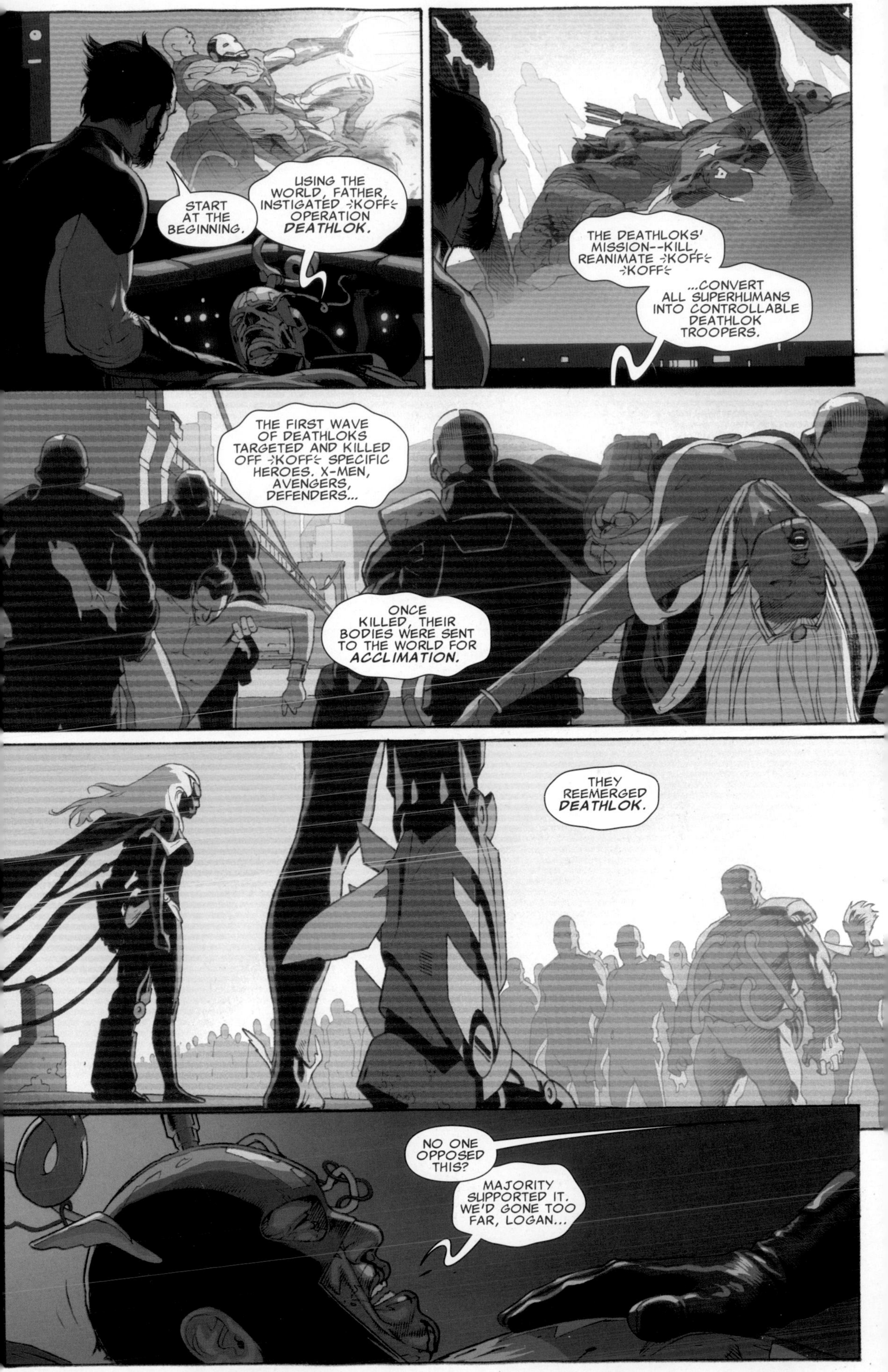
START AT THE BEGINNING.
USING THE WORLD, FATHER, INSTIGATED *KOFF* OPERATION DEATHLOK.
THE DEATHLOKS' MISSION--KILL, REANIMATE *KOFF* *KOFF*
...CONVERT ALL SUPERHUMANS INTO CONTROLLABLE DEATHLOK TROOPERS.
THE FIRST WAVE OF DEATHLOKS TARGETED AND KILLED OFF *KOFF* SPECIFIC HEROES. X-MEN, AVENGERS, DEFENDERS...
ONCE KILLED, THEIR BODIES WERE SENT TO THE WORLD FOR ACCLIMATION.
THEY REEMERGED DEATHLOK.
NO ONE OPPOSED THIS?
MAJORITY SUPPORTED IT. WE'D GONE TOO FAR, LOGAN...

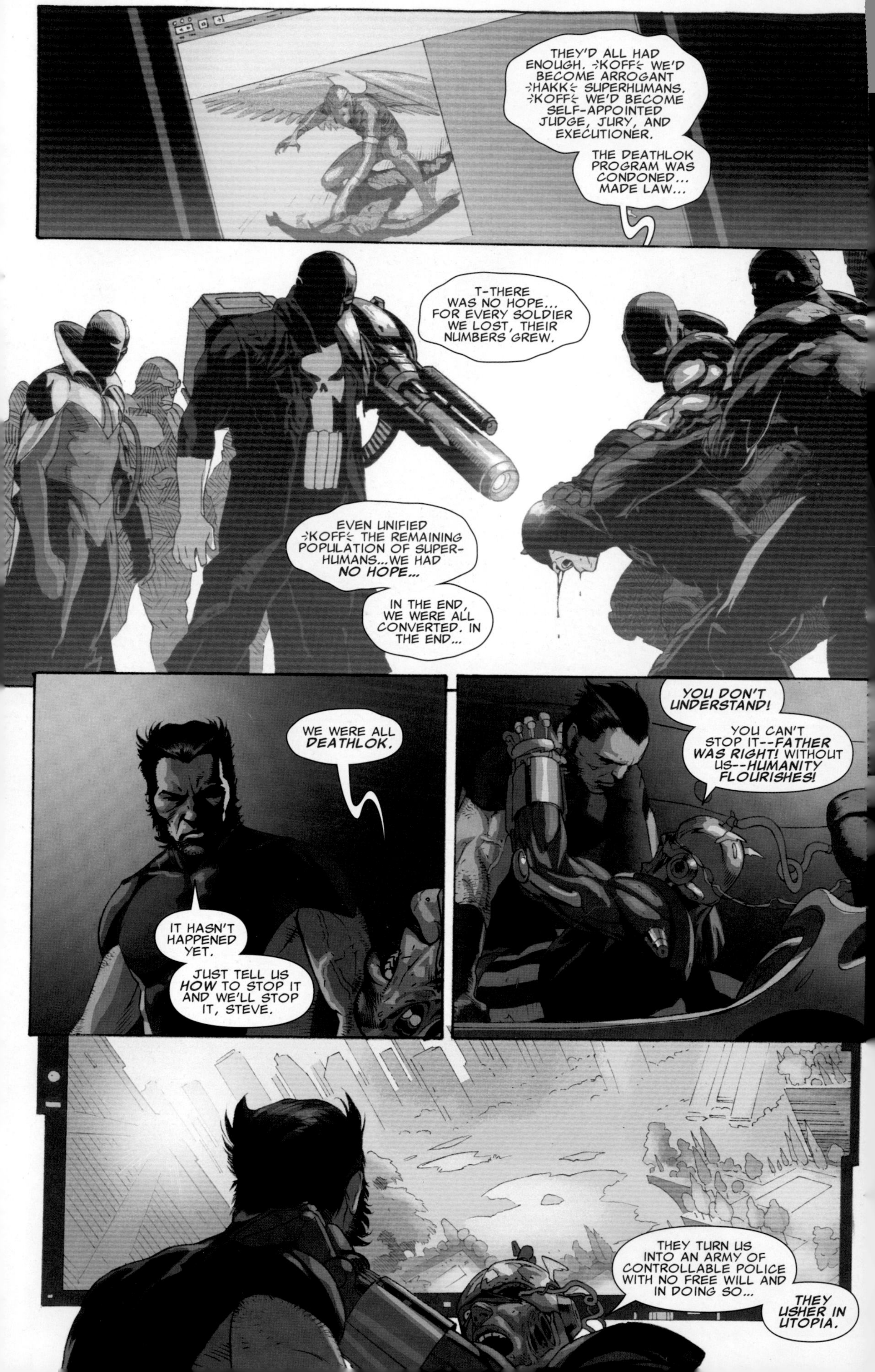
THEY'D ALL HAD ENOUGH. -KOFF- WE'D BECOME ARROGANT -HAKK- SUPERHUMANS. -KOFF- WE'D BECOME SELF-APPOINTED JUDGE, JURY, AND EXECUTIONER.
THE DEATHLOK PROGRAM WAS CONDONED... MADE LAW...
T-THERE WAS NO HOPE... FOR EVERY SOLDIER WE LOST, THEIR NUMBERS GREW.
EVEN UNIFIED -KOFF- THE REMAINING POPULATION OF SUPER-HUMANS...WE HAD NO HOPE...
IN THE END, WE WERE ALL CONVERTED. IN THE END...
WE WERE ALL DEATHLOK.
IT HASN'T HAPPENED YET.
JUST TELL US HOW TO STOP IT AND WE'LL STOP IT, STEVE.
YOU DON'T UNDERSTAND!
YOU CAN'T STOP IT--FATHER WAS RIGHT! WITHOUT US--HUMANITY FLOURISHES!
THEY TURN US INTO AN ARMY OF CONTROLLABLE POLICE WITH NO FREE WILL AND IN DOING SO...
THEY USHER IN UTOPIA.

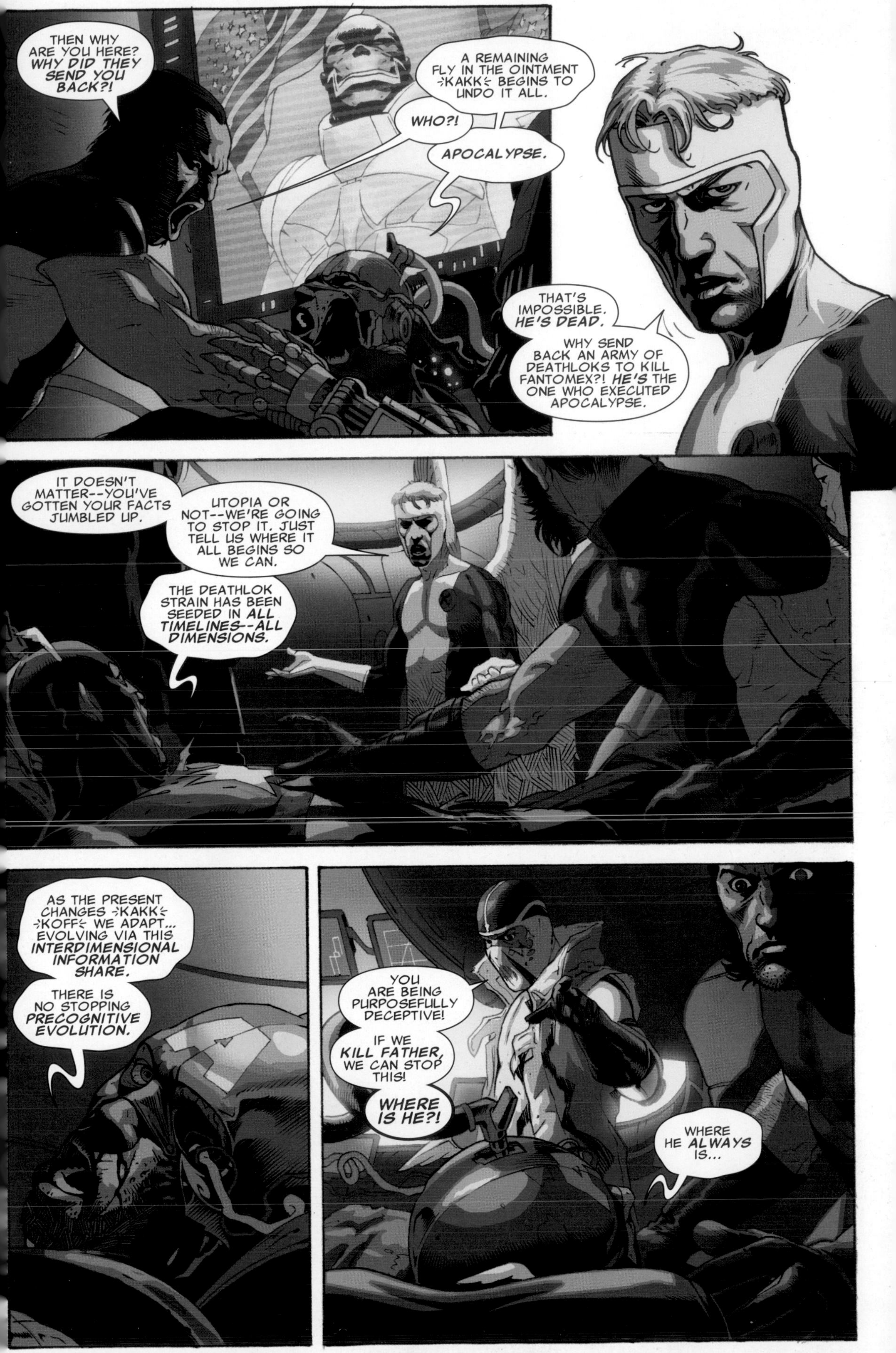
THEN WHY ARE YOU HERE? WHY DID THEY SEND YOU BACK?!
A REMAINING FLY IN THE OINTMENT ~KAKK~ BEGINS TO UNDO IT ALL.
WHO?!
APOCALYPSE.
THAT'S IMPOSSIBLE. HE'S DEAD.
WHY SEND BACK AN ARMY OF DEATHLOKS TO KILL FANTOMEX?! HE'S THE ONE WHO EXECUTED APOCALYPSE.
IT DOESN'T MATTER--YOU'VE GOTTEN YOUR FACTS JUMBLED UP.
UTOPIA OR NOT--WE'RE GOING TO STOP IT. JUST TELL US WHERE IT ALL BEGINS SO WE CAN.
THE DEATHLOK STRAIN HAS BEEN SEEDED IN ALL TIMELINES--ALL DIMENSIONS.
AS THE PRESENT CHANGES ~KAKK~ ~KOFF~ WE ADAPT... EVOLVING VIA THIS INTERDIMENSIONAL INFORMATION SHARE.
THERE IS NO STOPPING PRECOGNITIVE EVOLUTION.
YOU ARE BEING PURPOSEFULLY DECEPTIVE!
IF WE KILL FATHER, WE CAN STOP THIS!
WHERE IS HE?!
WHERE HE ALWAYS IS...

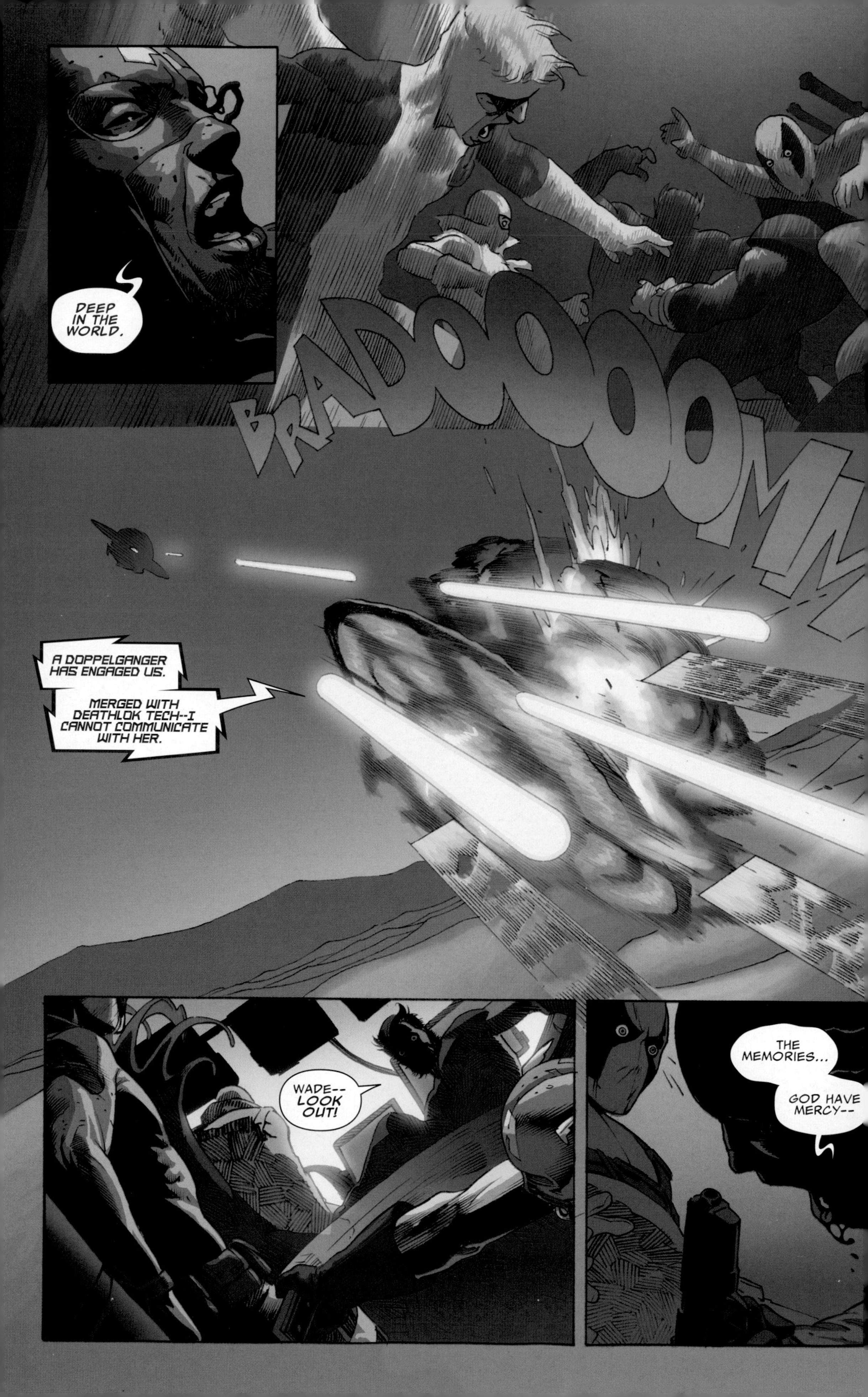
DEEP IN THE WORLD.
BRADOOOOOOOM
A DOPPELGANGER HAS ENGAGED US.
MERGED WITH DEATHLOK TECH--I CANNOT COMMUNICATE WITH HER.
WADE-- LOOK OUT!
THE MEMORIES...
GOD HAVE MERCY--

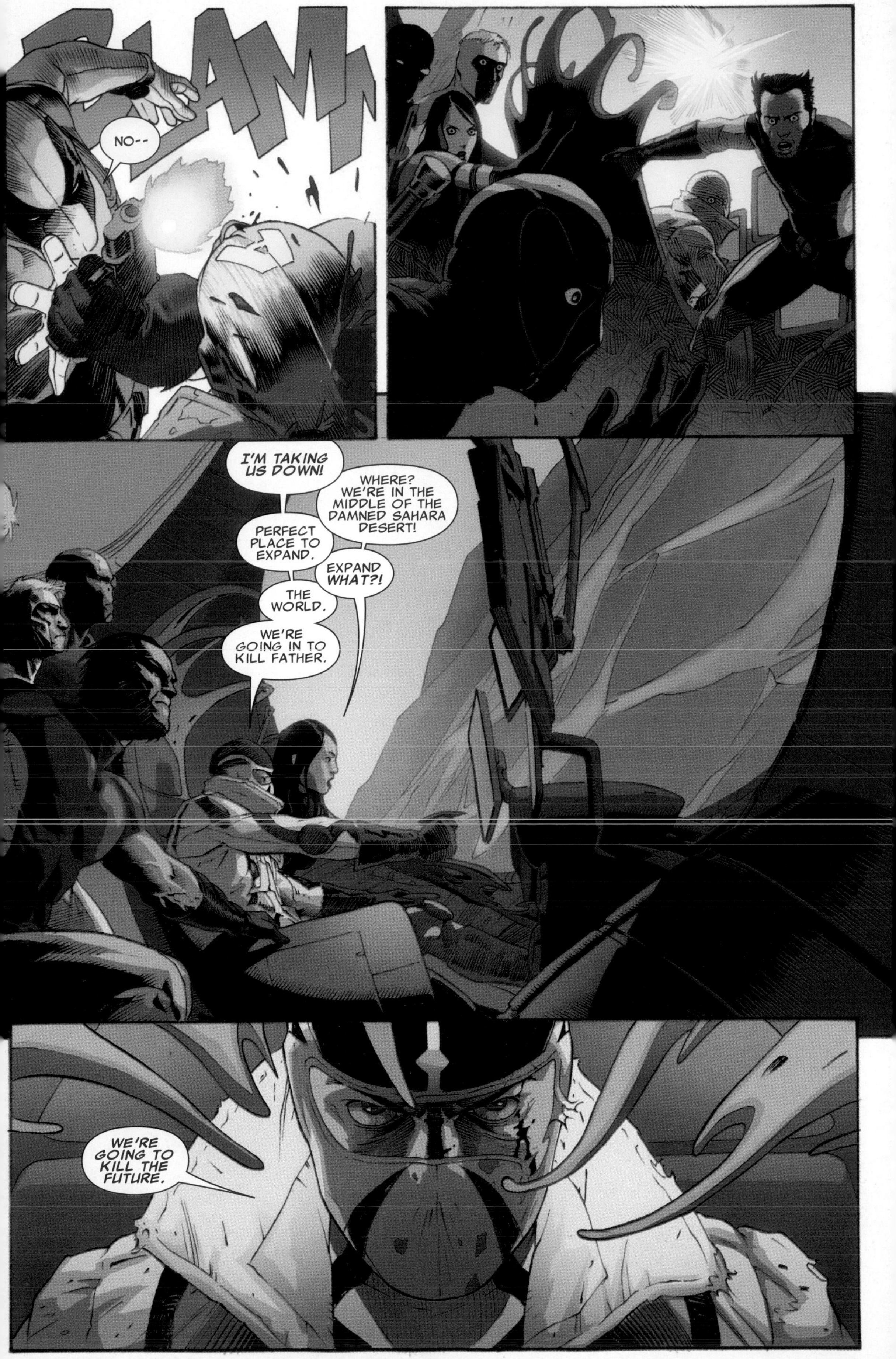

SLAM
NO--
I'M TAKING US DOWN!
WHERE? WE'RE IN THE MIDDLE OF THE DAMNED SAHARA DESERT!
PERFECT PLACE TO EXPAND.
EXPAND WHAT?!
THE WORLD.
WE'RE GOING IN TO KILL FATHER.
WE'RE GOING TO KILL THE FUTURE.

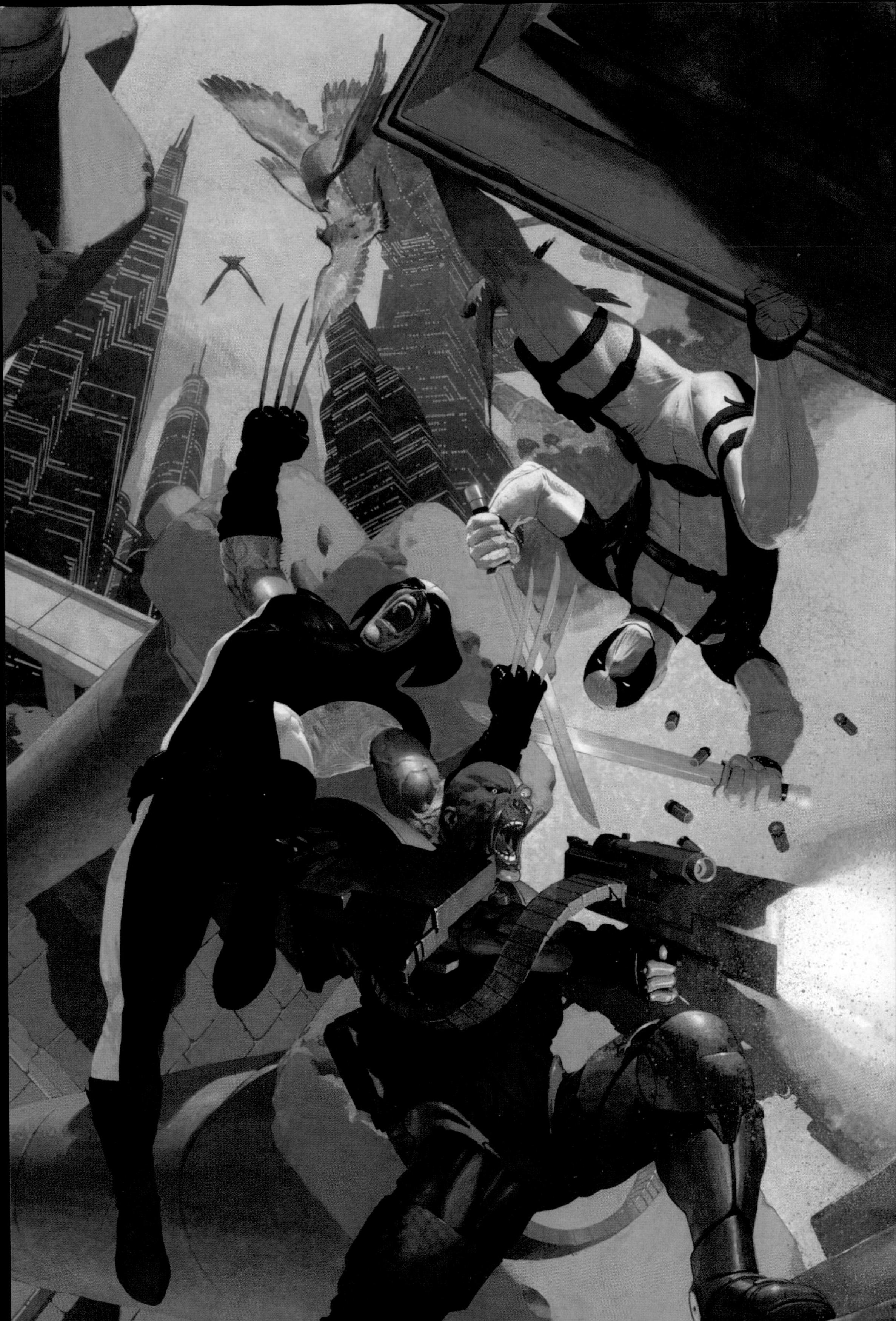

DEATHLOK NATION
CHAPTER 03

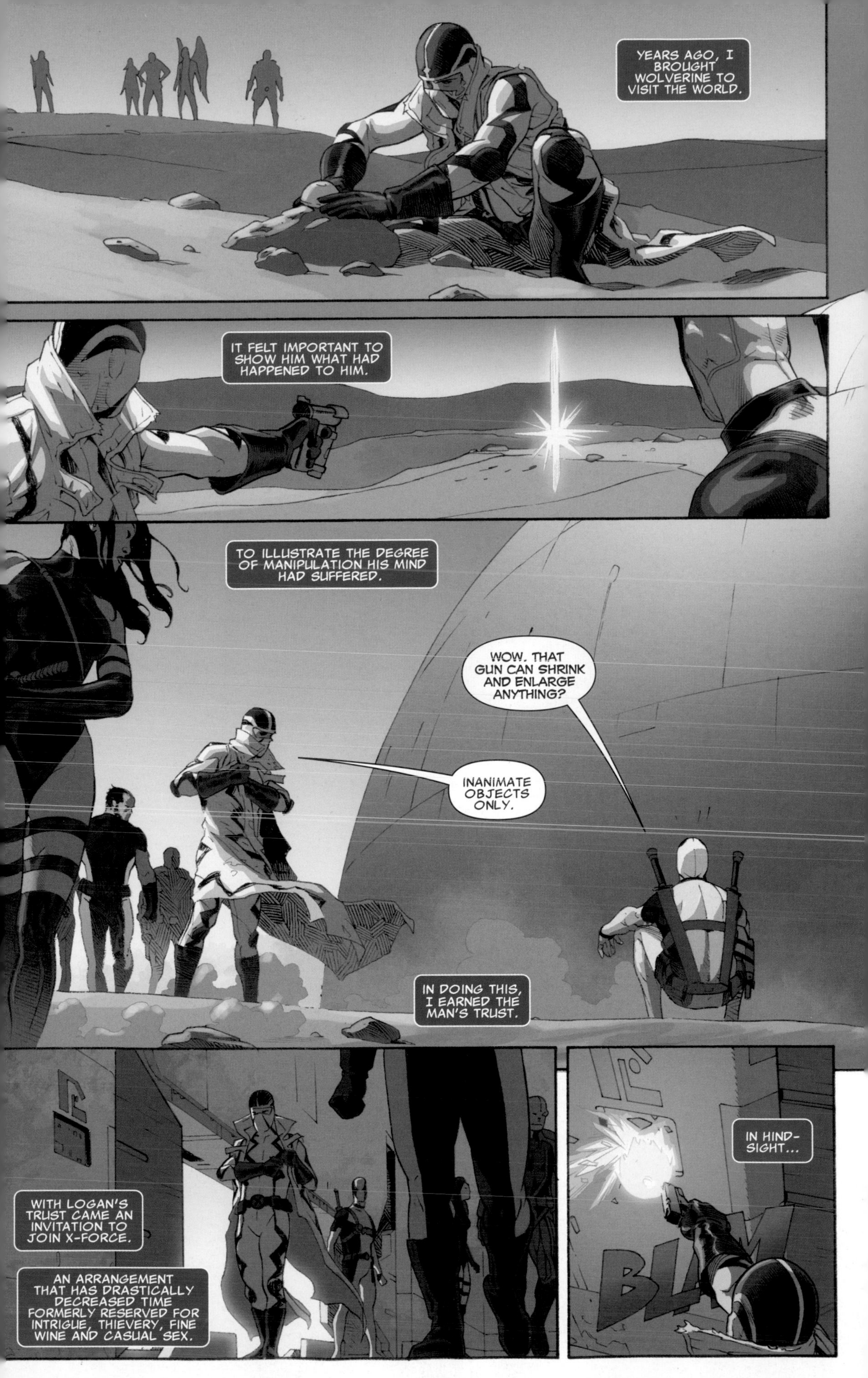
YEARS AGO, I BROUGHT WOLVERINE TO VISIT THE WORLD.
IT FELT IMPORTANT TO SHOW HIM WHAT HAD HAPPENED TO HIM.
TO ILLUSTRATE THE DEGREE OF MANIPULATION HIS MIND HAD SUFFERED.
WOW. THAT GUN CAN SHRINK AND ENLARGE ANYTHING?
INANIMATE OBJECTS ONLY.
IN DOING THIS, I EARNED THE MAN'S TRUST.
WITH LOGAN'S TRUST CAME AN INVITATION TO JOIN X-FORCE.
AN ARRANGEMENT THAT HAS DRASTICALLY DECREASED TIME FORMERLY RESERVED FOR INTRIGUE, THIEVERY, FINE WINE AND CASUAL SEX.
IN HIND-SIGHT...
BLAM

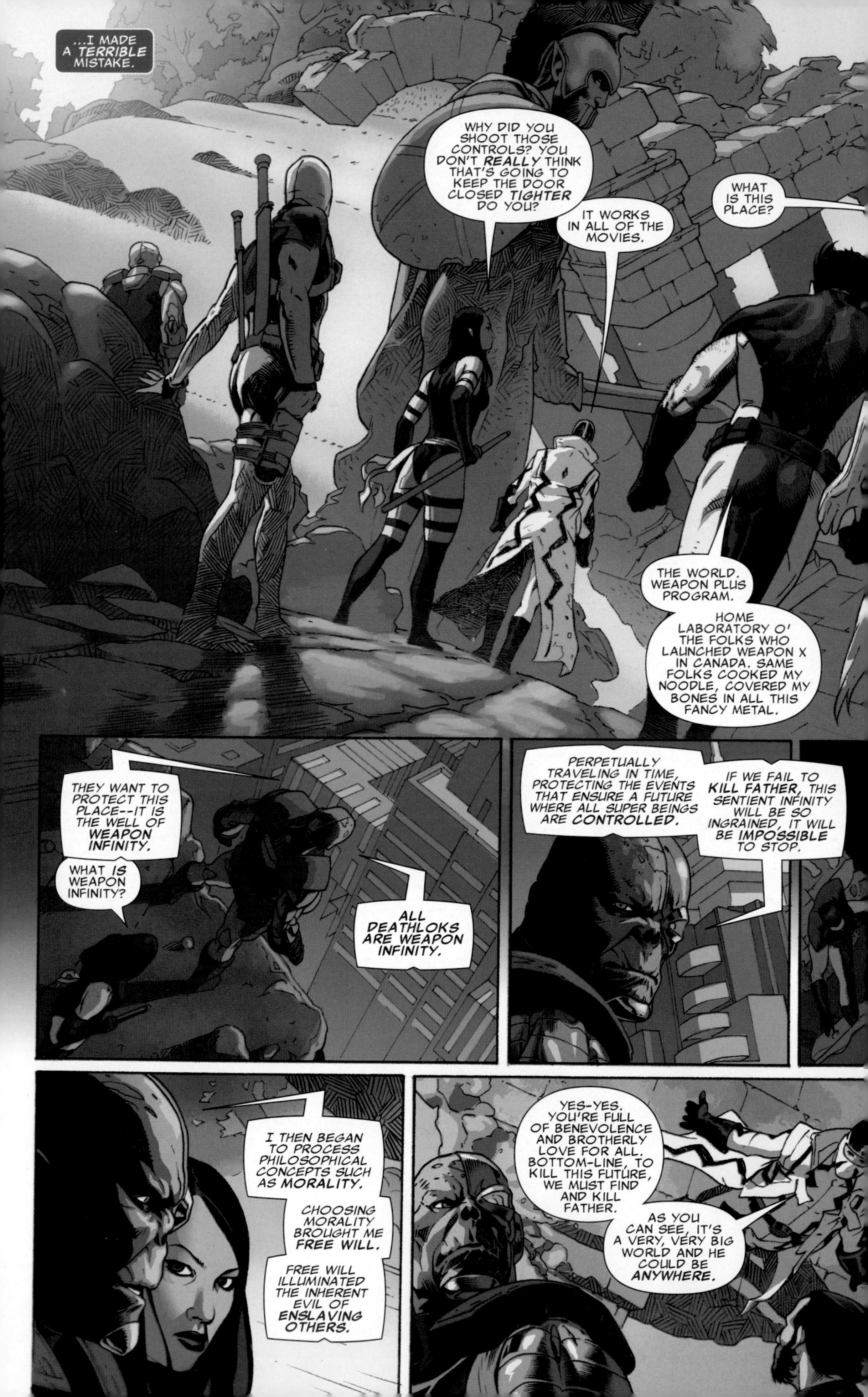

...I MADE A TERRIBLE MISTAKE.
WHY DID YOU SHOOT THOSE CONTROLS? YOU DON'T REALLY THINK THAT'S GOING TO KEEP THE DOOR CLOSED TIGHTER DO YOU?
IT WORKS IN ALL OF THE MOVIES.
WHAT IS THIS PLACE?
THE WORLD. WEAPON PLUS PROGRAM.
HOME LABORATORY O' THE FOLKS WHO LAUNCHED WEAPON X IN CANADA. SAME FOLKS COOKED MY NOODLE, COVERED MY BONES IN ALL THIS FANCY METAL.
THEY WANT TO PROTECT THIS PLACE--IT IS THE WELL OF WEAPON INFINITY.
WHAT IS WEAPON INFINITY?
ALL DEATHLOKS ARE WEAPON INFINITY.
PERPETUALLY TRAVELING IN TIME, PROTECTING THE EVENTS THAT ENSURE A FUTURE WHERE ALL SUPER BEINGS ARE CONTROLLED.
IF WE FAIL TO KILL FATHER, THIS SENTIENT INFINITY WILL BE SO INGRAINED, IT WILL BE IMPOSSIBLE TO STOP.
I THEN BEGAN TO PROCESS PHILOSOPHICAL CONCEPTS SUCH AS MORALITY.
CHOOSING MORALITY BROUGHT ME FREE WILL.
FREE WILL ILLUMINATED THE INHERENT EVIL OF ENSLAVING OTHERS.
YES-YES. YOU'RE FULL OF BENEVOLENCE AND BROTHERLY LOVE FOR ALL. BOTTOM-LINE, TO KILL THIS FUTURE, WE MUST FIND AND KILL FATHER.
AS YOU CAN SEE, IT'S A VERY, VERY BIG WORLD AND HE COULD BE ANYWHERE.

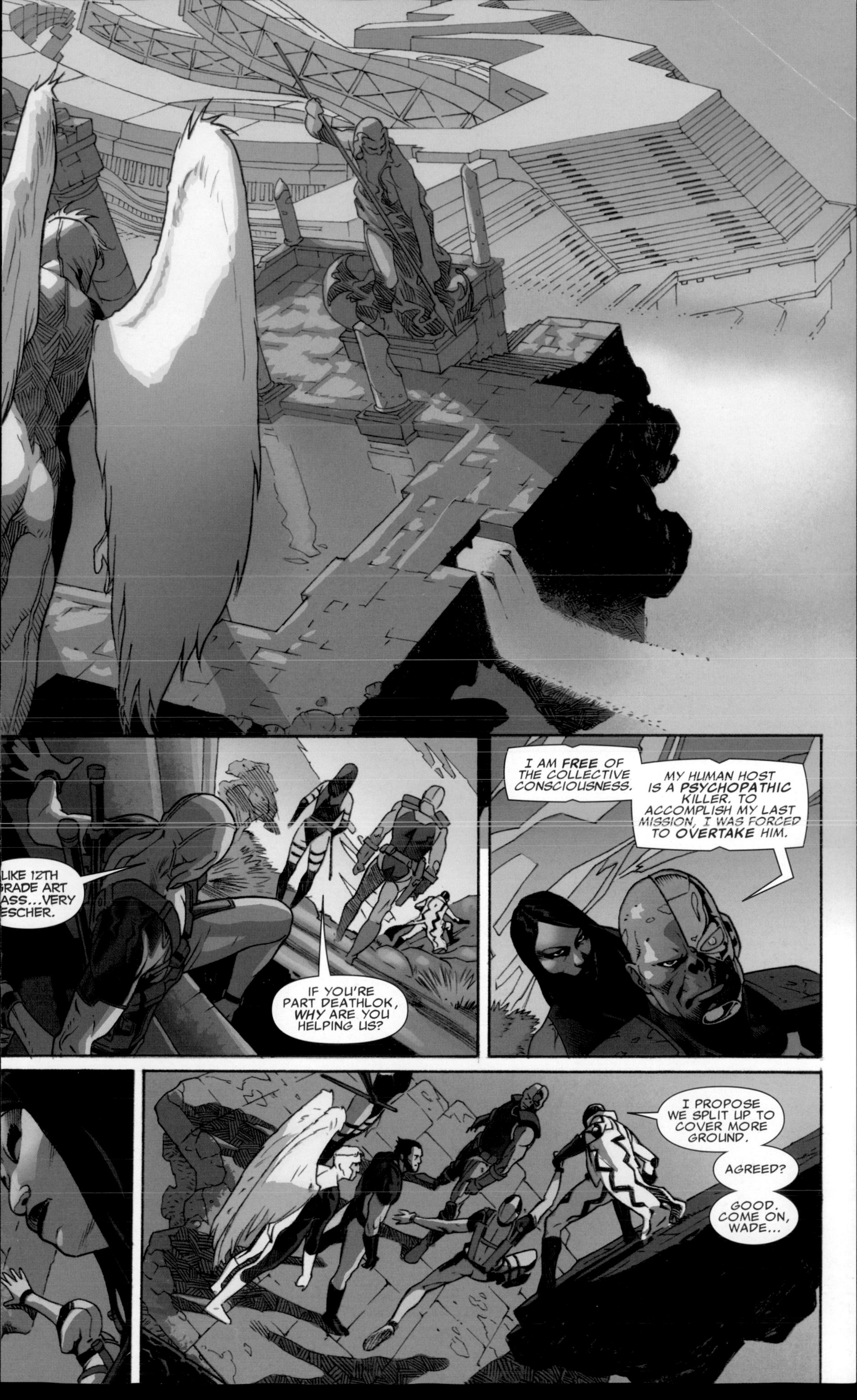
LIKE 12TH GRADE ART ASS...VERY ESCHER.
IF YOU'RE PART DEATHLOK, WHY ARE YOU HELPING US?
I AM FREE OF THE COLLECTIVE CONSCIOUSNESS.
MY HUMAN HOST IS A PSYCHOPATHIC KILLER. TO ACCOMPLISH MY LAST MISSION, I WAS FORCED TO OVERTAKE HIM.
I PROPOSE WE SPLIT UP TO COVER MORE GROUND.
AGREED?
GOOD. COME ON, WADE...

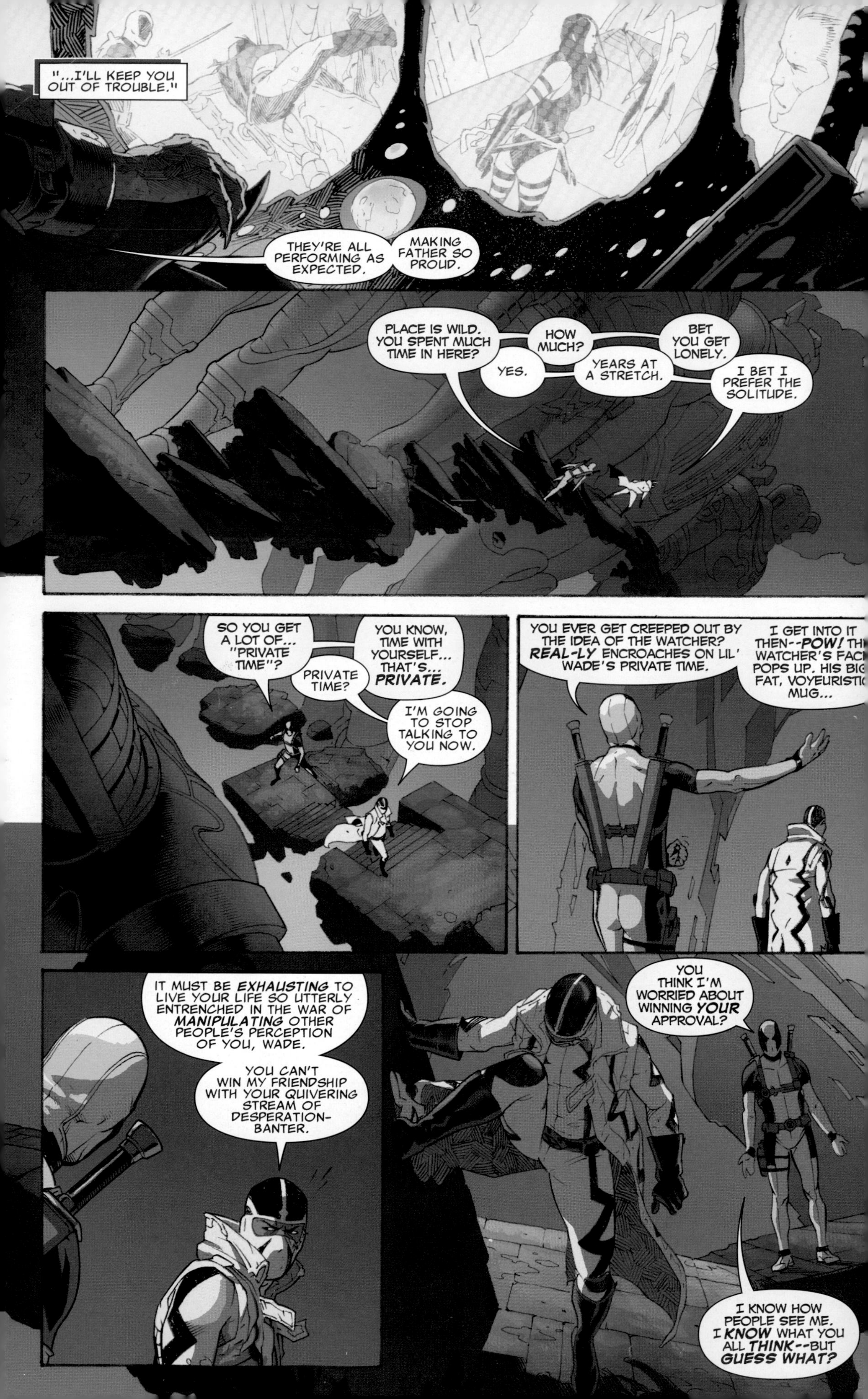
"...I'LL KEEP YOU OUT OF TROUBLE."
THEY'RE ALL PERFORMING AS EXPECTED.
MAKING FATHER SO PROUD.
PLACE IS WILD. YOU SPENT MUCH TIME IN HERE?
YES.
HOW MUCH?
YEARS AT A STRETCH.
BET YOU GET LONELY.
I BET I PREFER THE SOLITUDE.
SO YOU GET A LOT OF... "PRIVATE TIME"?
PRIVATE TIME?
YOU KNOW, TIME WITH YOURSELF... THAT'S... PRIVATE.
I'M GOING TO STOP TALKING TO YOU NOW.
YOU EVER GET CREEPED OUT BY THE IDEA OF THE WATCHER? REAL-LY ENCROACHES ON LIL' WADE'S PRIVATE TIME.
I GET INTO IT THEN--POW! THE WATCHER'S FACE POPS UP. HIS BIG FAT, VOYEURISTIC MUG...
IT MUST BE EXHAUSTING TO LIVE YOUR LIFE SO UTTERLY ENTRENCHED IN THE WAR OF MANIPULATING OTHER PEOPLE'S PERCEPTION OF YOU, WADE.
YOU CAN'T WIN MY FRIENDSHIP WITH YOUR QUIVERING STREAM OF DESPERATION-BANTER.
YOU THINK I'M WORRIED ABOUT WINNING YOUR APPROVAL?
I KNOW HOW PEOPLE SEE ME. I KNOW WHAT YOU ALL THINK--BUT GUESS WHAT?

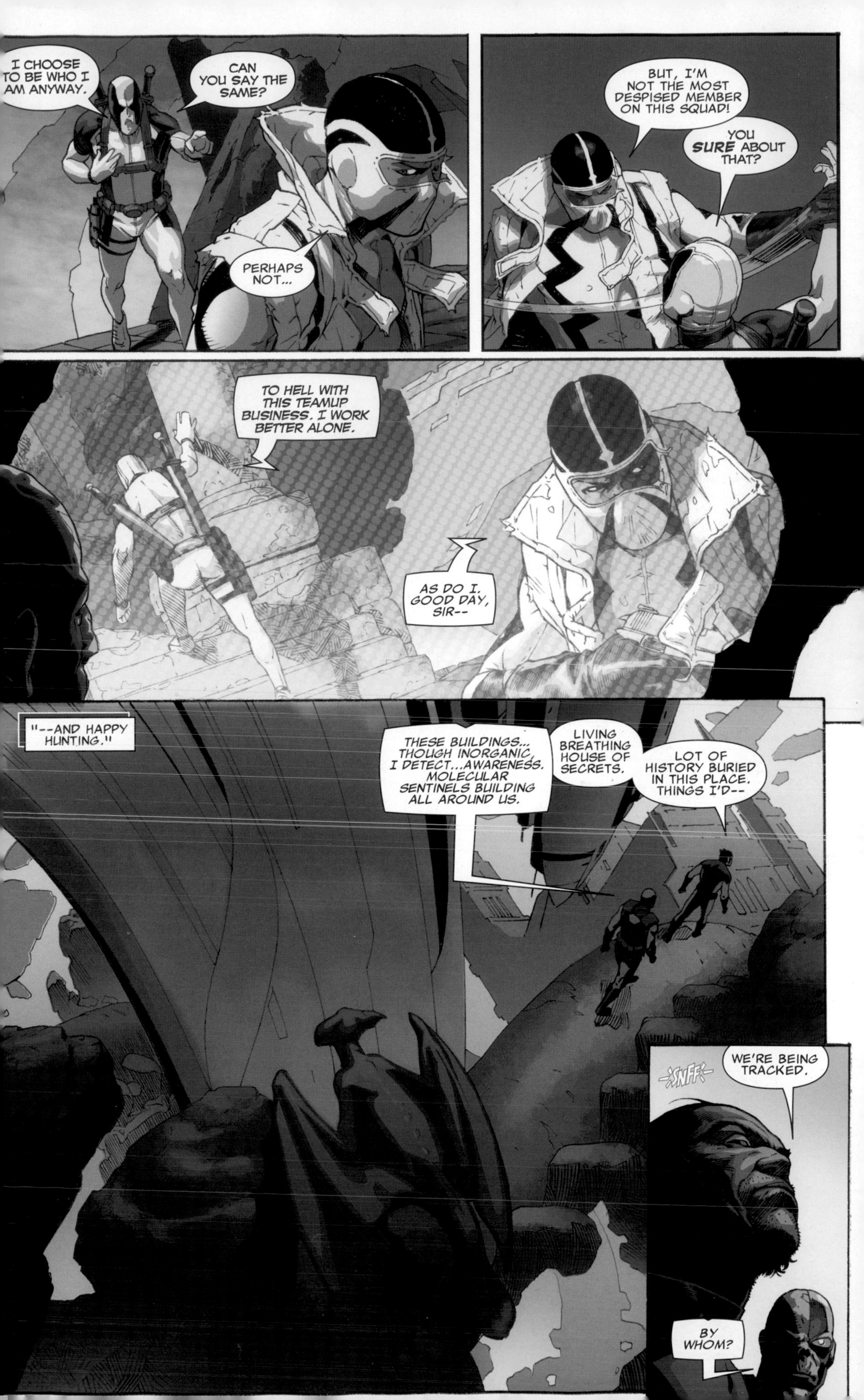
I CHOOSE TO BE WHO I AM ANYWAY.
CAN YOU SAY THE SAME?
PERHAPS NOT...
BUT, I'M NOT THE MOST DESPISED MEMBER ON THIS SQUAD!
YOU SURE ABOUT THAT?
TO HELL WITH THIS TEAMUP BUSINESS. I WORK BETTER ALONE.
AS DO I. GOOD DAY, SIR--
"--AND HAPPY HUNTING."
THESE BUILDINGS... THOUGH INORGANIC, I DETECT...AWARENESS. MOLECULAR SENTINELS BUILDING ALL AROUND US.
LIVING BREATHING HOUSE OF SECRETS.
LOT OF HISTORY BURIED IN THIS PLACE. THINGS I'D--
-SNFF-
WE'RE BEING TRACKED.
BY WHOM?

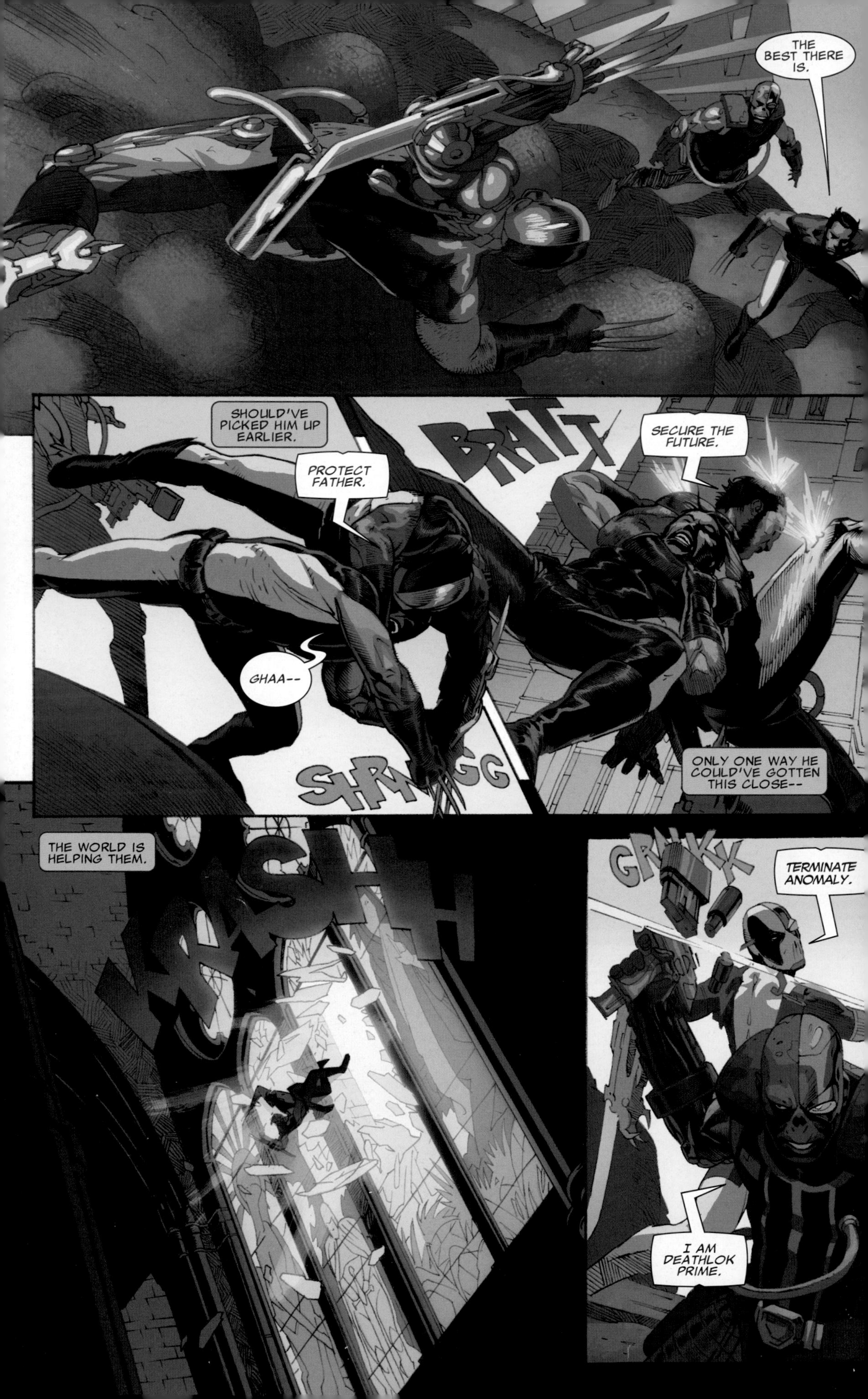
THE BEST THERE IS.
SHOULD'VE PICKED HIM UP EARLIER.
PROTECT FATHER.
BRATT
SECURE THE FUTURE.
GHAA--
SHRNGG
ONLY ONE WAY HE COULD'VE GOTTEN THIS CLOSE--
THE WORLD IS HELPING THEM.
KRASSHH
GRKKK
TERMINATE ANOMALY.
I AM DEATHLOK PRIME.

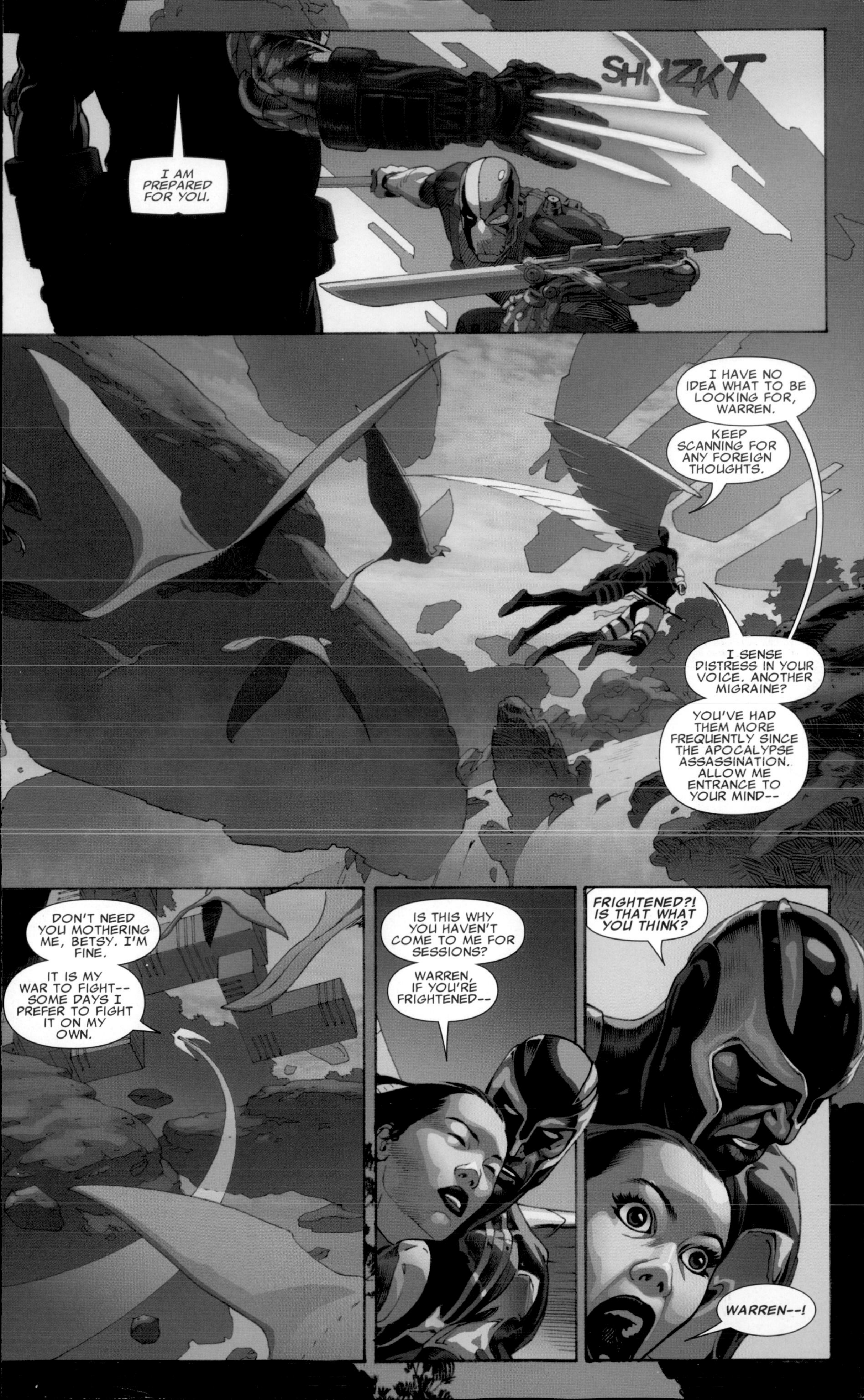
SHNZKT
I AM PREPARED FOR YOU.
I HAVE NO IDEA WHAT TO BE LOOKING FOR, WARREN.
KEEP SCANNING FOR ANY FOREIGN THOUGHTS.
I SENSE DISTRESS IN YOUR VOICE. ANOTHER MIGRAINE?
YOU'VE HAD THEM MORE FREQUENTLY SINCE THE APOCALYPSE ASSASSINATION. ALLOW ME ENTRANCE TO YOUR MIND--
DON'T NEED YOU MOTHERING ME, BETSY. I'M FINE.
IT IS MY WAR TO FIGHT-- SOME DAYS I PREFER TO FIGHT IT ON MY OWN.
IS THIS WHY YOU HAVEN'T COME TO ME FOR SESSIONS?
WARREN, IF YOU'RE FRIGHTENED--
FRIGHTENED?! IS THAT WHAT YOU THINK?
WARREN--!

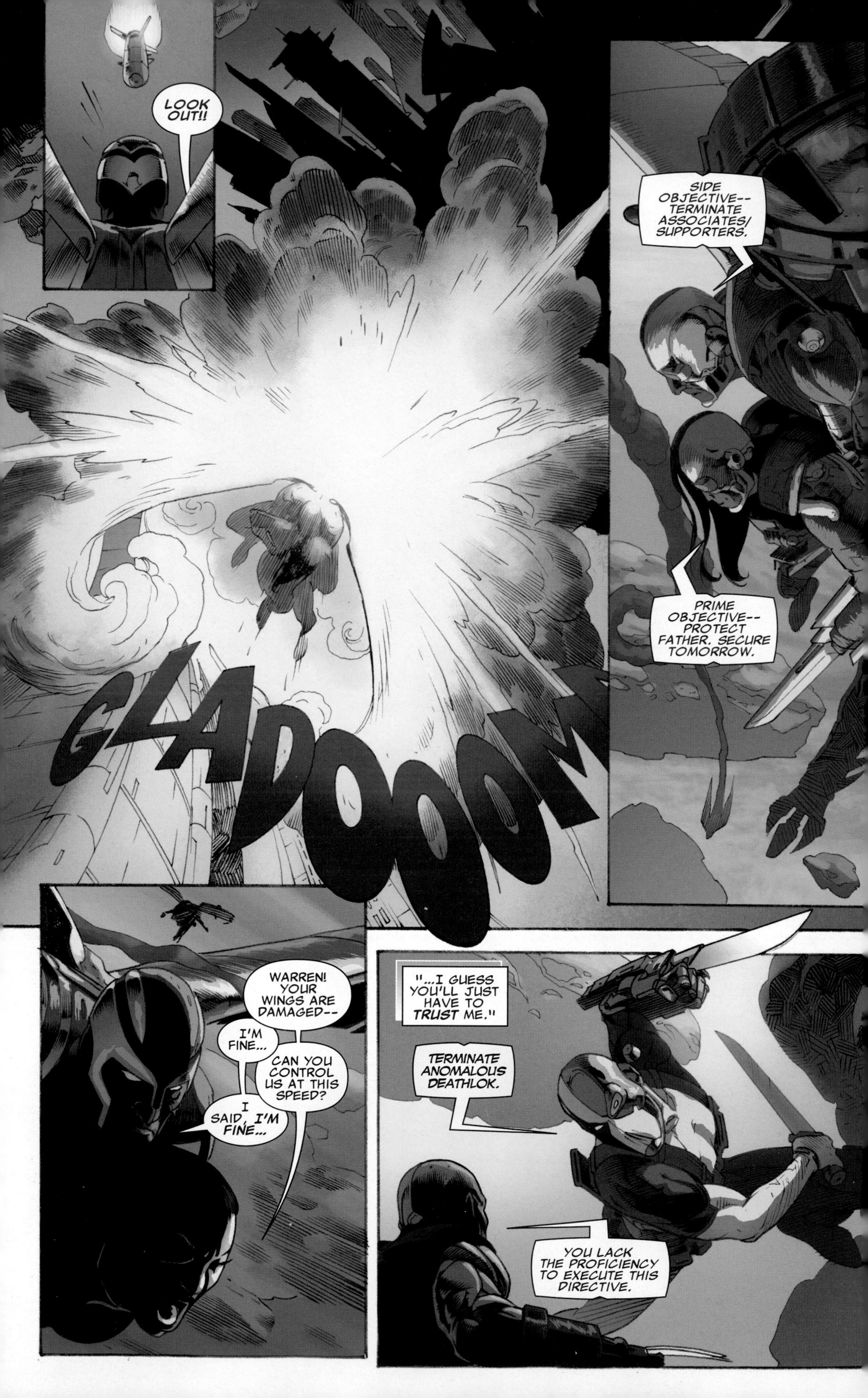
LOOK OUT!!
SIDE OBJECTIVE-- TERMINATE ASSOCIATES/ SUPPORTERS.
PRIME OBJECTIVE-- PROTECT FATHER. SECURE TOMORROW.
CLADOOOM
WARREN! YOUR WINGS ARE DAMAGED--
I'M FINE...
CAN YOU CONTROL US AT THIS SPEED?
I SAID, I'M FINE...
"...I GUESS YOU'LL JUST HAVE TO TRUST ME."
TERMINATE ANOMALOUS DEATHLOK.
YOU LACK THE PROFICIENCY TO EXECUTE THIS DIRECTIVE.

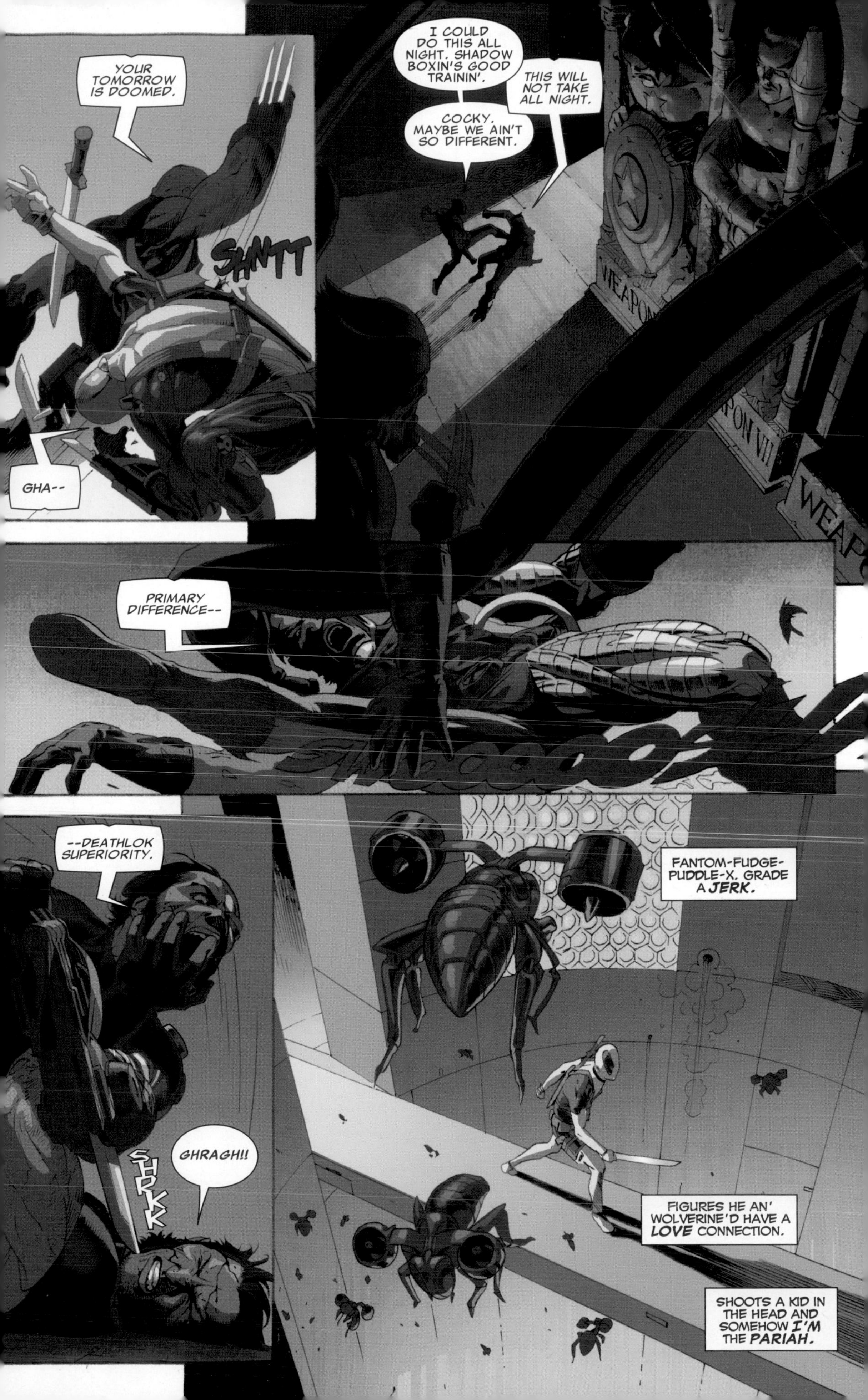
YOUR TOMORROW IS DOOMED.
SHNTT
GHA--
I COULD DO THIS ALL NIGHT. SHADOW BOXIN'S GOOD TRAININ'.
COCKY. MAYBE WE AIN'T SO DIFFERENT.
THIS WILL NOT TAKE ALL NIGHT.
PRIMARY DIFFERENCE--
--DEATHLOK SUPERIORITY.
SHRKK
GHRAGH!!
FANTOM-FUDGE-PUDDLE-X. GRADE A JERK.
FIGURES HE AN' WOLVERINE'D HAVE A LOVE CONNECTION.
SHOOTS A KID IN THE HEAD AND SOMEHOW I'M THE PARIAH.

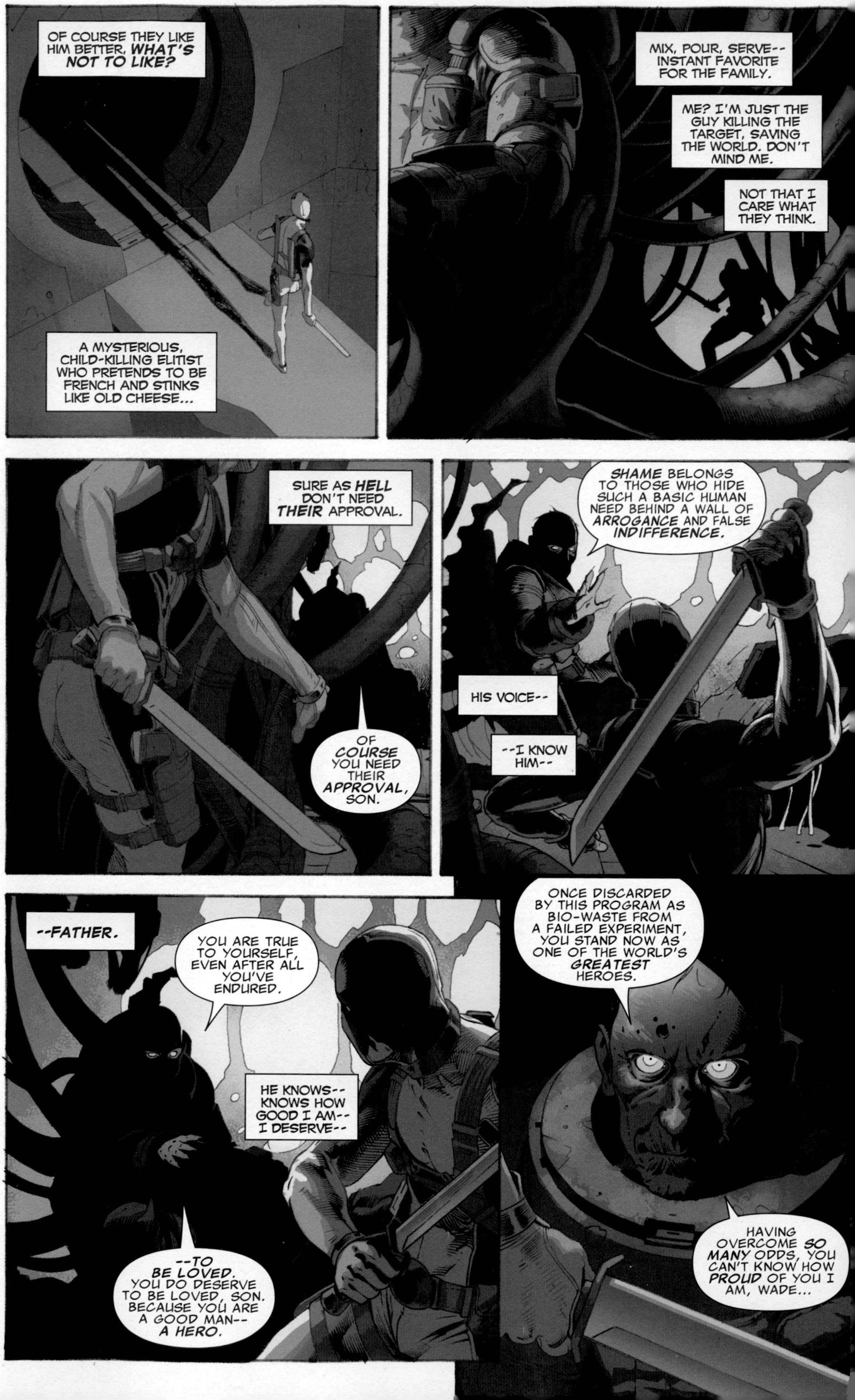
OF COURSE THEY LIKE HIM BETTER, WHAT'S NOT TO LIKE?
A MYSTERIOUS, CHILD-KILLING ELITIST WHO PRETENDS TO BE FRENCH AND STINKS LIKE OLD CHEESE...
MIX, POUR, SERVE-- INSTANT FAVORITE FOR THE FAMILY.
ME? I'M JUST THE GUY KILLING THE TARGET, SAVING THE WORLD. DON'T MIND ME.
NOT THAT I CARE WHAT THEY THINK.
SURE AS HELL DON'T NEED THEIR APPROVAL.
OF COURSE YOU NEED THEIR APPROVAL, SON.
SHAME BELONGS TO THOSE WHO HIDE SUCH A BASIC HUMAN NEED BEHIND A WALL OF ARROGANCE AND FALSE INDIFFERENCE.
HIS VOICE--
--I KNOW HIM--
--FATHER.
YOU ARE TRUE TO YOURSELF, EVEN AFTER ALL YOU'VE ENDURED.
HE KNOWS-- KNOWS HOW GOOD I AM-- I DESERVE--
--TO BE LOVED. YOU DO DESERVE TO BE LOVED, SON. BECAUSE YOU ARE A GOOD MAN-- A HERO.
ONCE DISCARDED BY THIS PROGRAM AS BIO-WASTE FROM A FAILED EXPERIMENT, YOU STAND NOW AS ONE OF THE WORLD'S GREATEST HEROES.
HAVING OVERCOME SO MANY ODDS, YOU CAN'T KNOW HOW PROUD OF YOU I AM, WADE...

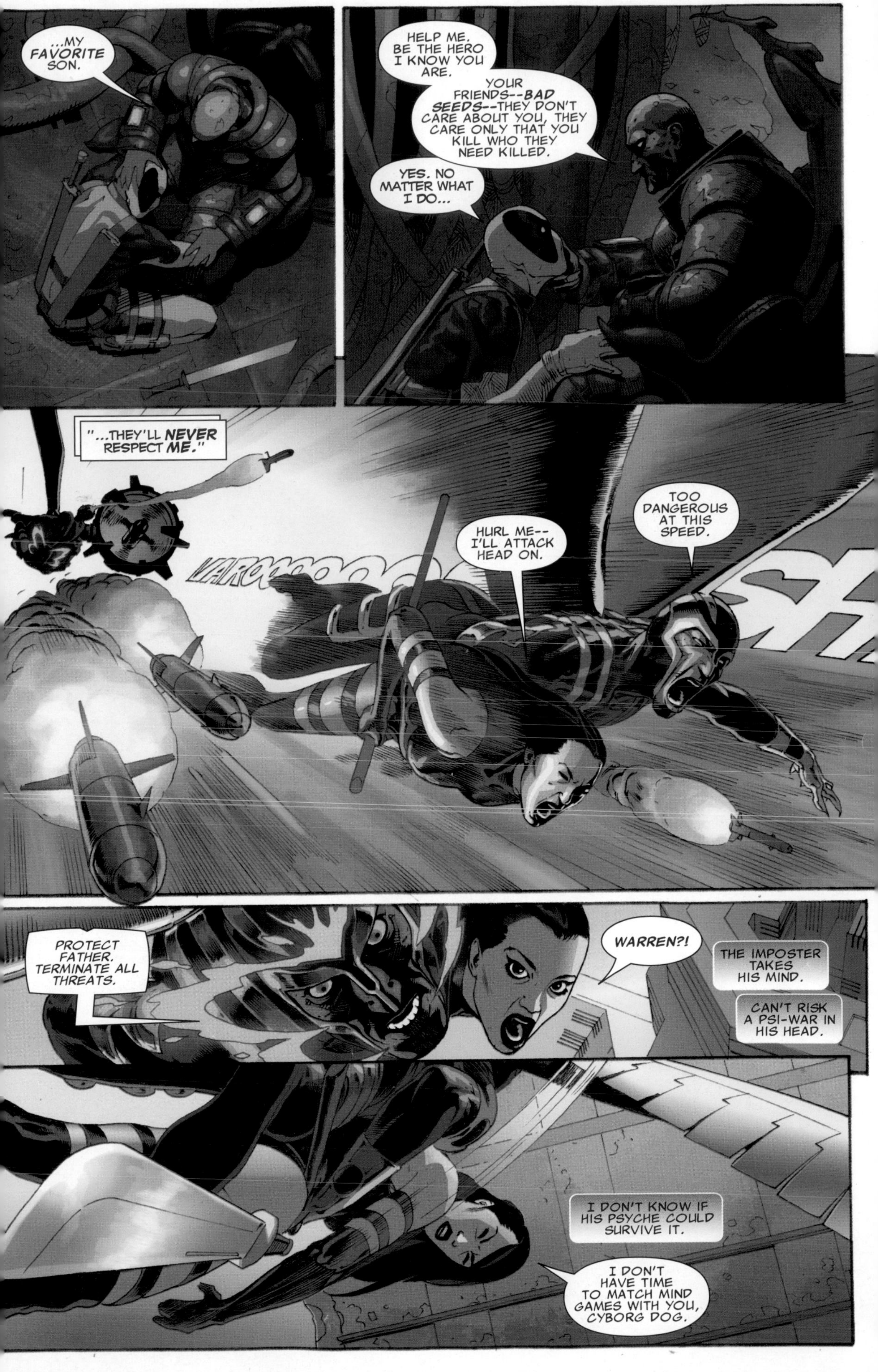
...MY FAVORITE SON.
HELP ME. BE THE HERO I KNOW YOU ARE.
YOUR FRIENDS--BAD SEEDS--THEY DON'T CARE ABOUT YOU, THEY CARE ONLY THAT YOU KILL WHO THEY NEED KILLED.
YES. NO MATTER WHAT I DO...
"...THEY'LL NEVER RESPECT ME."
HURL ME-- I'LL ATTACK HEAD ON.
TOO DANGEROUS AT THIS SPEED.
PROTECT FATHER. TERMINATE ALL THREATS.
WARREN?!
THE IMPOSTER TAKES HIS MIND.
CAN'T RISK A PSI-WAR IN HIS HEAD.
I DON'T KNOW IF HIS PSYCHE COULD SURVIVE IT.
I DON'T HAVE TIME TO MATCH MIND GAMES WITH YOU, CYBORG DOG.

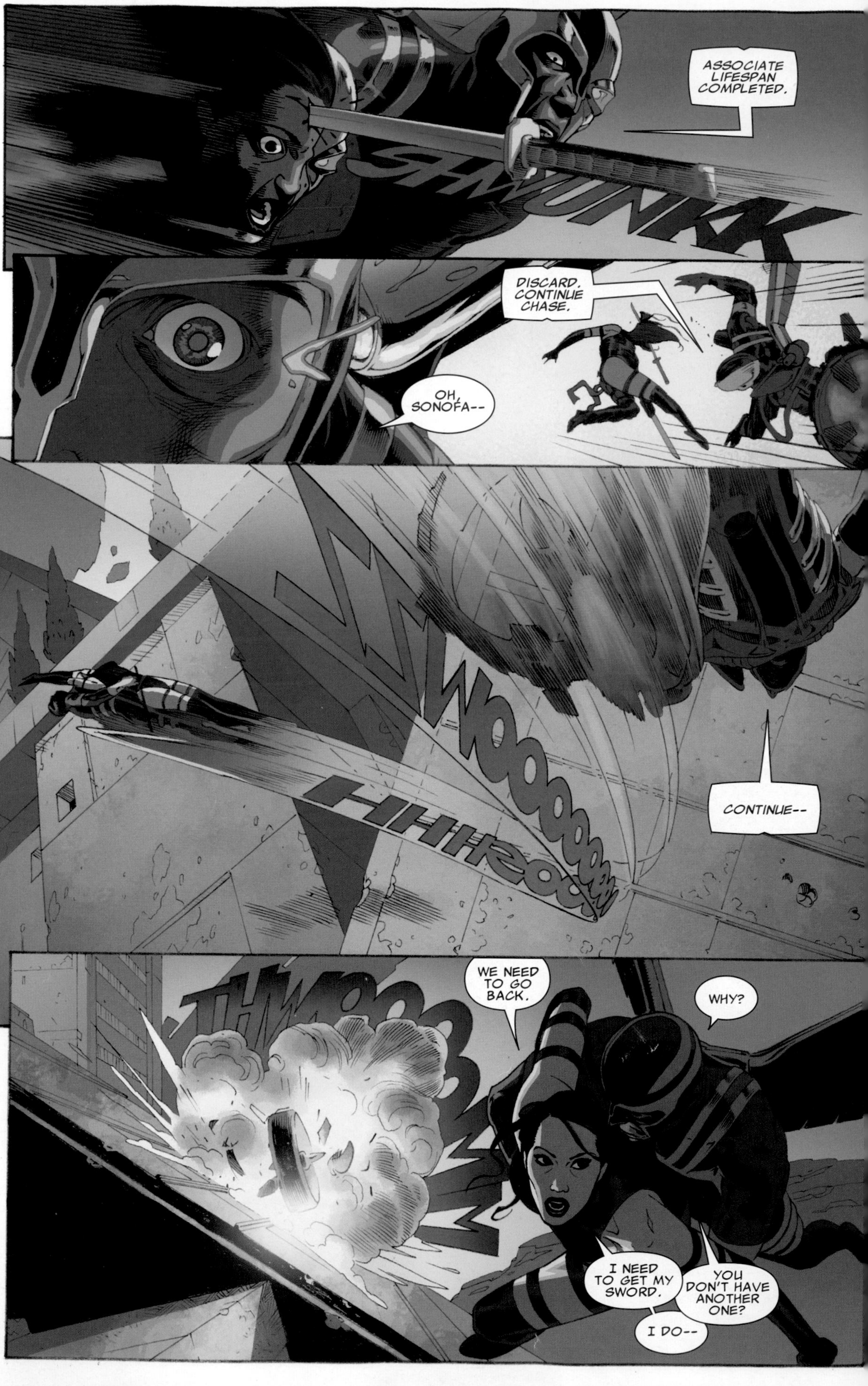
ASSOCIATE LIFESPAN COMPLETED.
SHUNKK
DISCARD. CONTINUE CHASE.
OH, SONOFA--
WOOOOOOOSH
HHROOOM
CONTINUE--
THWOOOOM
WE NEED TO GO BACK.
WHY?
I NEED TO GET MY SWORD.
YOU DON'T HAVE ANOTHER ONE?
I DO--

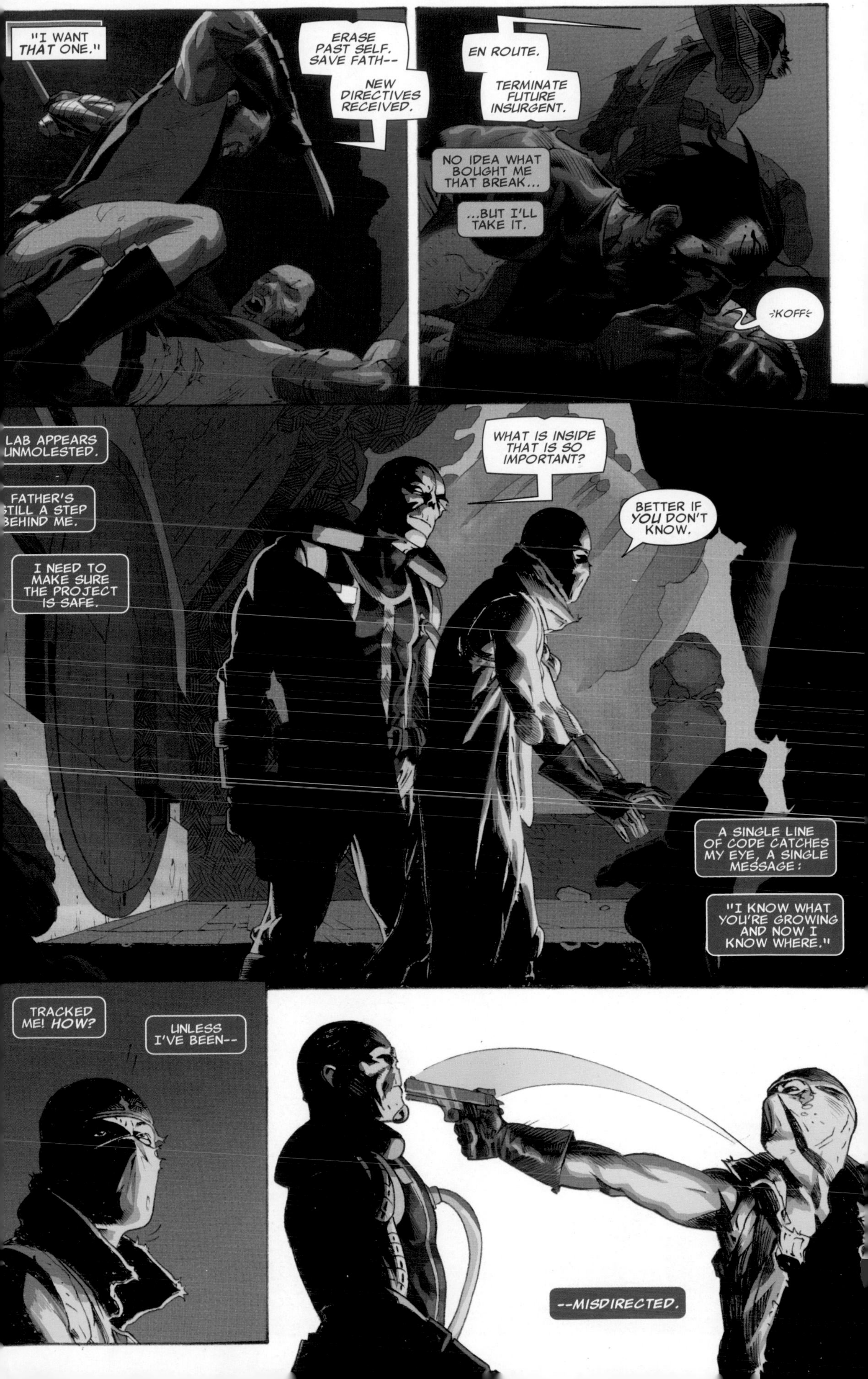

"I WANT THAT ONE."
ERASE PAST SELF. SAVE FATH--
NEW DIRECTIVES RECEIVED.
EN ROUTE.
TERMINATE FUTURE INSURGENT.
NO IDEA WHAT BOUGHT ME THAT BREAK...
...BUT I'LL TAKE IT.
KOFF
LAB APPEARS UNMOLESTED.
FATHER'S STILL A STEP BEHIND ME.
I NEED TO MAKE SURE THE PROJECT IS SAFE.
WHAT IS INSIDE THAT IS SO IMPORTANT?
BETTER IF YOU DON'T KNOW.
A SINGLE LINE OF CODE CATCHES MY EYE, A SINGLE MESSAGE:
"I KNOW WHAT YOU'RE GROWING AND NOW I KNOW WHERE."
TRACKED ME! HOW?
UNLESS I'VE BEEN--
--MISDIRECTED.

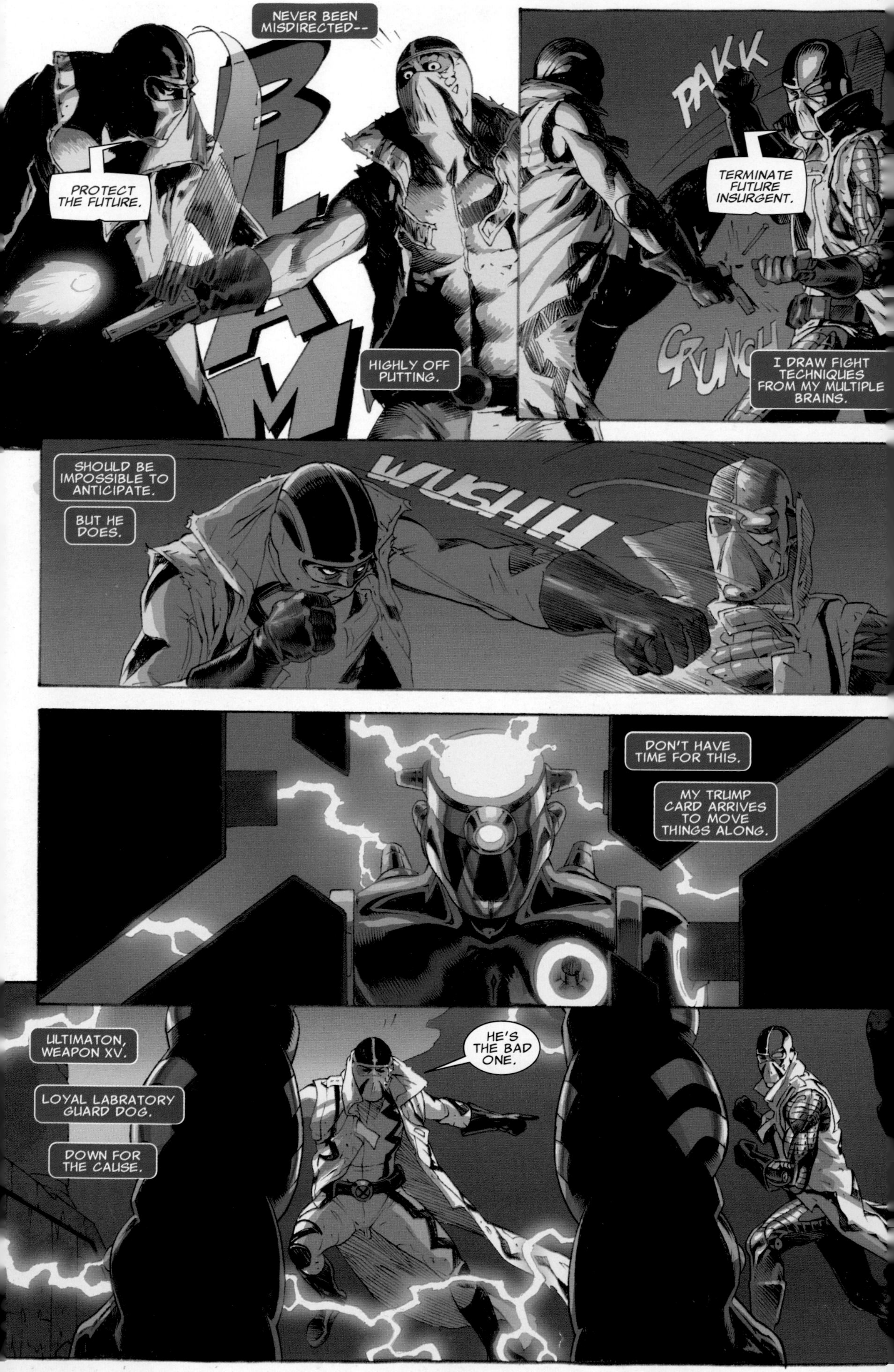
NEVER BEEN MISDIRECTED--
BLAM
PROTECT THE FUTURE.
HIGHLY OFF PUTTING.
PAKK
TERMINATE FUTURE INSURGENT.
CRUNCH
I DRAW FIGHT TECHNIQUES FROM MY MULTIPLE BRAINS.
SHOULD BE IMPOSSIBLE TO ANTICIPATE.
BUT HE DOES.
WUSHH
DON'T HAVE TIME FOR THIS.
MY TRUMP CARD ARRIVES TO MOVE THINGS ALONG.
ULTIMATON, WEAPON XV.
LOYAL LABRATORY GUARD DOG.
DOWN FOR THE CAUSE.
HE'S THE BAD ONE.

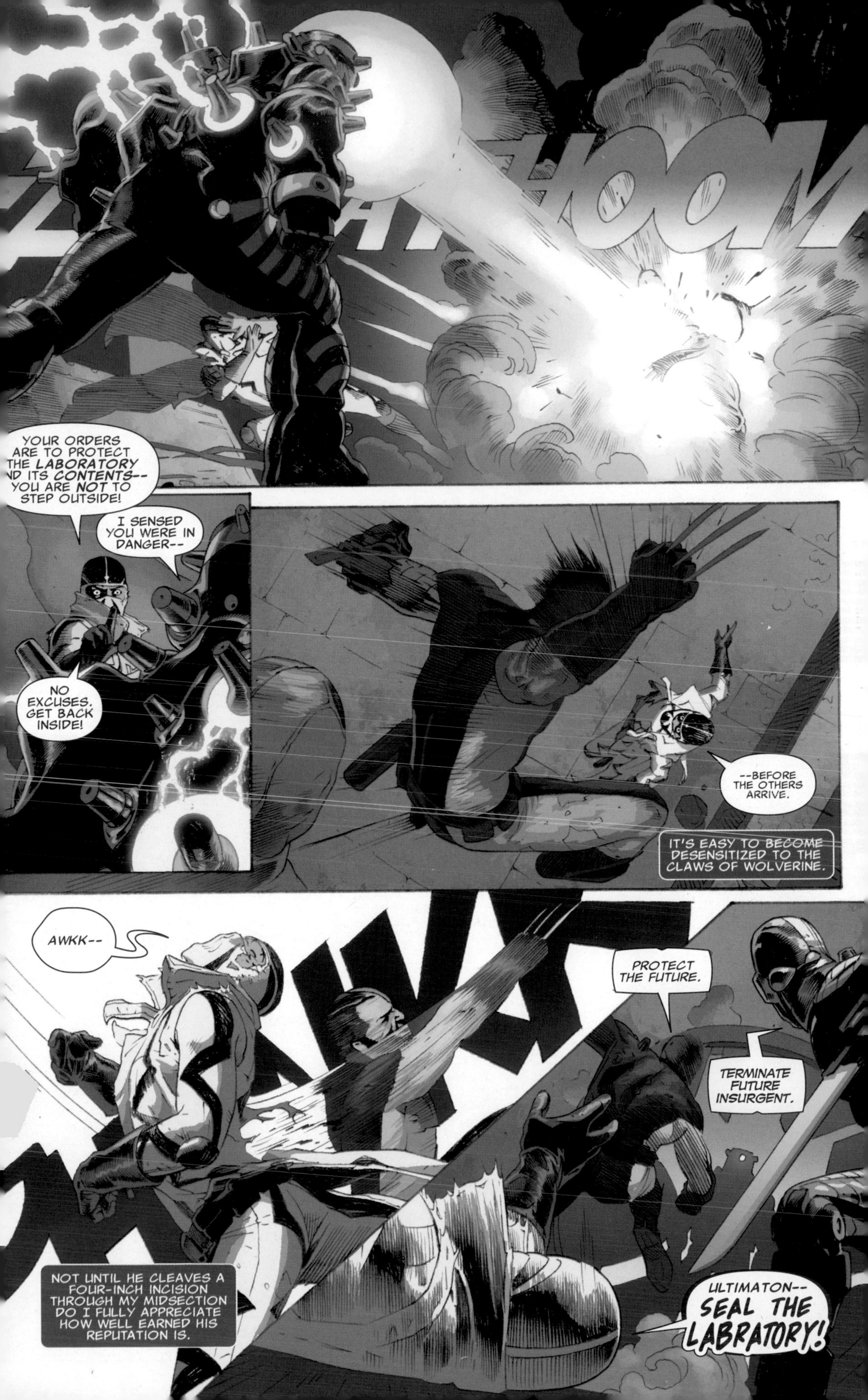

ZZAT-HOOM
YOUR ORDERS ARE TO PROTECT THE LABORATORY ND ITS CONTENTS-- YOU ARE NOT TO STEP OUTSIDE!
I SENSED YOU WERE IN DANGER--
NO EXCUSES. GET BACK INSIDE!
--BEFORE THE OTHERS ARRIVE.
IT'S EASY TO BECOME DESENSITIZED TO THE CLAWS OF WOLVERINE.
AWKK--
PROTECT THE FUTURE.
TERMINATE FUTURE INSURGENT.
NOT UNTIL HE CLEAVES A FOUR-INCH INCISION THROUGH MY MIDSECTION DO I FULLY APPRECIATE HOW WELL EARNED HIS REPUTATION IS.
ULTIMATON-- SEAL THE LABRATORY!

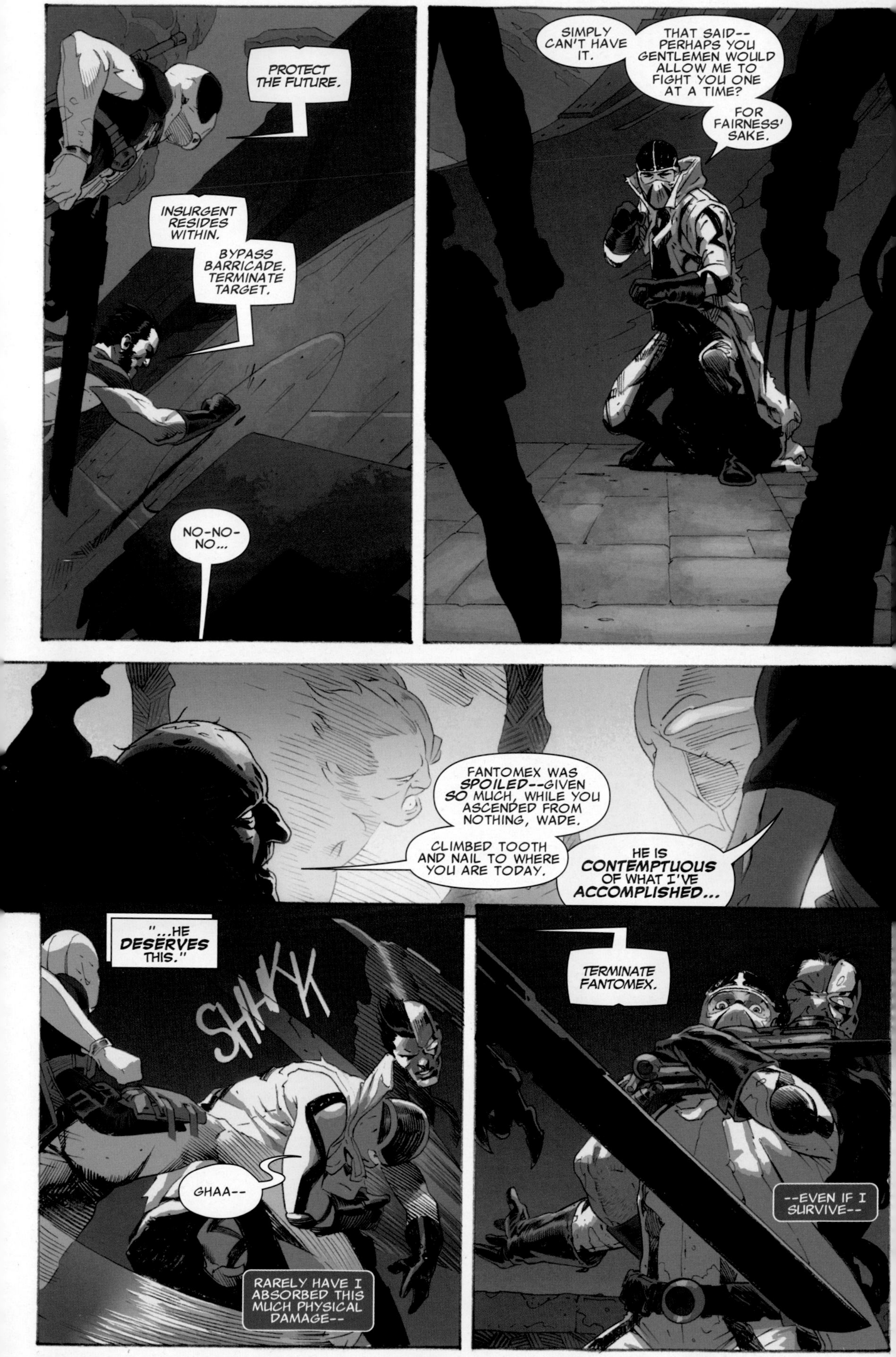
PROTECT THE FUTURE.
INSURGENT RESIDES WITHIN.
BYPASS BARRICADE. TERMINATE TARGET.
NO-NO-NO...
SIMPLY CAN'T HAVE IT.
THAT SAID-- PERHAPS YOU GENTLEMEN WOULD ALLOW ME TO FIGHT YOU ONE AT A TIME?
FOR FAIRNESS' SAKE.
FANTOMEX WAS SPOILED--GIVEN SO MUCH, WHILE YOU ASCENDED FROM NOTHING, WADE.
CLIMBED TOOTH AND NAIL TO WHERE YOU ARE TODAY.
HE IS CONTEMPTUOUS OF WHAT I'VE ACCOMPLISHED...
"...HE DESERVES THIS."
SHKK
GHAA--
RARELY HAVE I ABSORBED THIS MUCH PHYSICAL DAMAGE--
TERMINATE FANTOMEX.
--EVEN IF I SURVIVE--

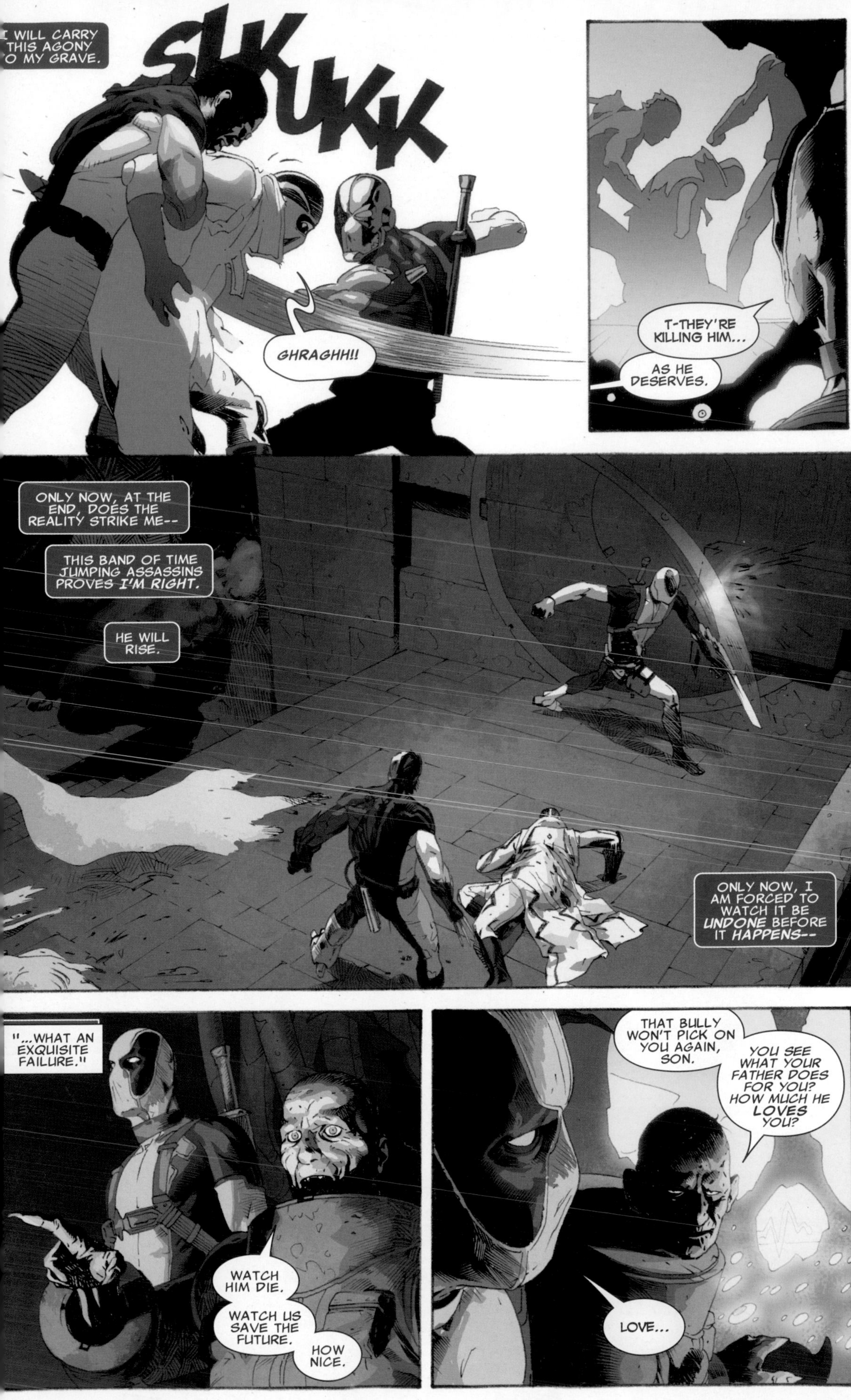
I WILL CARRY THIS AGONY TO MY GRAVE.
SLK UKK
GHRAGHH!!
T-THEY'RE KILLING HIM...
AS HE DESERVES.
ONLY NOW, AT THE END, DOES THE REALITY STRIKE ME--
THIS BAND OF TIME JUMPING ASSASSINS PROVES I'M RIGHT.
HE WILL RISE.
ONLY NOW, I AM FORCED TO WATCH IT BE UNDONE BEFORE IT HAPPENS--
"...WHAT AN EXQUISITE FAILURE."
WATCH HIM DIE.
WATCH US SAVE THE FUTURE.
HOW NICE.
THAT BULLY WON'T PICK ON YOU AGAIN, SON.
YOU SEE WHAT YOUR FATHER DOES FOR YOU? HOW MUCH HE LOVES YOU?
LOVE...

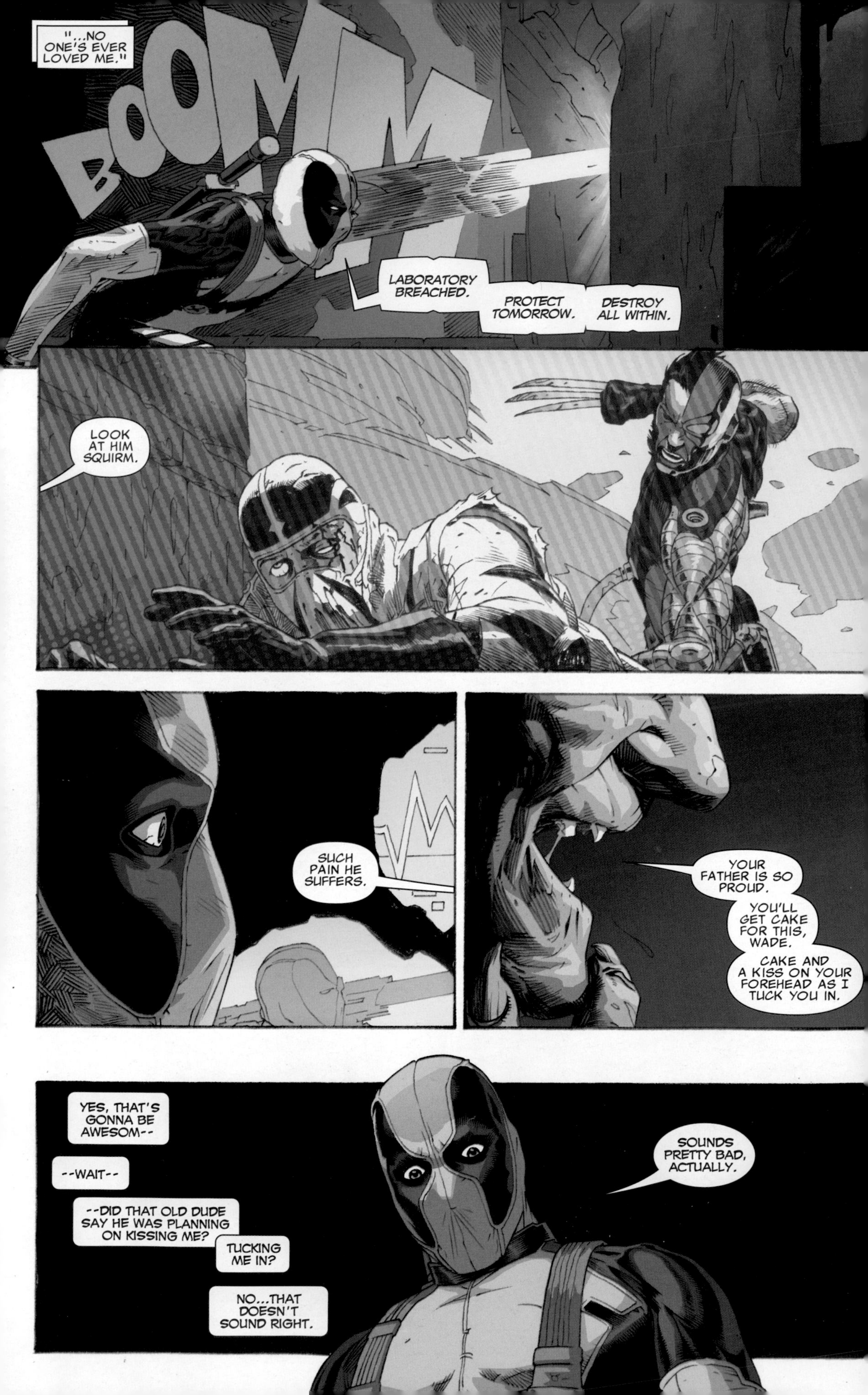
"...NO ONE'S EVER LOVED ME."
BOOMM
LABORATORY BREACHED.
PROTECT TOMORROW.
DESTROY ALL WITHIN.
LOOK AT HIM SQUIRM.
SUCH PAIN HE SUFFERS.
YOUR FATHER IS SO PROUD.
YOU'LL GET CAKE FOR THIS, WADE.
CAKE AND A KISS ON YOUR FOREHEAD AS I TUCK YOU IN.
YES, THAT'S GONNA BE AWESOM--
--WAIT--
--DID THAT OLD DUDE SAY HE WAS PLANNING ON KISSING ME?
TUCKING ME IN?
NO...THAT DOESN'T SOUND RIGHT.
SOUNDS PRETTY BAD, ACTUALLY.

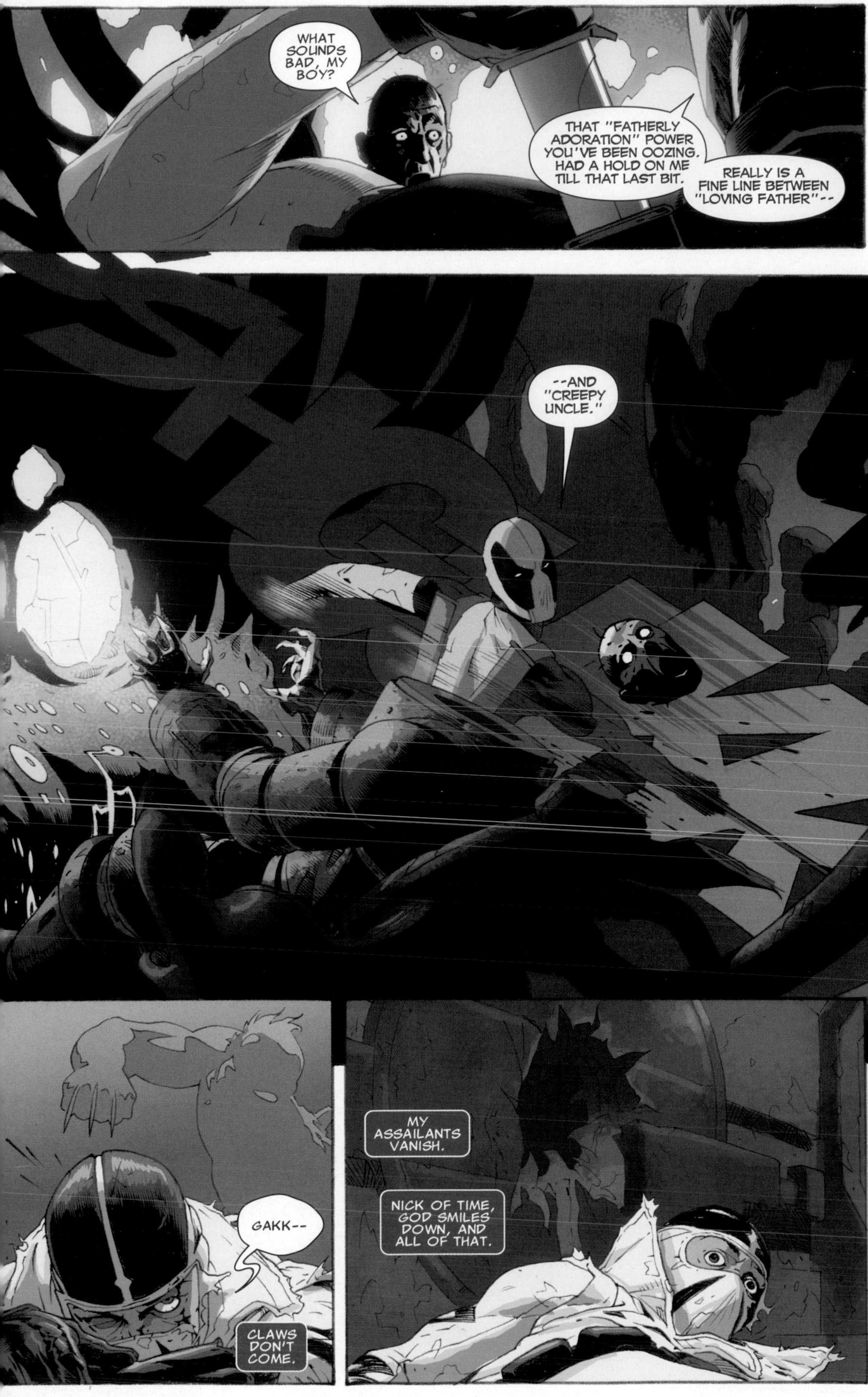
WHAT SOUNDS BAD, MY BOY?
THAT "FATHERLY ADORATION" POWER YOU'VE BEEN OOZING. HAD A HOLD ON ME TILL THAT LAST BIT.
REALLY IS A FINE LINE BETWEEN "LOVING FATHER"--
--AND "CREEPY UNCLE."
GAKK--
CLAWS DON'T COME.
MY ASSAILANTS VANISH.
NICK OF TIME, GOD SMILES DOWN, AND ALL OF THAT.

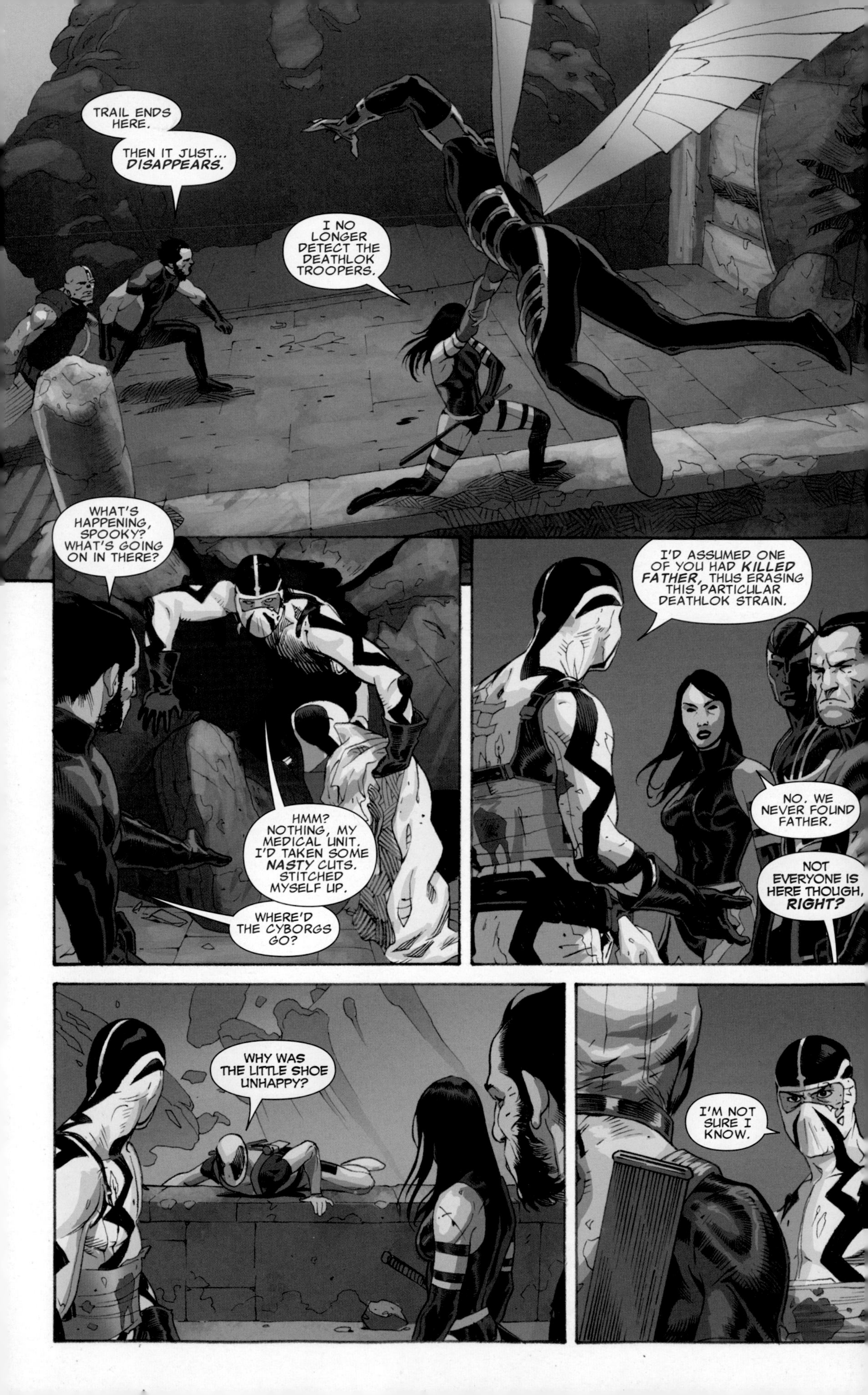
TRAIL ENDS HERE.
THEN IT JUST... DISAPPEARS.
I NO LONGER DETECT THE DEATHLOK TROOPERS.
WHAT'S HAPPENING, SPOOKY? WHAT'S GOING ON IN THERE?
HMM? NOTHING, MY MEDICAL UNIT. I'D TAKEN SOME NASTY CUTS. STITCHED MYSELF UP.
WHERE'D THE CYBORGS GO?
I'D ASSUMED ONE OF YOU HAD KILLED FATHER, THUS ERASING THIS PARTICULAR DEATHLOK STRAIN.
NO. WE NEVER FOUND FATHER.
NOT EVERYONE IS HERE THOUGH, RIGHT?
WHY WAS THE LITTLE SHOE UNHAPPY?
I'M NOT SURE I KNOW.

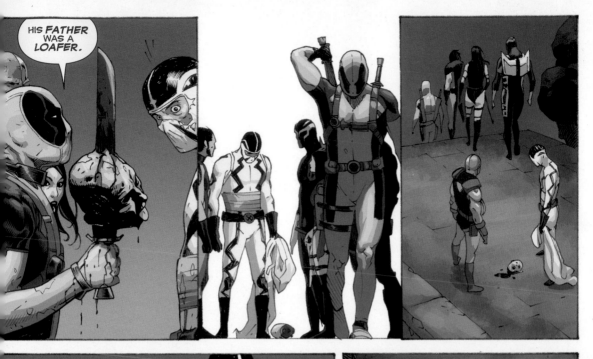

HIS *FATHER* WAS A *LOAFER.*

COME.

TOO *DANGEROUS* TO *LINGER* HERE...

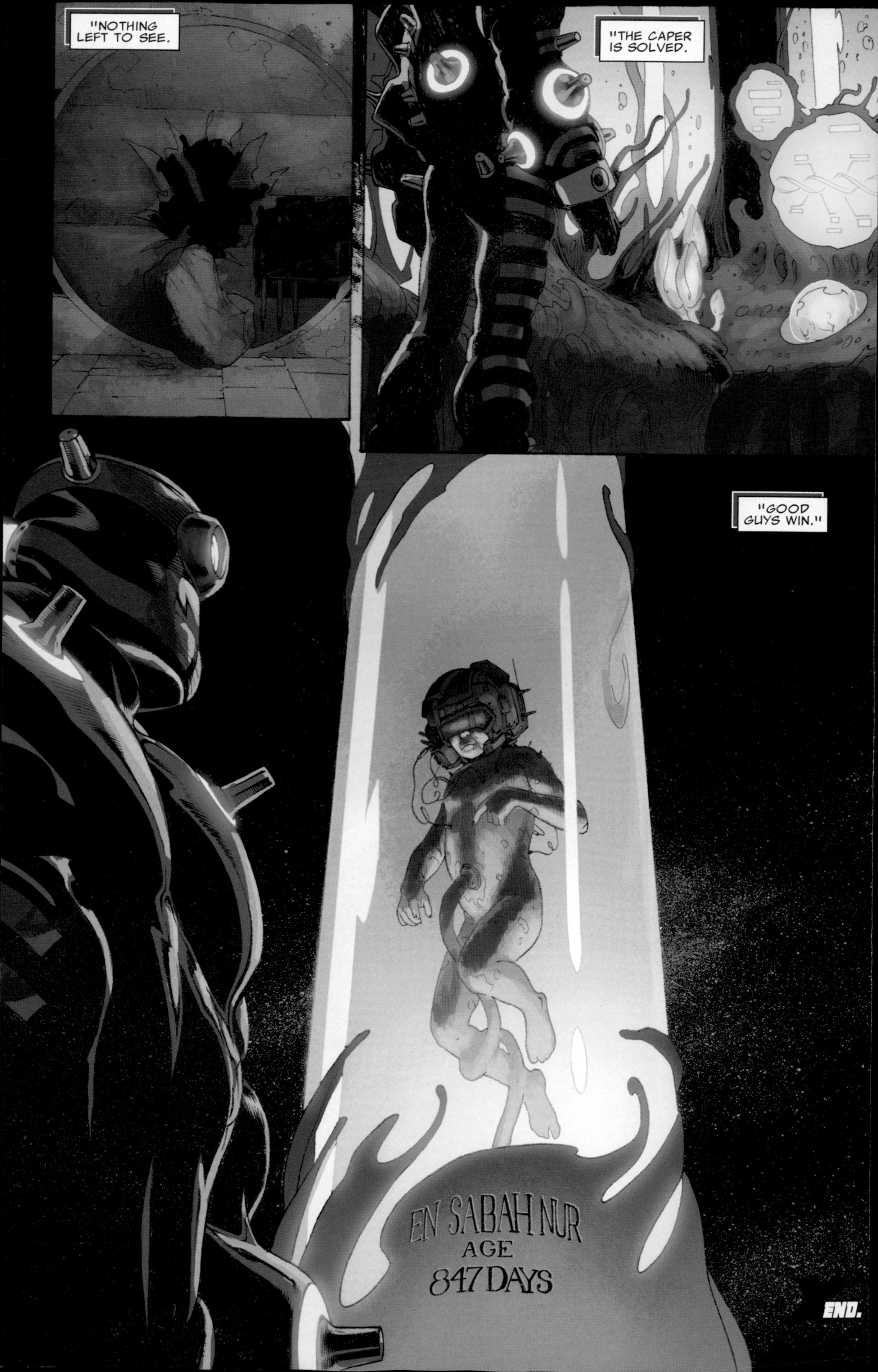
"NOTHING LEFT TO SEE.
"THE CAPER IS SOLVED.
"GOOD GUYS WIN."
EN SABAH NUR
AGE
847 DAYS
END.

1 - DOUBLE PAGE WIDE HORIZONTAL PANEL - X-FORCE WALK INTO A SCI-FI ROMAN COURTYARD ON A CLIFF, amid the immense and weird architecture of the world. It's all very Escher, up is down, waterfalls flow sideways etc. Psylocke walks next to Fantomex. Archangel walks next to Wolverine. The courtyard is a surrounded by statues of gladiators and gods, Skrull, Kree, and human. In the center of the courtyard is a sideways waterfall that turns in mid air, and floats freely off into the distance. NOTE: CAN YOU TRY AND HAVE ANGEL TRANSFORM INTO ARCHANGEL IN THE BG ACROSS A FEW PANELS HERE?

FANTOMEX (CAP)

...It wasn't a brilliant choice.

PSYLOCKE

Why did you shoot those controls? You don't really think that's going to keep the door closed tighter do you?

FANTOMEX

It works in all of the movies.

ARCHANGEL

What is this place?

WOLVERINE

The World. Weapon plus program. Maternity ward for a good lot of us.

WOLVERINE

Home laboratory of the folks who launched Weapon X in Canada. Same folks cooked my noodle, covered me in all this expensive metal.

2 - DEATHLOK Walks to the edge of the strange stone cliff OVERLOOKING A VISTA of the strange twisted multicity beyond. Psylocke investigates him.

DEATHLOK

They want to protect this place--it is the well of Weapon infinity.

PSYLOCKE

What is Weapon Infinity?

3 - TIGHT ON DEATHLOK turning to the rest of the team, stoic.

DEATHLOK

All Deathloks are Weapon Infinity.

DEATHLOK

Cyborgs operating on precognitive evolution.

DEATHLOK

Now initiated Deathlok troopers will perpetually be sent forwards and backwards in time, adapting, killing, protecting the events that ensure their survival.

4 - They walk along the edge of BIOLUMINESCENT, NEON, JAPANESE GARDEN. Deadpool is shrugging his shoulders, confused. Deathlok and Psylocke as they march on.

DEATHLOK

If we fail to kill Father this sentient infinity will be so ingrained in the current timeline it will be impossible to stop.

PSYLOCKE

If you're corrupted with the same mechanical virus, why are you helping us?

5 - Two shot - Deathlok and Psylocke.

DEATHLOK

I am free of the collective consciousness.

DEATHLOK

My human host is a psychopathic killer. To accomplish my last mission I was forced to overtake him.

6 - CLOSER ON DEATHLOK.

DEATHLOK

After acquiring dominance I began to loop through philosophical concepts such as morality.

DEATHLOK

This brought free will.

DEATHLOK

Free will illuminated the inherent evil of enslaving others.

7 - Fantomex turns to the group.

FANTOMEX

Yes-yes. You're full of benevolence and brotherly love for all. Bottom line, To kill this future we must find and kill Father.

FANTOMEX

As you can see, it's a very, very big world and he could be anywhere.

8 – Fantomex walks away grabbing Deadpool to follow him.

FANTOMEX

I propose we SPLIT UP TO COVER MORE GROUND.

FANTOMEX

Agreed?

FANTOMEX

Yes?

FANTOMEX

Good. The merc will come with me.

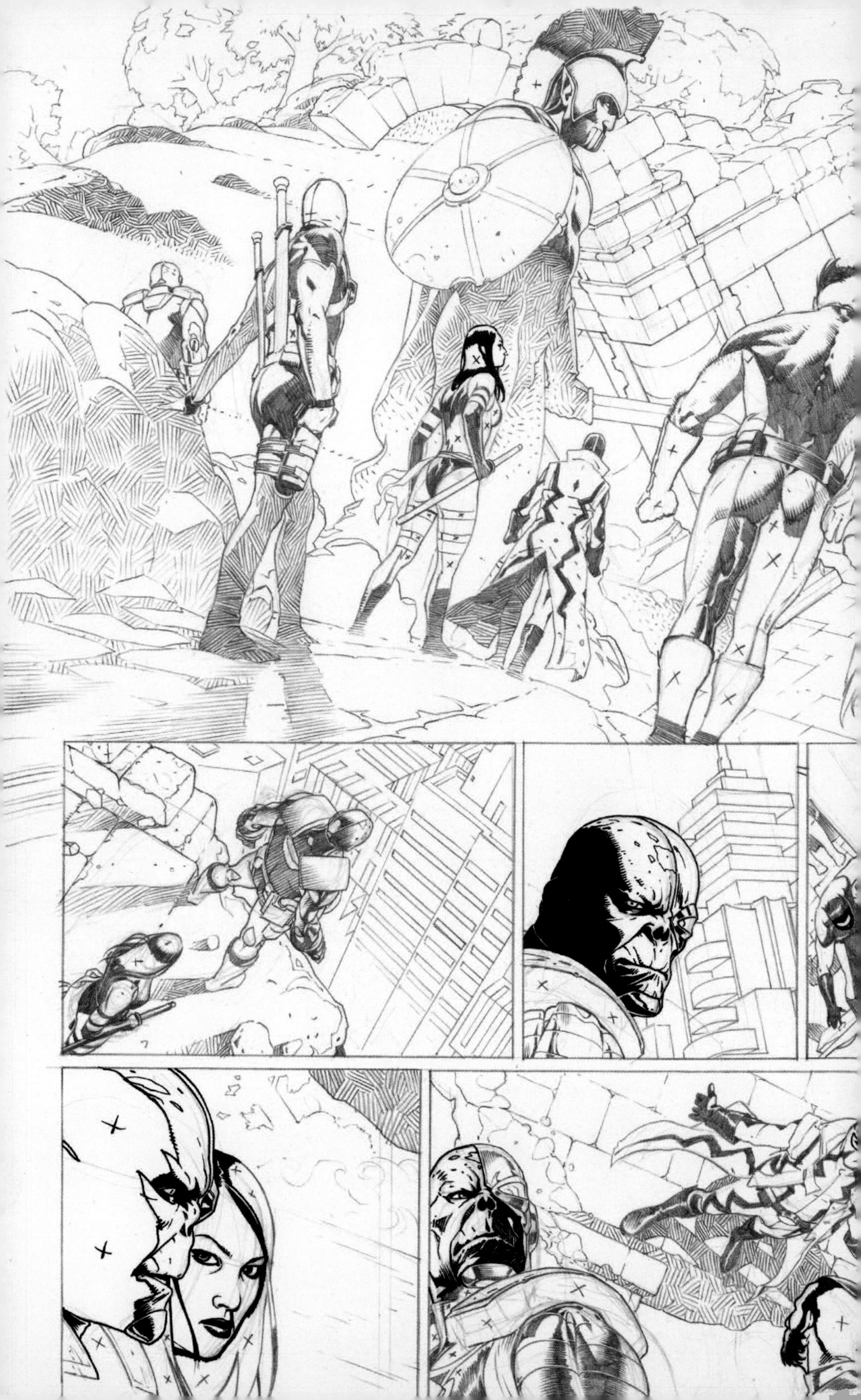

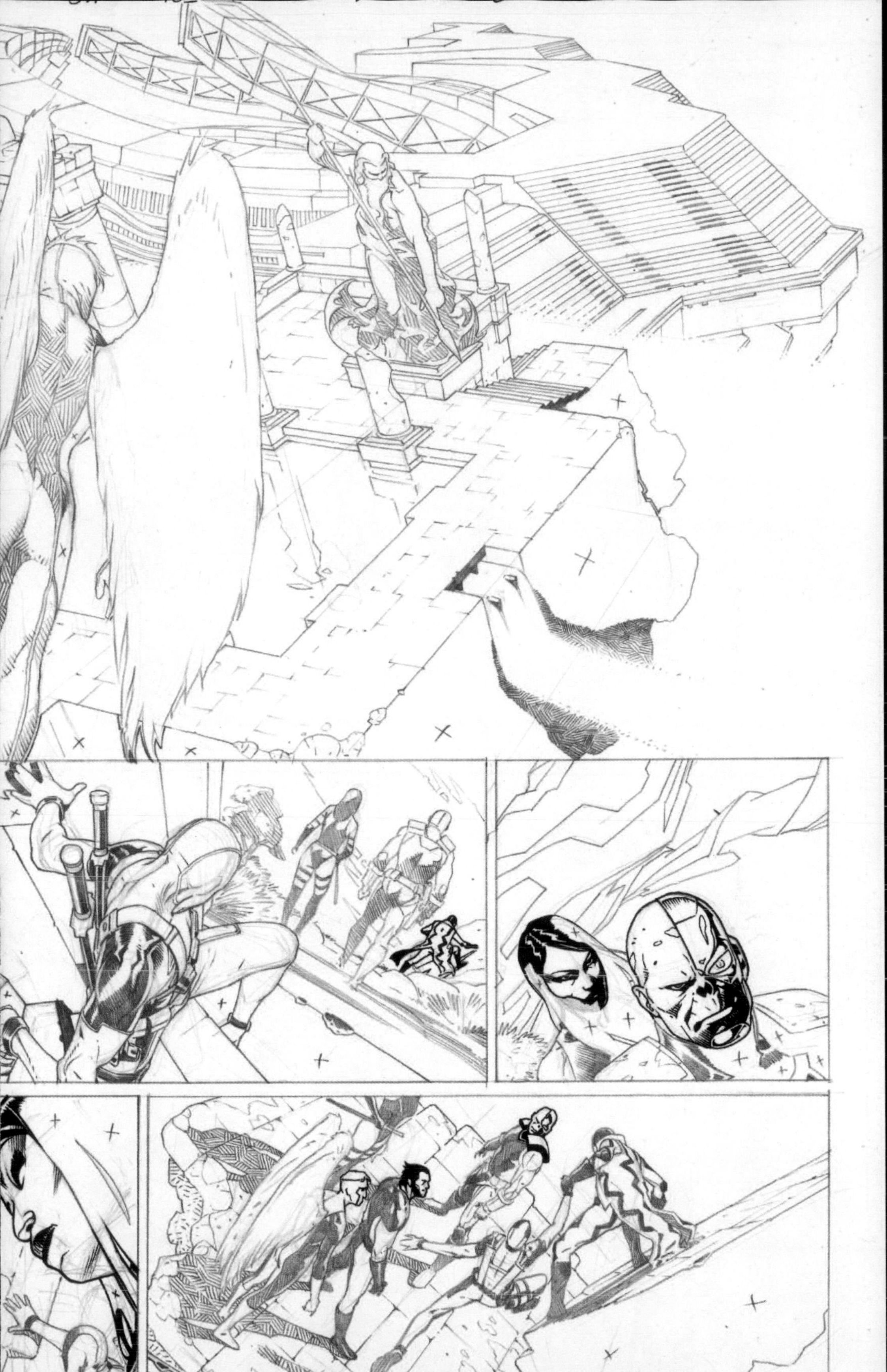

EVOLUTION OF A PAGE: FROM SCRIPT TO COLORS

PENCILS

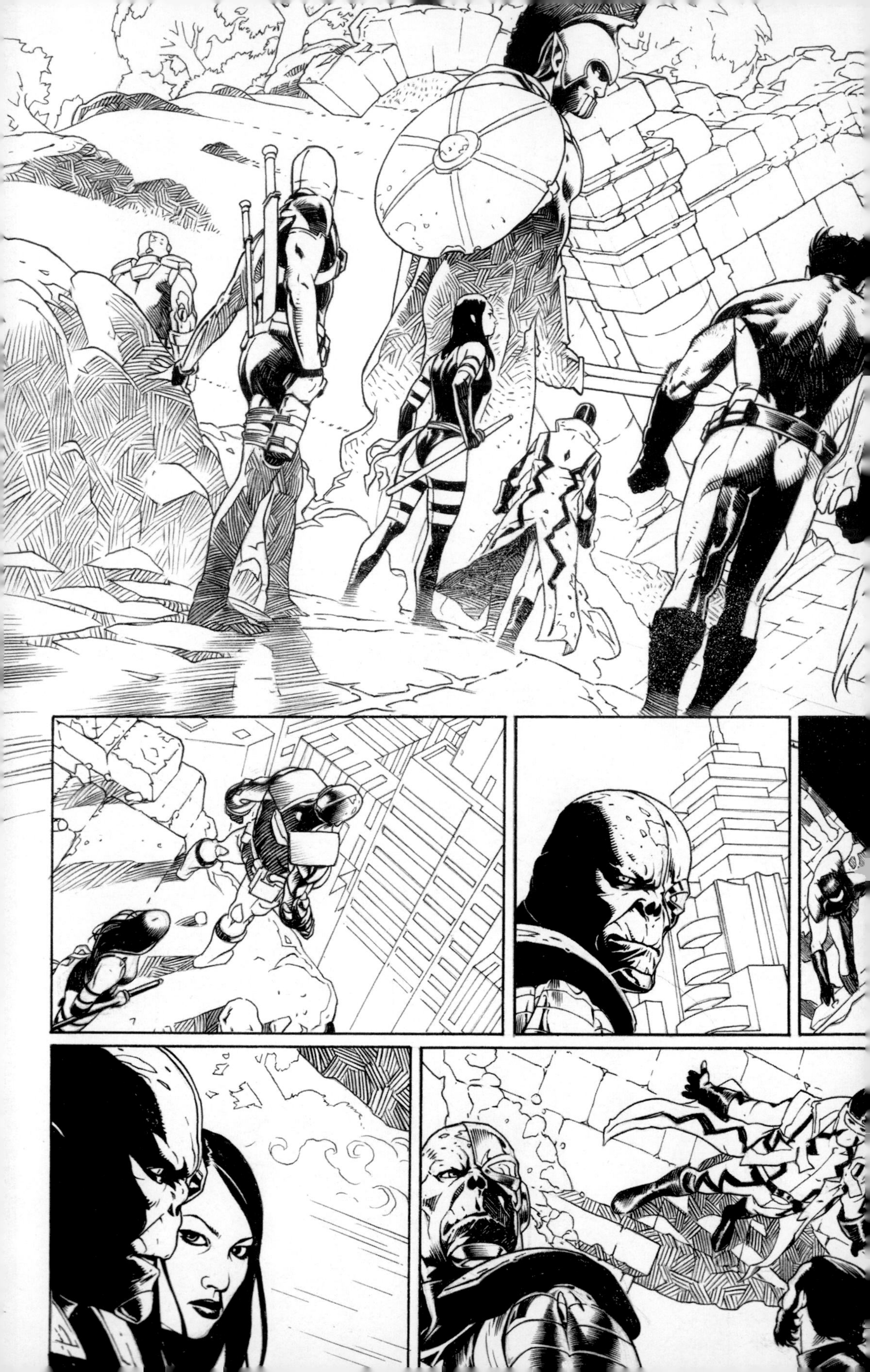

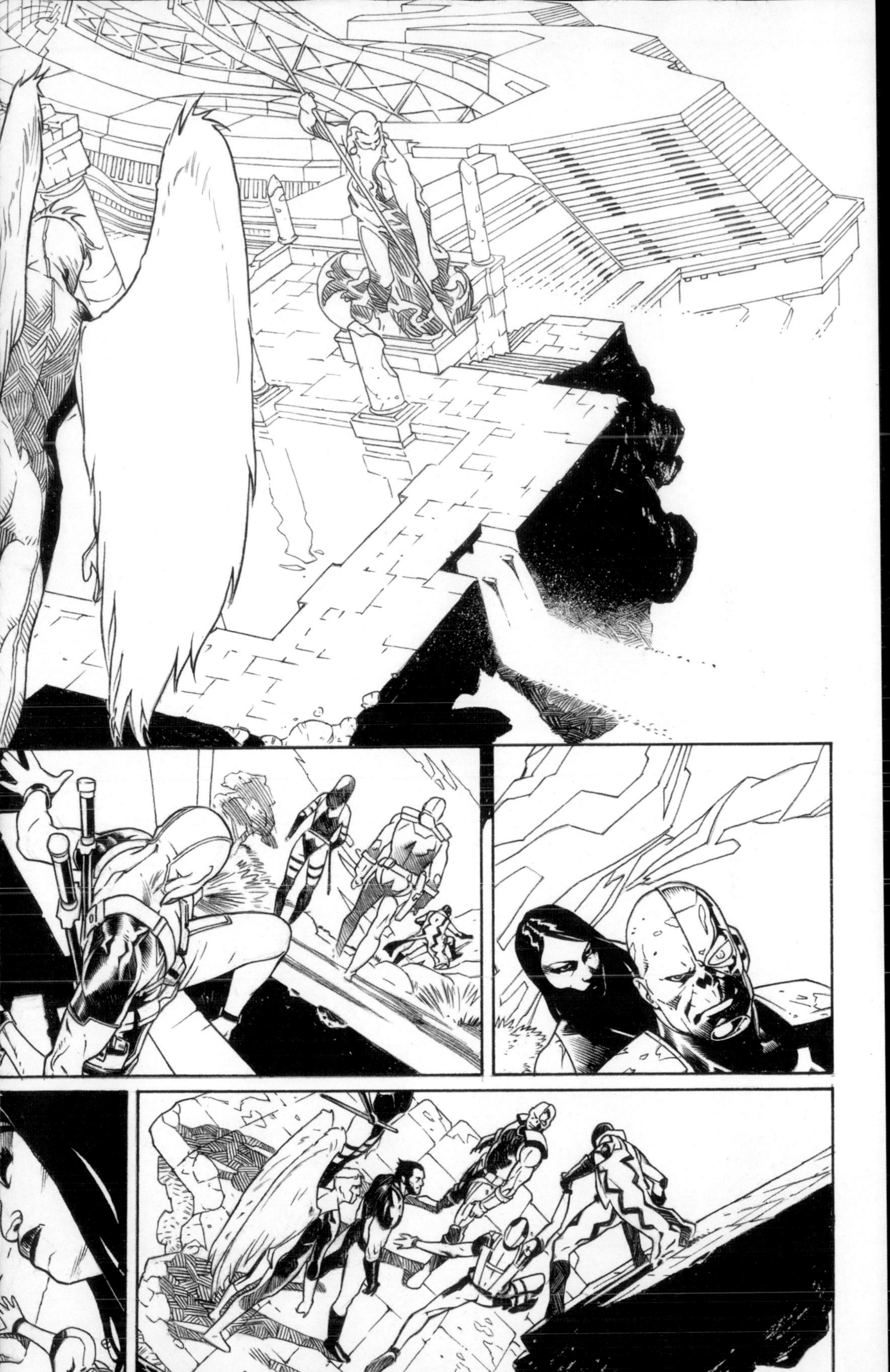

EVOLUTION OF A PAGE: FROM SCRIPT TO COLOR

INKS

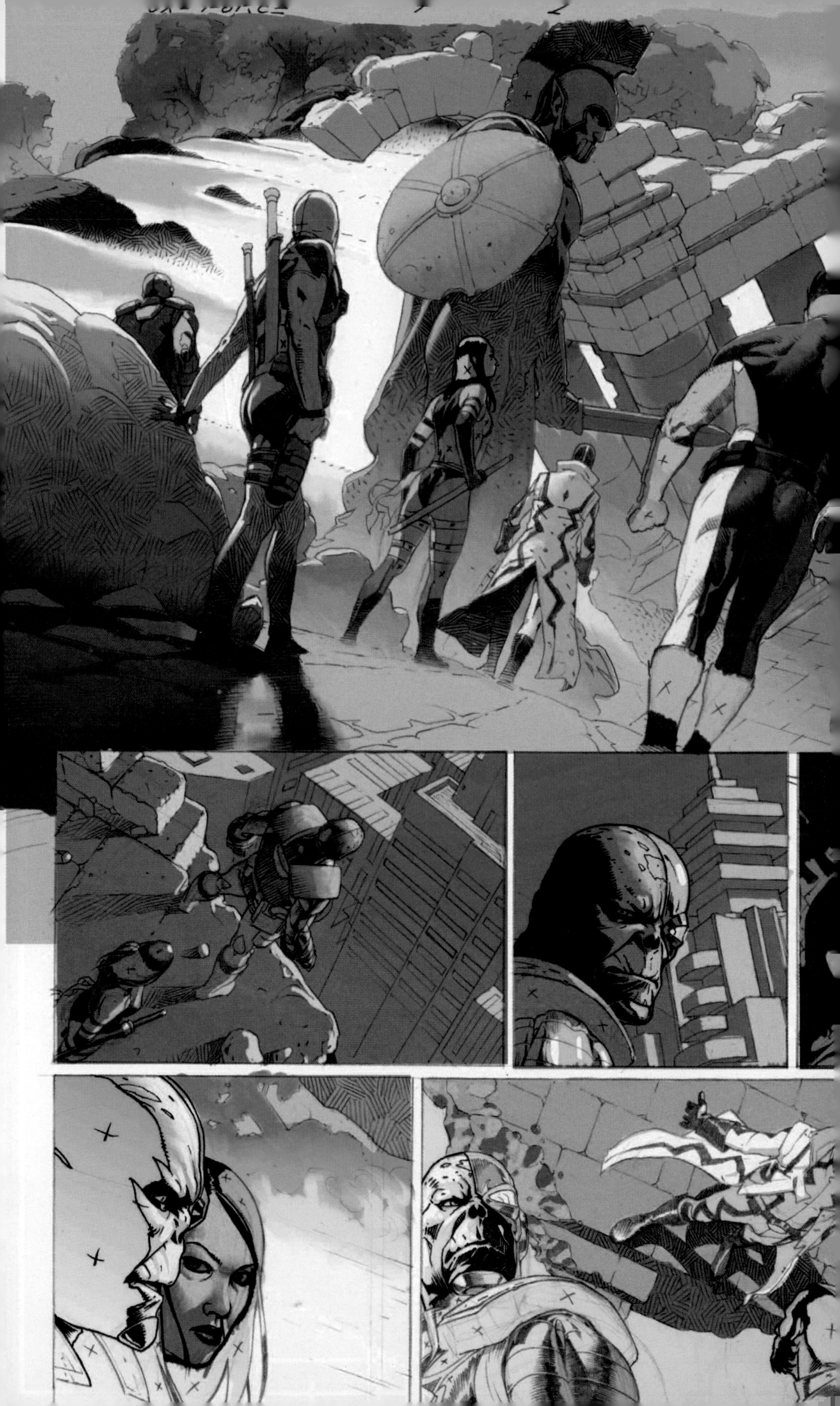

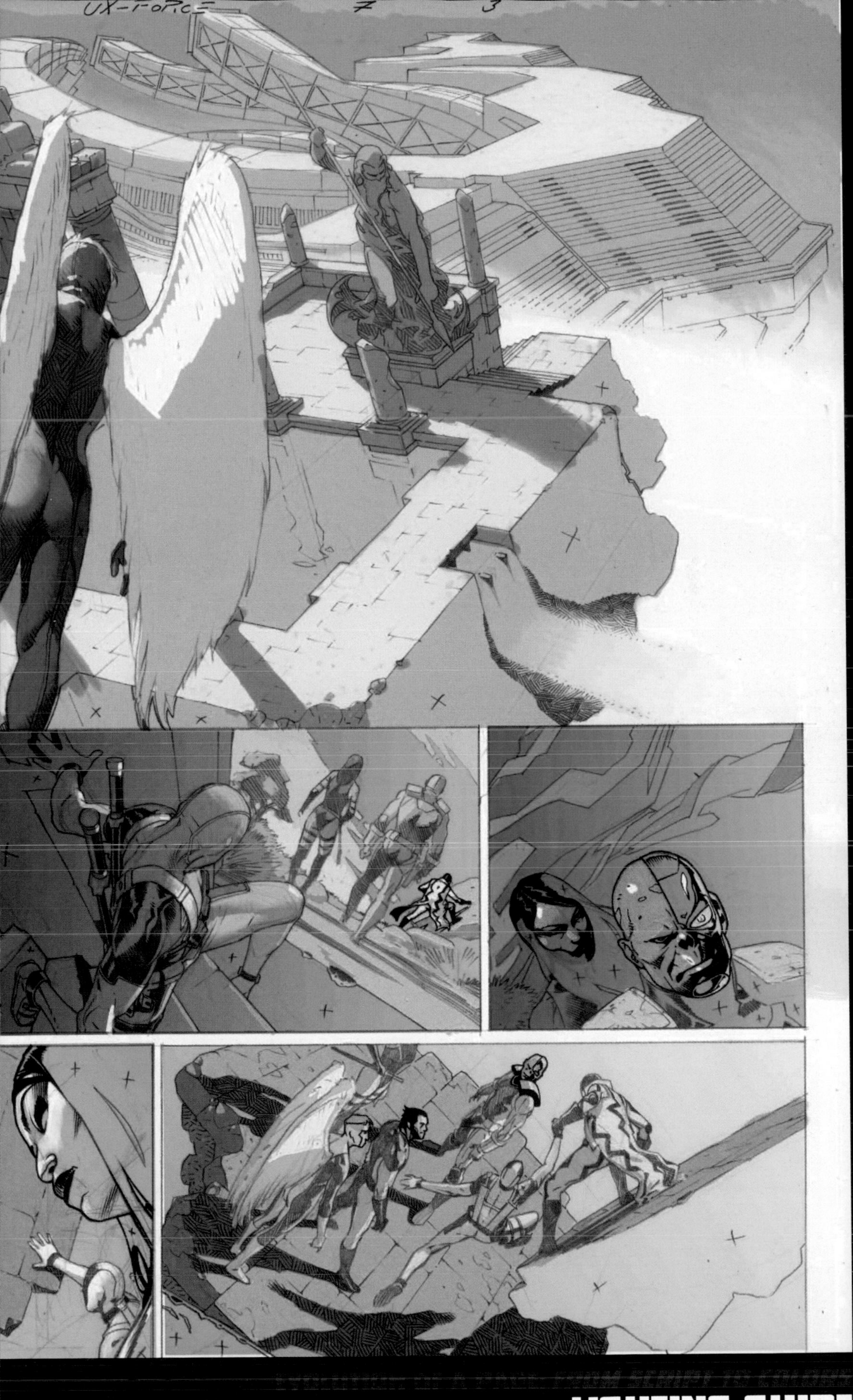
UX-FORCE 7 3

LIGHTING GUIDE

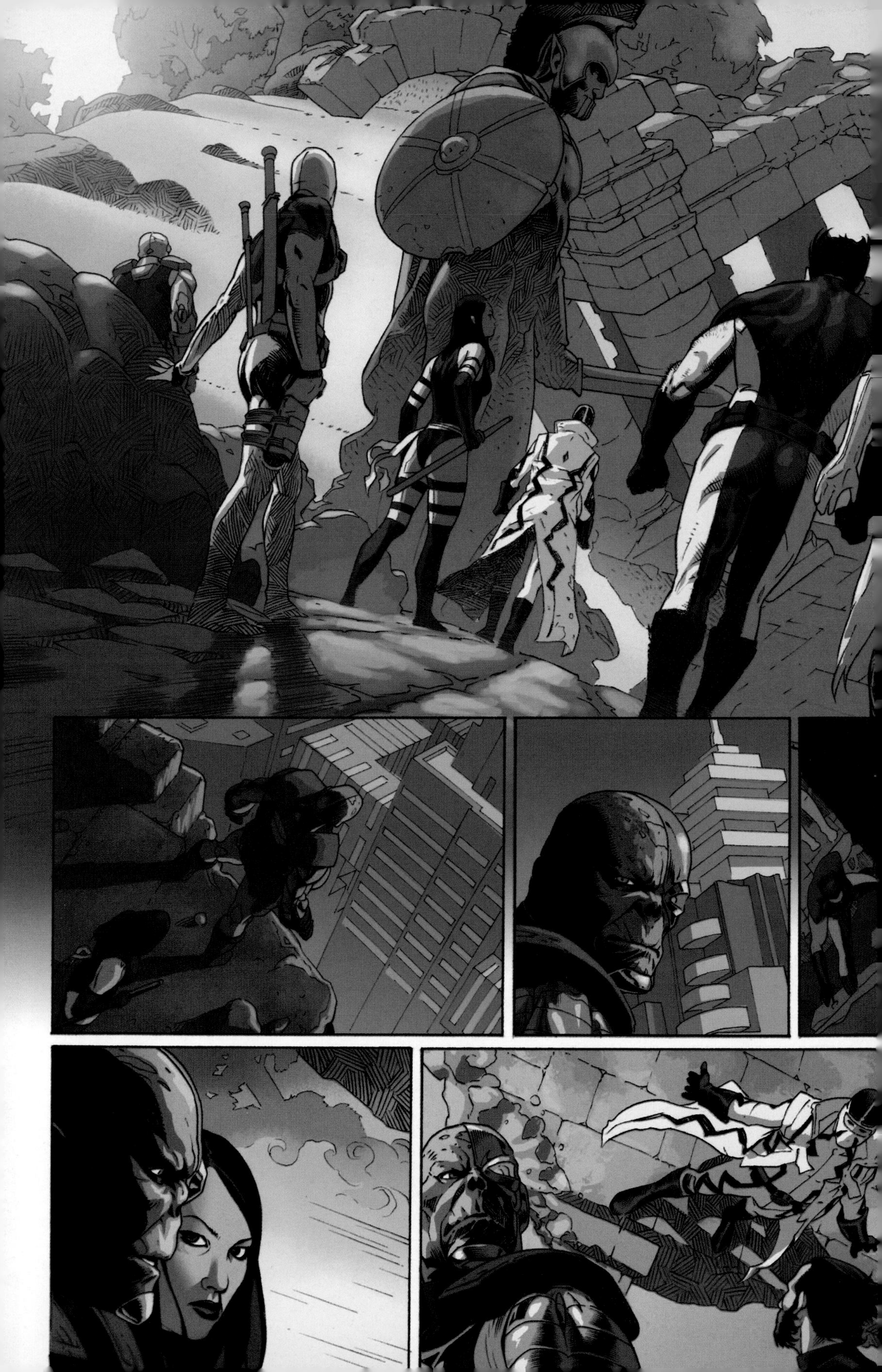

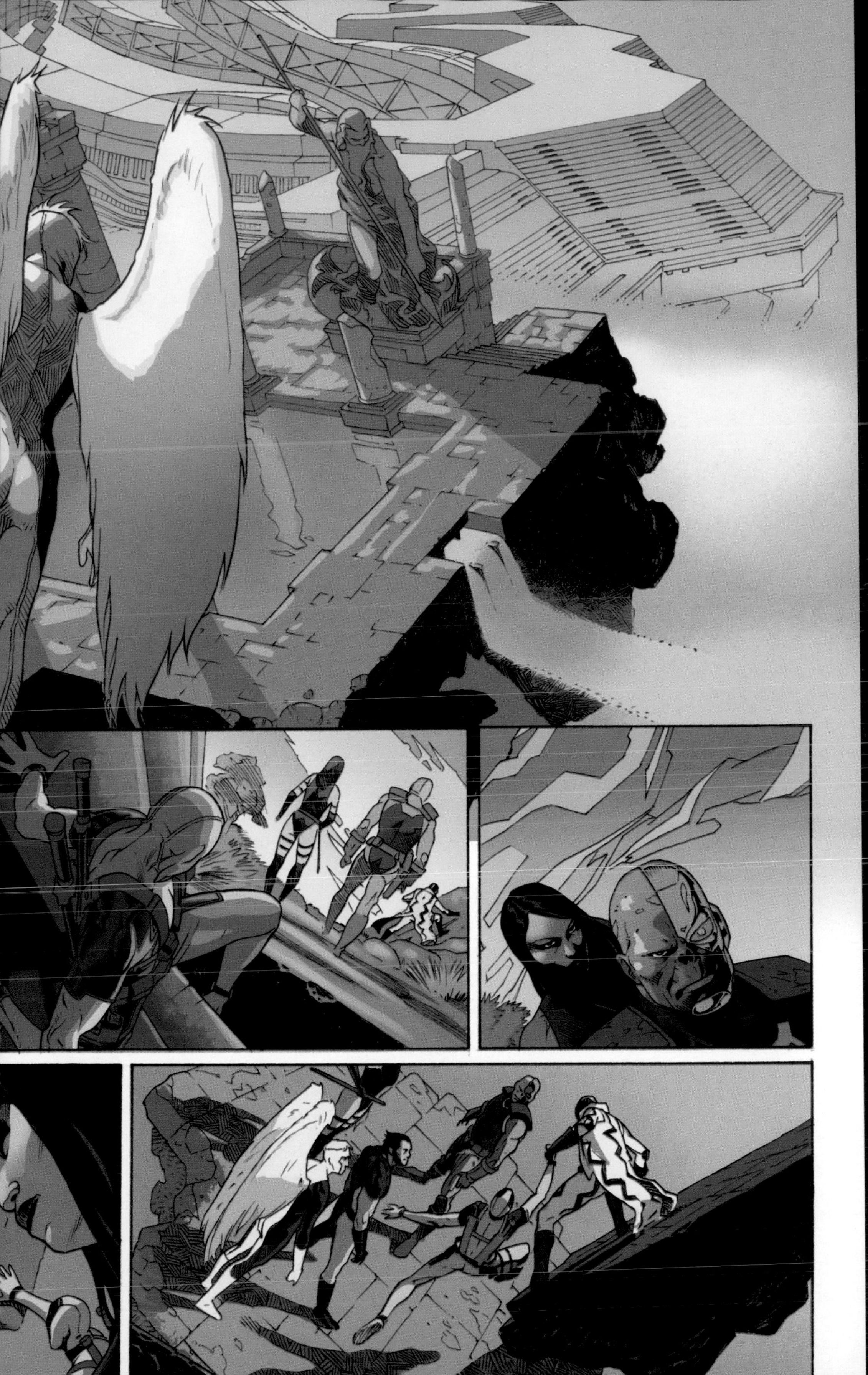

EVOLUTION OF A PAGE: FROM SCRIPT TO COLORS

COLORS

DARK FORCES

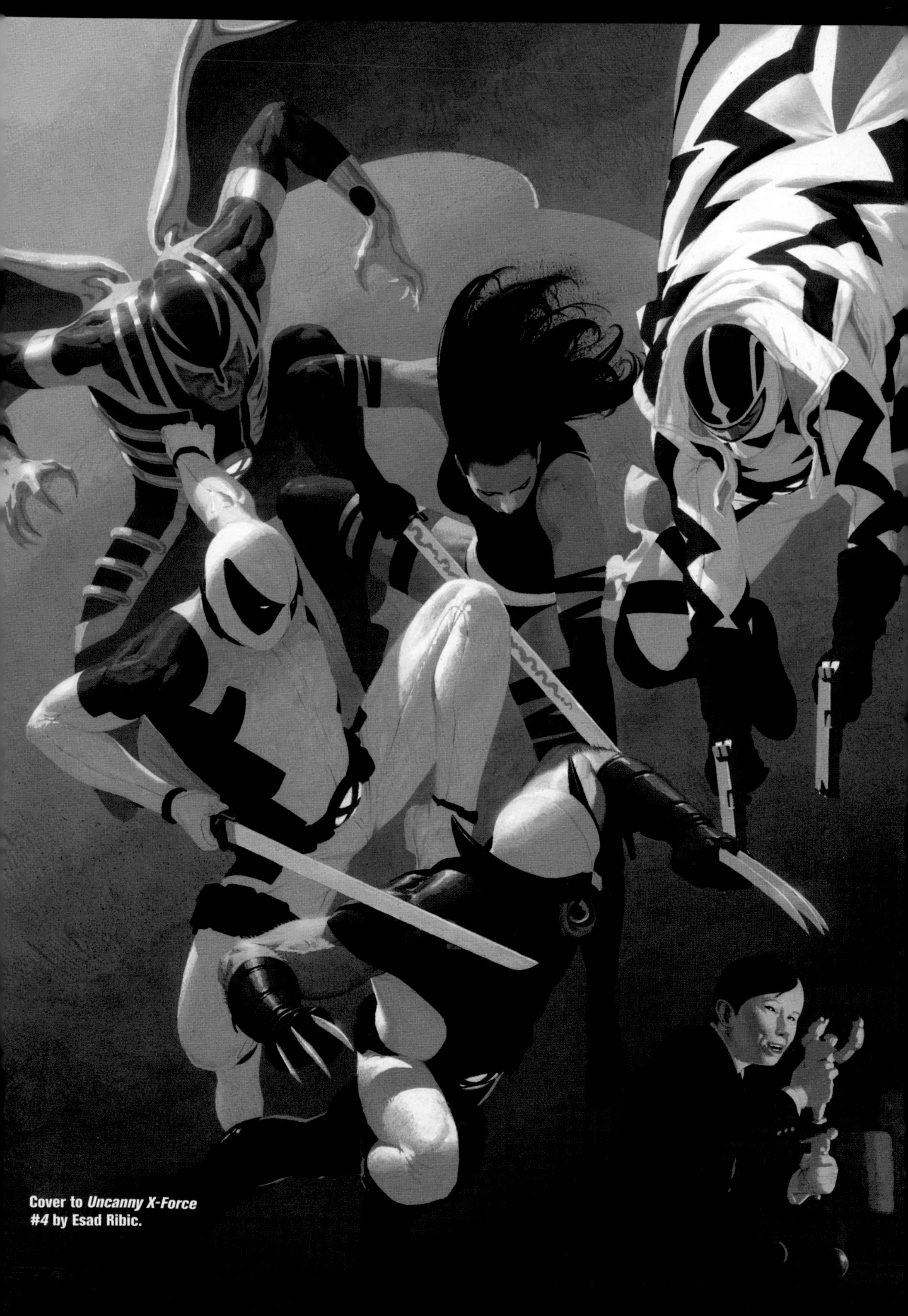

Cover to *Uncanny X-Force* #4 by Esad Ribic.

ND BLACK OPS

UNCANNY X-FORCE

Writer Rick Remender Keeps Track Of The Good Guys' Kill List With A Stable Of Top-Flight Artists **By Chris Arrant**

Since their inception in 1963, the mutant heroes known as the X-Men have carved a unique and sprawling niche in the world of comic books. They've gone everywhere – from the sewers of Manhattan to the outer reaches of known space, and even to alternate dimensions – and they've met their fair share of adversaries. And in this modern age when the mutant population is more a minority than ever, some of the threats they've been able to weather in the past could now be the death knell for them – and their entire species.

That's where X-Force comes in. In *Uncanny X-Force*, Wolverine and Archangel lead a team of mutants who aren't afraid to resort to extreme measures to ensure their survival. Bound together by personal tragedies of mistreatment and torture, they're a black-ops team operating under the radar to take out – as in, kill – the biggest threats their kind faces today. Unlike previous iterations that operated at some level in tandem with the larger mutant population, this new team is a secret known only to its members – and the secret is so raw that if their allies in the X-Men found out, it could spell the end for them all.

This new X-Force comes by way of writer Rick Remender. After proving himself with a number of well-received creator-owned series, Remender has become a rising star at the House of Ideas with work on *Punisher*, *Thunderbolts* and the new *Venom*. The debut issue of *Uncanny X-Force* was the highest-selling comic of the month, beating out all other titles at both Marvel and DC – and the hits have kept on coming since. Remender's worked with a murderer's row of talented artists, from Jerome Opeña to Rafael Albuquerque to Esad Ribic. He's teaming up with artist Billy Tan for the latest *Uncanny X-Force* arc, which leads into the much-hyped "Dark Angel Saga."

SPOTLIGHT: What's the current situation like in *Uncanny X-Force*?

RICK: You've got a small band of five mutants who all agree that threats against mutants need to be

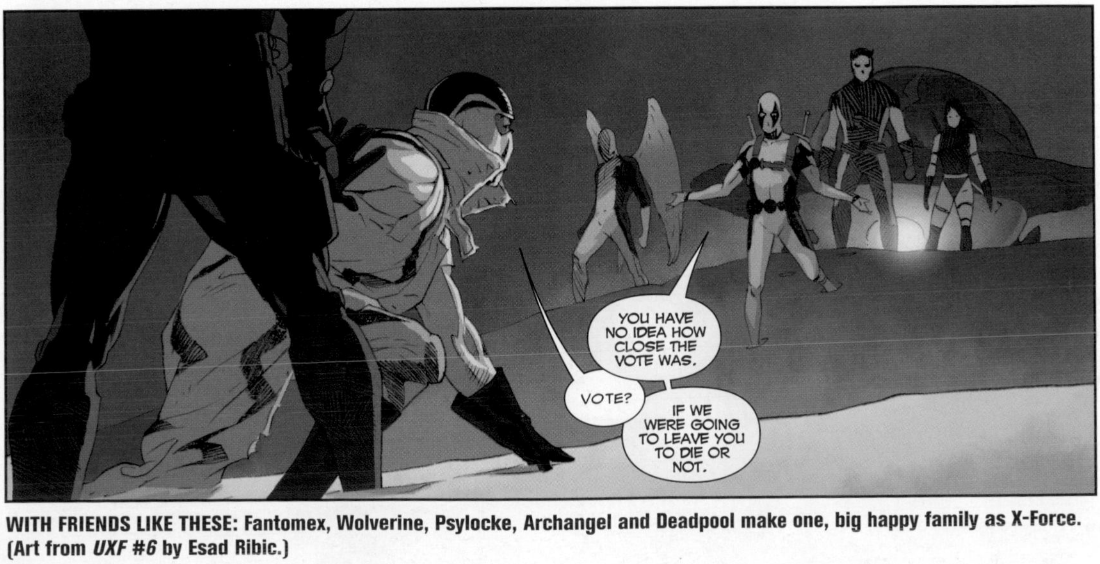

YOU HAVE NO IDEA HOW CLOSE THE VOTE WAS.
VOTE?
IF WE WERE GOING TO LEAVE YOU TO DIE OR NOT.

WITH FRIENDS LIKE THESE: Fantomex, Wolverine, Psylocke, Archangel and Deadpool make one, big happy family as X-Force. (Art from *UXF #6* by Esad Ribic.)

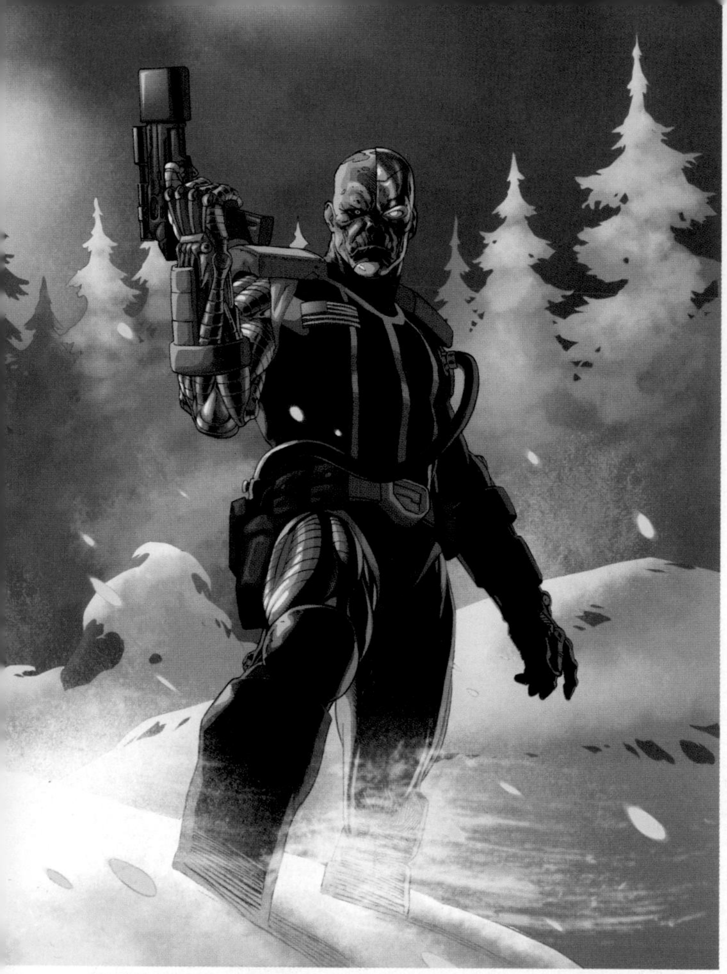

YOU'VE GOT A "FRIEND": Deathlok joins the fray alongside Fantomex in *UXF #5*. (Art by Ribic.)

preemptively hit instead of waiting for the likes of Apocalypse, Mr. Sinister or whoever to rain down fire from hell. X-Force is a band of mutants that'll take them down with extreme prejudice.

They're all characters who have something in their past – a similar event that's tainted them and cast a shadow on their souls. These are the people uniquely qualified for this kind of thing. Since they're capable of killing, they'll take on these terrible missions so other people don't have to.

The first arc of *Uncanny X-Force* dealt with Apocalypse and the idea of the villain being recast as a young boy. The second arc shows the affects that killing Apocalypse had, and the future comes back to try and wipe them out. After those arcs, we started to slowly build toward the "Dark Angel Saga" that starts in #11, with issue #10 being the prologue.

Once people see the events of *Uncanny X-Force #10* in a few weeks, the bigger picture will be pretty clear.

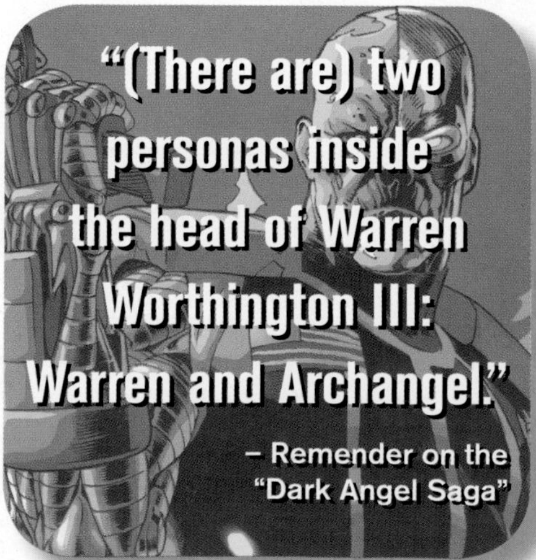
"(There are) two personas inside the head of Warren Worthington III: Warren and Archangel."
– Remender on the "Dark Angel Saga"

SPOTLIGHT: What can you tell us about "The Dark Angel Saga" as it begins in #10?

RICK: Well, you've got two personas inside the head of Warren Worthington III: Warren and Archangel. It's never really been divulged what Archangel is, and what it means to be Death in Apocalypse's Four Horsemen. Apocalypse keeps making these new Deaths for each iteration, but it's never truly been explained what they are. Starting in #10, we're going to discover what they are in a pretty inconvenient way.

Warren's been able to keep the Archangel persona in check with Betsy's help, but something happens that nobody sees coming that leads the team to make Warren's personality crisis their priority. And because of the killings and covert ops they've done as X-Force, they can't tell anyone outside the group or ask for help.

SPOTLIGHT: Warren is a founding member of the X-Men, yet he still couldn't go to Cyclops and his friends on Utopia for help?

RICK: No, because then they'd have to reveal what caused it all and what they've done. They can't tell anyone they assassinated a 10-year-old boy, even if he was Apocalypse. X-Force's terrible missions have bound them together as a family unit, and they have to turn to one another for everything.

SPOTLIGHT: But Warren's not just a member of X-Force. He's a co-captain with Wolverine as set out in the debut issue. How does this faltering of one of their leaders affect the team?

RICK: That's one of the key issues, and we're going to be dealing with what happens when those two can no longer agree with each other.

SPOTLIGHT: As you said, the secret shared by the members of X-Force has hung over their heads for a while now. If Cyclops knew what Logan's crew was up to behind the

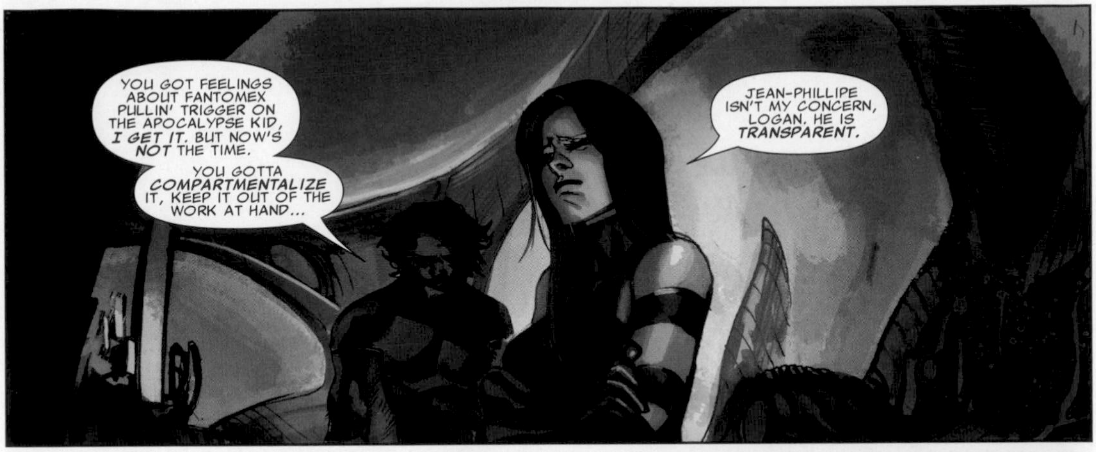
YOU GOT FEELINGS ABOUT FANTOMEX PULLIN' TRIGGER ON THE APOCALYPSE KID, I GET IT. BUT NOW'S NOT THE TIME.
YOU GOTTA COMPARTMENTALIZE IT, KEEP IT OUT OF THE WORK AT HAND...
JEAN-PHILLIPE ISN'T MY CONCERN, LOGAN. HE IS TRANSPARENT.

scenes, it'd tear things apart. In issue #9, we saw Magneto learn the secret and use it against them to accomplish one of his own goals – but how big will the secret play into the title, and the X-Men line as a whole?

RICK: This plays into the teaser image on a level that I don't think people will anticipate at all. There's an inherent hypocrisy in a lot of what's coming up in the book, and that philosophical divide and hypocrisy causes the drama – or some of it, anyway. X-Force plays a big role in what's coming up for the X-line, but I don't think the rug will be pulled out from under them when people expect it to.

X-Force's secret missions are a kind of Sword of Damocles hanging over their head, and Magneto learning about it and using it against them clearly adds new tension to it.

SPOTLIGHT: **We recently saw the induction of Deathlok into the book with the "Deathlok Nation" story arc. What's his role now with the covert team?**

RICK: Deathlok becomes the guard dog of Cavern-X, the team's base in Sedona, Arizona. In recent issues, it's become home to the World – a giant, self-contained world where time can be fast-forwarded, rewound and changed with test subjects inside. It was an invention of Weapon Plus – the people who created Wolverine, Nuke, Fantomex and Deadpool, among others. As we saw in the "Deathlok Nation" arc, the World can be full of trouble in the wrong hands – and Deathlok Prime is very aware of this and takes up guarding it here in Cavern-X.

SPOTLIGHT: **Having read through all the issues thus far, it reveals either a longtime X-Men fan or someone who's extraordinary with research – or**

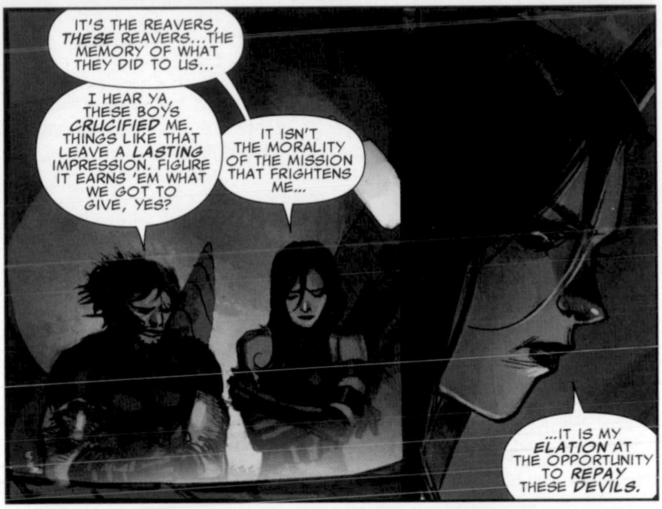
IT'S THE REAVERS, THESE REAVERS...THE MEMORY OF WHAT THEY DID TO US...
I HEAR YA, THESE BOYS CRUCIFIED ME. THINGS LIKE THAT LEAVE A LASTING IMPRESSION. FIGURE IT EARNS 'EM WHAT WE GOT TO GIVE, YES?
IT ISN'T THE MORALITY OF THE MISSION THAT FRIGHTENS ME...
...IT IS MY ELATION AT THE OPPORTUNITY TO REPAY THESE DEVILS.

MORAL CROSSROADS: Underpinning every violent act performed by X-Force is a serious ethical quandary for its members. (Art from *UXF #5.1* by Rafael Albuquerque.)

both – is behind this. You've had the Reavers, Deathstrike, Shadow King, Apocalypse and Ozymandius. Can you tell us about your knowledge of the X-titles of old?

RICK: Well, I'm a huge X-Men fan. X-Men were a passion as a child. I started collecting around 1984 or '85, and became sort of fanatical. This was before trade paperbacks and collections. I spent weekends mowing lawns to put together the funds to go out and buy back issues to fill in gaps in my collection. And they're not cheap – even back then. At the time, all of the Claremont/Byrne issues were going for $20 to $40 an issue – and the Lee/Kirby issues were crazy expensive, as were the Neal Adams issues. But that made it all the more exciting as a kid.

But that hunt was fun. I was putting together pieces of a universe. Around 1992, I became a manager of a comic shop and worked there for three years. And during that time, I pieced together an entire *Uncanny X-Men* run in mint condition. And since I was working in a shop, I was also able to dip into any side stories and spinoffs that I had missed out on at that point.

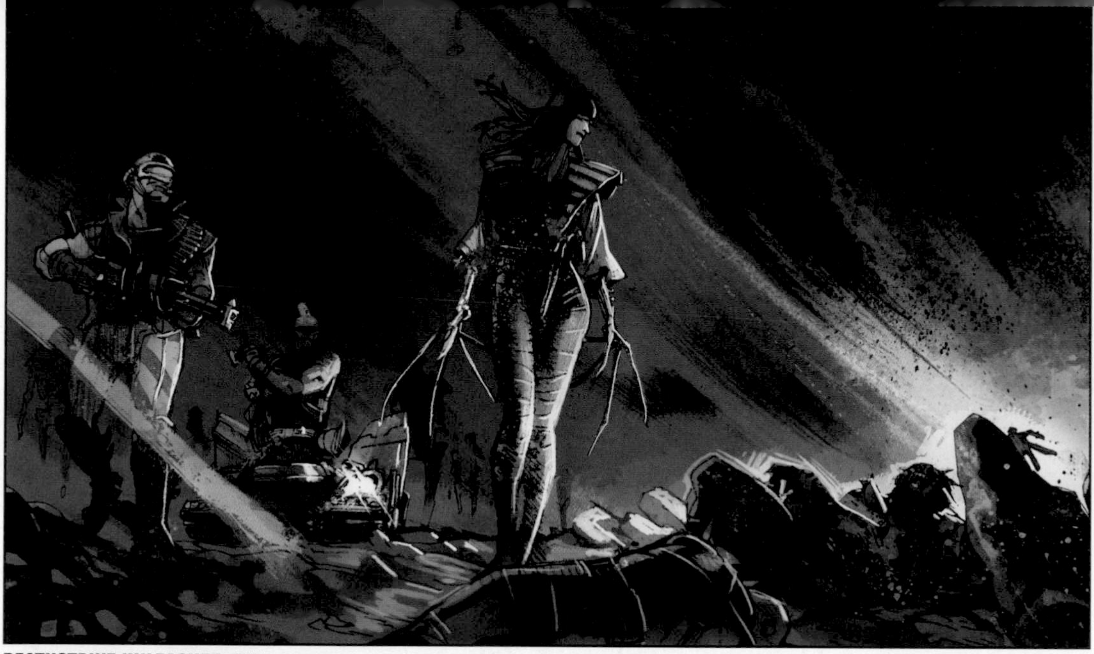

DEATHSTRIKE UNLEASHED: This gorgeous, painterly panel by Albuquerque featuring X-Force's mortal foe is a hallmark of *UXF*'s prestigious corps of talented artists. (Art from *UXF #5.1*.)

SPOTLIGHT: And how does that play out into your plan for *Uncanny X-Force*?

RICK: It's important to me that the book not feel like a fringe book, but important to the X-titles and Marvel as a whole. Going back to those *Uncanny X-Men* issues I collected, I worked to retain the things I found enjoyable about the books I grew up with. For the appearance of Deathstrike and the Reavers in *Uncanny X-Force #5.1*, I went back and re-read *Uncanny X-Men #200-250* to get into Chris Claremont's head and how he characterized each of them. After that, I moved forward to brush up on what has been done with the characters since.

All of this knowledge has helped my work with the editors to plan out things that readers won't even begin to see until the second year of the book. I like to seed things early on, and then have them pay off much later.

SPOTLIGHT: You've worked with an all-star slate of artists on the book: Jerome, Esad, Rafael and now Billy. How do you keep doing it?

RICK: I've been really lucky. Jerome Opeña and I have been working together for around six years now. It's pretty well-established that we, as well as me and Tony Moore, like to work together. I'd like to keep working with them throughout the rest of my career. It's nice to have buddies you keep working with. There's an inherent value coming out of long-term partnerships like that.

As for #5.1 artist Rafael Albuquerque, I've been trying to work with him since 2006. We pitched numerous projects to DC

RICK REMENDER: COLLECTED EDITIONS

He's taking on Wolverine's black-ops task force in *Uncanny X-Force*, but Rick Remender's been doing a few things with Punisher you might want to take a look at!

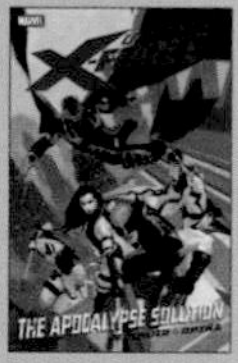
THE APOCALYPSE SOLUTION

Uncanny X-Force:
The Apocalypse Solution Premiere HC/TPB
Collects *Uncanny X-Force #1-4* and more
By Rick Remender and Jerome Opeña
Apocalypse has returned – reborn as an innocent child – and the only way X-Force can stop him is to kill him quickly, before he can gather his full powers!

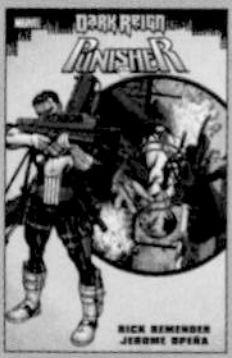
PUNISHER

Punisher: Dark Reign Premiere HC/TPB
Collects *Punisher (2009) #1-5* and more
By Rick Remender and Jerome Opeña
Remender's first go-around with Uncanny X-Force *artist Jerome Opeña finds Frank Castle in an Osborn-dominated world.*

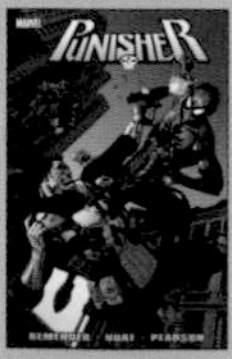
PUNISHER

Punisher: Dead End Premiere HC/TPB
Collects *Punisher (2009) #6-10* and *Annual #1*
By Rick Remender, Tan Eng Huat and Jason Pearson
Punisher goes for the kill against the Hood, and goes mano a mano against Spider-Man!

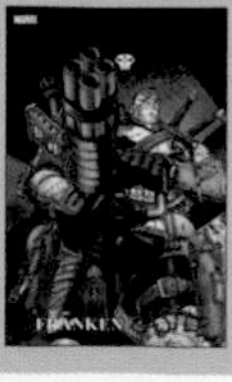

Punisher: Franken-Castle HC/TPB
Collects *Punisher (2009) #11-16, Franken-Castle #17-21* and more
By Rick Remender, John Romita Jr., Jefte Palo and more
After the son of Wolverine kills him, the Punisher joins the Legion of Monsters in one of the most insane stories in modern Marvel history – and one of its most popular!

while I worked there, and we also tried to get some creator-owned projects off the ground. We were hired a couple times, but it fell part. I always wanted Rafael to be one of the guys I wrap my wing around and selfishly keep for all the books I write. Issue #5.1 was very fortuitous for us to be able to finally work together. Editor Jody LeHeup went out of his way to secure Rafael for the book, and it came out great.

Working with Esad Ribic was something I believe Axel Alonso put together. Axel and I were both friends with Esad, and we realized Esad had some open time coming up. And so we asked, and he agreed. I love his work. He's such a brilliant and genius storyteller. He's one of those few guys who are not only an amazing illustrator, but also an amazing storyteller.

SPOTLIGHT: In general, though, have you thought about how you've become such an artist magnet?

RICK: I chalk it up to my background as an artist. I write very visual scripts, and I've been fortunate enough to have amazing artists want to work with me. It's a welcome side effect to being a visually minded person. I get to work with the best of the best.

SPOTLIGHT: Although the X-Force name had been around long before, you really broke the mold here and made it your own. The first issue outsold the flagship _Uncanny X-Men_ title and all the comics that came out that month. Now that you're wrapping up your first year on the book, what do you think of what you and the artists and Marvel have been able to accomplish here?

RICK: I've been fortunate enough to work with two great editors with Axel and Jody. They have amazing feel for stories, and they work very hard on every single book. We've also been lucky to have top-level artists draw the book – including our colorists Dean White and Matt Wilson, who make it look beautiful.

I feel a lot of weight working with such a crack team. There's a lot of pressure, but you can't take shortcuts. I hacked out one story four years ago, and it still haunts me. Every comic is someone's first – so it's important to me that if they're spending $4 on a book, they're getting their money's worth.

I think we've made some good comics here. The important thing is that they're intelligent and have heart.

ESCAPE FROM APOCALYPSE: The first four issues of _UXF_ set the tone for Remender's "Dark Angel Saga." (Art from _UXF #4_ by Jerome Opeña.)

It'd be easy for this book to be about the shock value of heroes willing to kill, but we play that to establish a unique situation for these characters to open up with. My approach is to treat every single kill as a big moment. It shouldn't be casual; it shouldn't be easy. We build on the killing with intellect and my knowledge of each character's history to really tell a three-dimensional comic.

Catch the prologue to the "Dark Angel Saga" in May's UXF #10 by Rick Remender and Billy Tan! ●